JUAN GREGORIO PALECHOR

A BOOK IN THE SERIES

Latin America in Translation / En Traducción / Em Tradução

Sponsored by the Duke–University of North Carolina Program in

Latin American Studies

Narrating Native Histories

Narrating Native Histories aims to foster a rethinking of the ethical, methodological, and conceptual frameworks within which we locate our work on Native histories and cultures. We seek to create a space for effective and ongoing conversations between North and South, Natives and non-Natives, academics and activists, throughout the Americas and the Pacific region.

This series encourages analyses that contribute to an understanding of Native peoples' relationships with nation-states, including histories of expropriation and exclusion as well as projects for autonomy and sovereignty. We encourage collaborative work that recognizes Native intellectuals, cultural interpreters, and alternative knowledge producers, as well as projects that question the relationship between orality and literacy.

JUAN GREGORIO PALECHOR

The Story of My Life

by Myriam Jimeno

Translated by Andy Klatt · Foreword by Joanne Rappaport

DUKE UNIVERSITY PRESS DURHAM AND LONDON 2014

Designed by Amy Ruth Buchanan
Typeset in Quadraat by Tseng Information Systems, Inc.

This translation was funded by the Duke/UNC Consortium
for Latin America in Translation.

Library of Congress Cataloging-in-Publication Data
Jimeno, Myriam.
[Juan Gregorio Palechor. English]
Juan Gregorio Palechor : the story of my life / by Myriam Jimeno ;
translated by Andy Klatt ; foreword by Joanne Rappaport.
pages cm — (Narrating native histories) (Latin America
in translation/en traducción/em tradução)
Includes bibliographical references and index.
ISBN 978-0-8223-5522-9 (cloth : alk. paper)
ISBN 978-0-8223-5537-3 (pbk. : alk. paper)
1. Palechor, Juan Gregorio, 1923–1992. 2. Yanaconas—
Biography. 3. Peasants—Political activity—Colombia.
I. Jimeno, Myriam. Juan Gregorio Palechor. Translation of:
II. Title. III. Series: Narrating native histories. IV. Series:
Latin America in translation/en traducción/em tradução.
F3429.3.Y3P35513 2014
986.106′35—dc23
2013026437

CONTENTS

ix   Foreword by Joanne Rappaport

xiii   Preface

xv   Acknowledgments

1   Introduction

Part 1. Narrations, Life Stories, and Autobiographies

10   For Those Who Come After

12   The Anthropological Narrative as Dialogue

14   Life Stories, Biographies, and Autobiographies

17   Recovering the Subaltern Vision

19   Reality, Experience, and Expression:
     The Authorship of Oral Histories

22   Debates on Technique in Life Stories

**Part 2. Juan Gregorio Palechor:
Between the Community and the Nation**

28   Identity and Ethnic Re-creation

35   Ethnicity as a Social Relation

37   The Limits of Diversity and Ethnic Recognition

44   Juan Gregorio Palechor: Between the Community
     and the Nation

54   Cauca, the *Resguardo* of Guachicono, and
     Indigenous Movements

60   Identity and the Struggle for the Resguardo

65   A Politics of Our Own and the Reinvention of Identity

Part 3. Juan Gregorio Palechor: The Story of My Life

76 Where I Come From: Five Generations of the Macizo Colombiano and Guachicono

78 Recognizing the Way of the World and Observing the Weather

80 Life on the Resguardo

88 Our Nervousness about School and What We Were Taught

92 The Harshness of Family Life and the Art of Agriculture

96 When I Was Conscripted

102 Learning New Things

104 Public Life and Political Violence

110 During the Violence, I Was Forced by Necessity to Work as a Tinterillo

119 The Formation of Community Action Committees: The Liberal Revolutionary Movement and the National Front

124 Religion, Money, and Politics

131 Working with the MRL and the Political Parties

135 The Management Class of the Catholic Religion

138 Looking for an Organization: The Campesino Association and the Indigenous Organization

143 My Work in CRIC

148 The Struggles of CRIC and Indigenous Traditions

156 Politiqueros and Their Empty Words

158 Why an Organization of Indigenous People?

163 Appendix: CRIC Documents

191 Glossary

195 Notes

215 References

225 Index

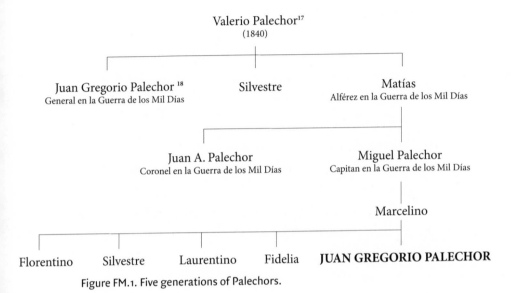

Valerio Palechor[17]
(1840)

Juan Gregorio Palechor [18]
General en la Guerra de los Mil Días

Silvestre

Matías
Alférez en la Guerra de los Mil Días

Juan A. Palechor
Coronel en la Guerra de los Mil Días

Miguel Palechor
Capitan en la Guerra de los Mil Días

Marcelino

Florentino   Silvestre   Laurentino   Fidelia   **JUAN GREGORIO PALECHOR**

Figure FM.1. Five generations of Palechors.

FOREWORD

Joanne Rappaport

Juan Gregorio Palechor: The Story of My Life is the product of a collaborative dialogue between Juan Gregorio Palechor, a native Yanacona from southern Cauca and a founder of the Regional Indigenous Council of Cauca (CRIC), Colombia's oldest and most influential indigenous organization, and Myriam Jimeno, a distinguished member of the anthropology faculty at the National University of Colombia and a longtime activist in solidarity with the Colombian indigenous movement. In its Spanish original, this volume was copublished by a series of academic presses and CRIC, a decision that underlines Jimeno's commitment to the usefulness of research in indigenous organizing and to what in the United States we now call "public anthropology" or "engaged anthropology," but which Jimeno envisions with somewhat more urgency as an ethnography that is simultaneously an exercise in citizenship.[1]

Juan Gregorio Palechor's life history was published in 2006, just after Lorenzo Muelas Hurtado, a Guambiano leader and member of the Constituent Assembly that wrote Colombia's 1991 constitution, wrote his own autobiography in collaboration with archaeologist Martha Urdaneta Franco—it began as a narrated life history but ultimately incorporated Muelas's own research into his oral history of his sharecropper antecedents.[2] *Juan Gregorio Palechor* was followed four years later by another indigenous autobiography, this time by Trino Morales (with the assistance of French sociologist Christian Gros), Guambiano, and cofounder of CRIC and member of the international Barbados Group comprised of Native leaders and Latin American public intellectuals who advocated for indigenous sovereignty in the 1970s.[3] As a whole, this corpus opens a new window into the nature of the indigenous movement at the moment of its founding, when young unschooled indigenous farmers began to organize to reclaim lands stolen from them in the nineteenth century and to incorporate these territories into communal reservation landholdings.

Jimeno juxtaposes Palechor's life history with a series of key documents for the study of indigenous organizing in Cauca, as well as two perceptive critical essays on the historical development of Native activism and the problematic nature of testimonial literature. The three parts of the book complement one another, juxtaposing distinct approaches to the history of CRIC, a narrative that unfolds as a conversation among three different voices whose combination is mutually enriching and multidimensional. Palechor's voice anchors the book, detailing his experiences of the early years of the indigenous movement, a time very different from today's organizations whose leaders articulate indigenous demands with those of Colombian society, not only through mobilization but also through the exercise of public administration at the local, regional, and national levels. Palechor's objectives were different: to reclaim lands in order to sustain an autonomous indigenous government independent of the Catholic Church and traditional political parties.

Palechor's voice conveys his own historically grounded political sophistication and a familiarity with the dreams of many of his non-indigenous compatriots. He narrates his participation in other social movements that united Colombians. Palechor admired the populist Liberal leader and presidential candidate Jorge Eliécer Gaitán, whose 1948 assassination provoked the decade-long wave of unrest called "La Violencia" that still clouds the Colombian conflict. He was an activist affiliated with the left wing of the Liberal Party, the Revolutionary Liberal Movement (MRL), and later joined the National Association of Peasants (ANUC), Colombia's peasant movement, which also sought the return of lands to those who worked them (to appropriate ANUC's own slogan). So, while Palechor's narrative conveys to us his indigenous dreams of autonomy and territory, it also forces us to contextualize his objectives within the larger set of aspirations of popular sectors in Colombia, which have fought to build a more equitable and democratic society in the face of a conflict that for six decades has deterred such dreams. In other words, Juan Gregorio Palechor's autobiography is at once the voice of an indigenous Colombian and a life history in which many Colombians of his generation might recognize themselves—in effect, a dramatic example of how ethnography can be an exercise in citizenship.

What, then, does this book achieve for English-speaking readers? Our intention in editing *Narrating Native Histories* was to reconceptualize the study of indigenous society in Latin America, North America, and the Pacific by offering readers the chance not only to familiarize themselves with pathbreaking contributions from academics in the English-speaking world, but also to become acquainted with the distinct approaches of academics from the global South, as well as the insightful analyses of Native peoples themselves. *Juan Gregorio Palechor* achieves these objectives simultaneously: at the same time that it problematizes the nature of indigenous organizing in the Americas by historicizing the dreams that have accumulated over the past four decades, it pointedly reminds us that indigenous politics is at once a fundamental concern of Native peoples and a process that is deeply rooted in the aspirations of their cocitizens who are not indigenous.

PREFACE

A final message to the cabildos: Pay close attention to the organization and its struggle. The Executive Committee should forge a closer relationship with indigenous communities because it's with them and for them that we struggle. This is my recommendation. . . . that the Cabildos take to heart the great authority they've been given to defend the indigenous communities. The Executive Committee named by the indigenous communities should use their knowledge to prepare themselves for private life, but for public life as well, because that's what we seek. . . . We lack knowledge because unfortunately no government has made the attempt to civilize us, to educate us, and that's why we struggle; that's what I want . . . Compañeros: ask many more questions in order to develop yourselves, so the communities understand a little better, and avoid personal conflicts, because sometimes people fight over things that aren't worth it. . . . We have to struggle and fight for both long- and short-term policies. As for those of us who've already been working for a long time and who may die, we leave you others a door that is now wide open so that indigenous people can continue working, following the path of what we've accomplished over the last twenty years.

—Message of Juan Gregorio Palechor
on the twenty-second anniversary of CRIC.

ACKNOWLEDGMENTS

I began the first phase of this project during a 1991 sabbatical year from the National University of Colombia, with support from the Bank of the Republic's Foundation for the Promotion of Research and Technology. I worked out of the Center for Social Studies at the Faculty of Human Sciences of the National University of Colombia. Martha Novoa transcribed the text, noted omissions and errors, and provided commentaries. Thanks to the support of the British Council in Colombia, the Foundation for Higher Education, and anthropologist Stephen Hugh-Jones. I had the opportunity to consult bibliographic materials as a Visiting Scholar at the Faculty of Anthropology, Kings College, University of Cambridge. The comments of Dr. Hugh-Jones were extremely helpful as were those of sociologists Pedro Cortés and Teresa Suárez, both extraordinarily knowledgeable about indigenous organizations and the situation of indigenous people in Cauca.

More recently, I am grateful to anthropologist Andrés Salcedo, who helped me see the text through new eyes and whose enthusiasm for the project inspired me to take it up again and make some necessary changes. I thank María Lucía Sotomayor for her invaluable help in producing the Spanish-language edition, which was published in 2006 with the support of the Center for Social Studies at the National University of Colombia, the Regional Indigenous Council of Cauca—CRIC, the Colombian Institute of Anthropology and History, and the University of Cauca. Many thanks to Andy Klatt for his careful translation. The text has been enriched thanks to his attention to detail and his observations, notes, and comments along the way.

Though he was ill, Juan Gregorio Palechor read the text and enthusiastically approved of it. Unfortunately, though, he didn't live to see it published. I share the sentiments expressed by Avelina Pancho and Elizabeth Castillo at Palechor's funeral on February 13, 1992. He built "a great house for all Indians, a house that is open and has many inhabitants . . . we Indians and friends of the Indians . . . we your friends have come to say thank you for your life."

INTRODUCTION

In January 1979, word spread throughout Colombia of another audacious operation by the M-19 guerrillas. They had stolen five thousand firearms from the *Cantón Norte*, the army's principal arsenal in the capital city of Bogotá. This time, their daring act had a significant consequence: the government of President Julio César Turbay (1978–82) made an all-out effort to capture the guerrillas who had made the army look so incompetent.

Within days, telephones began ringing in the offices of those of us who were working in solidarity with the indigenous movement in Cauca and in the offices of legal advocacy groups like FUNCOL,[1] with news that indigenous leaders belonging to the Regional Indigenous Council of Cauca (*Consejo Regional Indígena del Cauca*—CRIC), as well as their advisors, were being rounded up in Cauca, accused of belonging to the M-19 guerrillas. Regional Indigenous Council of Cauca president Marcos Avirama was arrested and tortured, as was his brother Edgard, the organization's secretary, and leaders Taurino Ñuscué, Miguel Ñuscué, and Mario Escué. Before long several nonindigenous advisors including Guillermo Amórtegui, Graciela Bolaños, Luis Ángel Monroy, and Teresa Suárez met the same fate.

On February 3, pistol-wielding assassins killed Paez leader Benjamín Dindicué in the settlement of Irlanda on the *resguardo* of Huila in the region of Tierradentro. Within the space of a few months, others including Dionisio Hipia, Avelino Ul, and Julio Escué were killed on different *resguardos* in Cauca. CRIC leaders not in captivity, such as Juan Gregorio Palechor and Manuel Trino Morales, went into hiding and sought the help of solidarity networks formed by intellectuals in Bogotá. I helped establish a small group that later adopted the name *Yaví* for the Amazonian shamans who take on the form and assume the powers of the jaguar. With legal assistance from FUNCOL and the help of a few intellectuals, we undertook to inform international human and indigenous rights organizations about what was happening. Help was urgently needed to protect the lives of prisoners and put an end to the torture that many of them were suffering. Working intensively over the course of several months we held meetings, organized forums and debates, and produced pamphlets and posters designed to turn domestic and international opinion against the repression that had driven indigenous leaders underground, including Juan Gregorio Palechor, Trino Morales, and Jesús Avirama of CRIC and Adolfo Poloche of the Regional Indigenous Council of Tolima (*Consejo Regional Indígena del Tolima*). They were men who had defended the positions of the indigenous movement and struggled against increased repression. It was at this time and in this context that I began to record Palechor's story.

In those days CRIC was breaking new ground as a political and ideological phenomenon.[2] In general it was viewed with a great deal of suspicion by the government and by regional party leaders, hacienda owners, the police, and even by leftist groups whose political orthodoxies downplayed the importance of the indigenous population. I began to have informal conversations with Palechor in this tense and polarizing atmosphere as part of a research project on relations between the state and the indigenous population.[3] Palechor liked the idea of relating his life story since as the oldest of the indigenous leaders at that time he wanted to express his views on some earlier stages of our national history that he had personally experienced.

In 1980 we agreed to a few initial taping sessions at his modest home in a rural part of Timbío, a peaceful town near Popayán where our isolation allowed us to talk without interruption. At that time CRIC was still viewed with suspicion. Some members of its leadership were in jail and others like Palechor were compelled to be discreet about their identities and restrict their movements lest they too be detained and tortured. We taped part of his narrative, which was later transcribed. Palechor's native language was Spanish, since the communities in the south of Cauca where he was born had adopted the colonial language early on.

The plan was simple: to discuss the trajectory of his life with a focus on his development as a leader. I was familiar with a few indigenous biographies, particularly *Crashing Thunder*,[4] *Black Elk Speaks*,[5] and *Juan Pérez Jolote*,[6] and my primary goal was to get him to speak as freely as possible. The idea of recording the life history of Juan Gregorio Palechor attracted a lot of young indigenous activists who had come into contact with him in Cauca in the mid-1970s. His lively and expressive speaking style as well as his eloquence and wry sense of humor made him exceptionally charismatic, and he was respected for his important role in building an indigenous organization that brought Native issues into the open where they could no longer be ignored. He was well known for his activism in the 1970s peasant movements and for persevering in CRIC for more than twenty years despite the poverty and personal danger that this entailed.

When I first met Palechor in Cauca in 1976, CRIC was part of a broader panorama of rural unrest,[7] but the organization would go on to consolidate itself as an indigenous organization with its own particular demands and its own outspoken leadership.[8] Up until that time few indigenous movements in Colombia had gone beyond local demands. The most important such movement had been led decades earlier by indigenous leader Manuel Quintín Lame, first between 1910 and 1921 as an uprising in Cauca and then between 1922 and 1967 as a nationwide movement for indigenous rights.[9] After the 1980 recording session it was hard to find another place and time to meet. The greatest obstacle, though, was tension stemming from the close relationship between CRIC and the M-19 guerrilla movement, and work on the narrative was suspended for almost ten years. In 1990 I tried to take up the project again with the help of the National University of Colombia and the Bank of the Republic's Foundation for the Promotion of Research and Technology. In 1991 Palechor and I revised the existing text, and he provided additional narrative material with the same autobiographical approach. In 1990 and 1994, with the help of the British Council Colombia and anthropologist Stephen Hugh-Jones of the University of Cambridge, I was able to use some of my time during two stints as a Visiting Scholar in Cambridge to produce a complete transcript of what we had on tape. Back in Colombia, Palechor read the transcript and added comments.

Palechor and I had agreed from the start that the narrative would be chronological. I formulated open and general questions in order to elicit his biography with an emphasis on life on the resguardo where he was born, his contact with local and national institutions, and his political activity. While I was also interested in the history of CRIC, Palechor had a number of reasons on this occasion as on others for not focusing excessively on that aspect of his life.

We continued to develop the project as a dialogue, so the transcription reflects his narrative on one hand, and my interpretation on the other. This kind of work is complicated and brings up a lot of problems that I will discuss in greater depth below. But at this point I would like to address what the work consists of and what can be expected from it. This is Palechor's life history, narrated in the form of an autobiography. He was comfortable with this format and it allowed him to speak in a free-flowing fashion. His narrative was transcribed literally using his own expressions and colloquialisms, and events are presented in the same sequence in which they were narrated. I added section titles, established the punctuation, and eliminated some repetitions and habitual but semantically empty expressions. But in order to preserve the documentary nature of the work I did not, strictly speaking, rewrite any part of it. Palechor did not indulge in superfluous anecdotes and he did not portray his life as being particularly perilous. It is really a straightforward story, so much so that it might disappoint readers expecting to hear about extraordinary events, compelling indigenous myths, or ecosophical paradigms.

Despite the strongly documentary character of this testimony, it was the collaboration between the researcher and the narrator that made a certain kind of creative process and product possible. The potential reader was implicitly present as a third party throughout the collaborative process as well, and I believe that Palechor always worked with this future reader in mind as the recipient of his historical testimony. In this sense—and I will come back to this point in part one—the text is faithful to its nature as first-hand testimony, which makes it anthropologically interesting. But at the same time it is a specific construction within which the author retrieves and relates his lived memories in order to share them with others. And the narration is mediated by my presence, the necessarily active presence of an anthropologist.

Finally, as specialists in the field know, all memory is selective and reiterative, and is employed to reinterpret lived experience. As Okely points out, the anthropologist and the research subject jointly produce the ethnographic context, and both parties are needed to do so.[10] Each of them defines and chooses with whom they will speak and what they will speak about, producing a dialogue in the form of an apparent monologue. By listening I elicited information, at times as an agent of the nonindigenous world.[11] Our dialogue was possible not only because both of us had experienced the historical forces that dominated our time and we shared many of its discursive practices and narrative structure, but also because we identified with the same cause.[12]

This book is divided into three parts. In part one I will discuss autobiography as an anthropological tool and in part two I will offer my conceptual perspective on ethnic struggles and some elements of the sociohistorical context of Cauca and the indigenous movement there. Part three is Palechor's narrative.

The text has no literary pretensions: it is intended to accord with the interests of social scientists. It is not, however, an indigenous ethnography. It does not examine any particular indigenous group, it does not describe indigenous characteristics or cultural institutions, and it does not establish an indigenous prototype. There are no descriptions of indigenous mythology or explorations of symbolism in any rituals, aspects of some texts that often lead to stereotyped views of indigenous people. It is not that kind of text because Palechor wasn't that stereotypical indigenous "type." Palechor's autobiography reflects the collective experience of his people, their way of life, customs, and struggles, but it is the view of one author based on his individual life experience. His was a life directly tied to the indigenous peasantry and to agrarian conflicts on the national level. His testimony does not represent the experience of an isolated individual or that of a Native isolated from

Figure Intro.1. Third Indigenous Encounter of Cauca, June 15–17, 1973. The sign reads "IKAS and people of Cauca: Thinking clearly we get organized." Photo from CRIC Archives.

the larger society by his indigeneity. The cultural activity he describes does not markedly differ from that of the mestizo peasants who were his neighbors. His life was that of a rural leader involved in political activity with a particular vision of this experience. It was a profoundly contemporary life that reflected the dominant conflicts and the options available to him. He consistently identified as indigenous, a historical identity that he shared with his group of origin on the resguardo of Guachicono, deep in the mountains of the Colombian Massif in the department of Cauca.

The culture of this region reflects the rapid disappearance of its own pre-Hispanic population and its replacement by a wave of indigenous immigrants who have been given the generic name of Yanacona.[13] This population adopted nonindigenous cultural elements including the use of Spanish hundreds of years ago. To this day, however, the people of the region retain the organizational form of the indigenous resguardo, they self-identify as indigenous, and they defend the indigenous cause. That is why this work does not depict a native person with highly "traditional" cultural characteristics, a romantic figure inhabiting a natural paradise, or an individual who is marginalized from our national history. On the contrary, Palechor's experience, like that of the resguardo of Guachicono itself and many other indigenous areas of Cauca and of Colombia, is closely linked to the country's institutions, beliefs, practices, and images, albeit transformed, reinterpreted, integrated, and lived out in different ways always tied to the changing historical context.

This text can not be considered a traditional indigenous narrative. As Arnold Krupat has pointed out, an indigenous autobiography "is a contradiction in terms. Indian autobiographies are collaborative efforts, jointly produced by some white who ultimately determines the form of the text in writing."[14] The genre of the self-written life story is a recent phenomenon with European origins. In addition, its organizing principles are European in nature: egocentric individualism, historicism, and the written word.[15] Swann and Krupat report that the autobiographical form was unknown in the oral cultures of North America and that the first of them were produced by Indians who had been converted to Christianity.[16]

The social relations in which Juan Gregorio Palechor participated were by their very nature bicultural. His personal experience was also multicultural, due among other things to his contact with political parties and movements, his travels around the country (although not mentioned in this autobiography), his abiding consciousness of national history and the active role of the individual in national construction. If there are underlying themes in his account, they are the responsibility of the individual to the collectivity and the demand for the nation to recognize the justice of the indigenous cause and act on it.

When I finished the second version of the text, I made a modest attempt to get it published, but it was poorly received by a number of readers and by several colleagues, and publishers were unwilling to consider it. Another decade passed while unrelated events led me to conduct research in other areas, especially on the topic of violence and social conflict. Palechor's death in Popayán on February 12, 1992 may have been another reason for the lack of progress in producing this book.

This is my third attempt to publish Palechor's accounting of his life. I've made some structural changes in the text, written a new introduction, and slightly updated the bibliography. I was greatly helped in this undertaking by Andrés Salcedo, a young colleague at the Department of Anthropology of the National University of Colombia in Bogotá. His reading notes helped me make some necessary changes, and the text was so new, surprising, and interesting to him that he helped me see it through new eyes. He enthusiastically helped me select the accompanying illustrations from among my disorganized pile of documents and his comments helped me understand what Gabriel García Márquez meant when he said: "When we find ourselves at the mercy of nostalgia, we may turn to writing as a means to struggle against forgetting."

PART 1

....

Narrations, Life Stories, and Autobiographies

In these memoirs or recollections there are
gaps here and there, and sometimes they
are also forgetful, because life is like that.
—**Pablo Neruda,** *Memoirs*

THE USE OF NARRATIVE to learn about particular people and historical periods is as old as the western historiographic tradition, dating from the times of Herodotus and Thucydides. David Bynum asserts that all past and present historians have had to accept oral evidence, whatever their qualms about oral sources.[1] Since its earliest days, anthropology has used narrative as a fundamental resource for understanding societies lacking a written language. Since the end of the nineteenth century, the basic methods of collecting anthropological field data have been to elicit and record narratives along with the systematic observation and questioning of subjects. As we shall see, though, the use of narrative evidence has been the subject of careful consideration, much theorizing, and many debates.

For Those Who Come After

At the beginning of the twentieth century, there was a surge of historical and ethnological interest in the indigenous cultures in the United States that had been militarily defeated by federal troops and white settlers. As a result, several examples of indigenous oral literature and a number of indigenous autobiographical narratives were put into writing. In 1906, a student of "Indian sociology" S. M. Barrett published a book called Geronimo's Story of His Life. In his own book For Those Who Come After: A Study of Native American Autobiography,[2] Arnold Krupat has shown that the public was not primarily interested in Geronimo's Story of His Life as the biography of an individual, although Geronimo was a great Apache leader who had been defeated by the U.S. military after a protracted conflict. The public was more interested in Apache life, its cultural prototype, and in a culture on the verge of disappearing. The nineteenth-century interest in the individual and what made him or her unique had given way to a twentieth-century desire to establish culture as an object of scientific study; but in order to do so it was necessary to provide a body of information about "vanishing" societies.[3]

At that time, academic anthropology in the United States was evolving under the influence of Franz Boas. In a clean break with earlier practices, there was a new emphasis on collecting objective data in the field without the need for immediate interpretation. Cushing and Boas in the United States and Malinowski in Britain produced a documentary corpus and formulated methods for anthropological fieldwork based on the collection of testimony from cultural protagonists.[4] Knowledge about indigenous cultures was considered important, and they had come to be studied as individual societies rather than representing stages in an evolutionary process toward modern civilization. The Boasian School assigned a central role to the indigenous point of view with respect to their own cultures, and collected narratives that were believed to be "objective" records of indigenous peoples' own perspectives and of their "cultures," without the interpretations of others looking in from the outside[5] Boas himself believed that autobiography was too subjective to be considered scientific.

Nevertheless, the first professional anthropologist to produce an indigenous autobiography was Paul Radin, one of Boas's disciples. It was called Crashing Thunder: The Autobiography of an American Indian, and was published in 1926.[6] Radin's goal was to "obtain an 'inside view' of another culture told in the words of a member of that culture, in order to rescue all the subjective value associated with the events related."[7]

Paul Radin presented himself in the introduction as a simple editor. He made a point of stating that his role in producing the text was minimal, limited to contextualizing cultural references through footnotes and incorporating elements of text previously dictated by "Crashing Thunder," the pseudonym of Winnebago Indian Sam Blowsnake. On the book's last page the autobiography states that Crashing Thunder wrote the book with the "help" of his brother, and that he did it for the benefit of "those who come after me." But as Krupat comments, those who came after Crashing Thunder turned out to be critical of Paul Radin with respect to his role in the autobiography, his real degree of participation, and his influence over the narrative as well as its character as a work of art or science.[8] This discussion tells us that autobiography is a complex cultural product and that the process by which it is composed is subject to examination and to controversy. In addition, it clearly demonstrates that these narratives are intended for the readers of years to come.

Today it would be difficult to do anthropology in a way that obscured its own role in the product and presented texts as distant cultural artifacts, pretending that the anthropologist's own cultural perspective could be ignored, that the anthropologist could be a passive recipient of information, and that research subjects simply pass along that information.

The Anthropological Narrative as Dialogue

In recent years, many anthropologists have discussed the relationship between the anthropologist and his or her object of study, and the effects of this relationship on research results, in order to emphasize the dialogic nature of research.[9]

Some authors discuss the difficult interaction established between the researcher and the informant and the unavoidable and complex negotiation of a common terrain, which is subject to reexamination throughout the research process. They also discuss the bias that results when the anthropologist makes himself or herself invisible in the research results.[10] But beyond the general categories within which anthropologists and research subjects must negotiate, several levels of individual exchange and reciprocity are produced. Anthropologists' accounts of their own fieldwork illustrate how others have related to them and made an ethnographic context possible.[11] They also expose the inevitable contention for power that influences the choices made by researchers and research subjects alike, choices that entail a series of implications.[12] In the words of Françoise Morin, "far from being a monologue that relegates the observer to a marginal role . . . , it is based on a dialogue in which the ethnologist is one of the agents of the outside world."[13]

Anthropologists choose their subjects, but subjects also choose the anthropologists with whom they want to share their lives. Anthropologists inevitably train people to describe their lives in their own terms. "Consequently, the data we collect is doubly mediated, first by our own presence and then by the second-order self-reflection we demand from our subjects."[14] This double mediation produces an interpretation not only of the culture under study but of the anthropologist's culture as well, since it is the anthropologist to whom the research subject presents his or her life story.[15]

Edward Bruner stresses that all researchers begin to work with preconceived narratives that structure their field observations.[16] With this preexisting narrative as a starting point, the anthropologist engages in a complex set of exchanges with the informant in the search for information. But the most relevant aspect is that the anthropologist and the research subject share a common terrain composed of the same narratives and "the discursive practices of our time." To magnify the distinction between the anthropologist as subject and the indigenous person as object is to obscure what they have in common, the historical forces and certain contemporary narrative structures that are common to both, making the anthropologist more of an author of what is produced than he or she may think and making the subject of the investigation less naïve about the relations established in the course of the research.[17] This suggests the need for a more dialogic and interpretive approach that would require negotiations with the research subject and self-reflection on the part of the anthropologist.

Watson and Watson-Frank further argue that autobiography is the result of a confluence and even a blending of the consciousness of the researcher with that of the subject "to the point that it is no longer possible to disentangle them."[18] In the words of Derrida, "the ego is always mediated by the other, which makes the autobiographical enterprise into something paradoxical in which the author, far from being self-sufficient, is in fact tied to the dynamic defined by the name and the signature that define him as a result of this detour through the other. Autobiography can never be self sufficient because the ego is incapable of presenting itself fully to itself."[19]

Thus it is important for the researcher to present not only the life story of a person as it was related to him or her but also to discuss his or her own assumptions that contributed to the final construction of the text.[20] The researcher must describe the immediate conditions that influenced both the person who related the life story and the person who elicited and recorded it. Along the same lines, it is helpful to know what part of the material was volunteered spontaneously and what information was offered as a result of the persuasive efforts of the researcher. Finally, it is important to note the extent to which the final text was edited and what aspects of the original narrative were eliminated.

These narratives also point to a renovation now taking place in anthropological methodology that recovers the value of unique, subjective expressions used by the subject to culturally define his or her world.[21] They inform us about the version of world seen through the eyes of the subject at a particular moment in time.[22]

Life Stories, Biographies, and Autobiographies

With the above in mind, life stories, biographies, and autobiographies merit new interest not only as a resource for the study of nonliterate cultures, nor only as a tool for anthropologists. Biographies and life stories have also been used in the humanities, psychology, medicine, and several social sciences for different purposes and with varying degrees of success.[23] Their use dates back to the development of salvationist religions, particularly Christianity, with "meaning attached to the Life of Christ and the Way of the Cross."[24] They came to be spread more widely in the Middle Ages and were "brought to fruition with the application of pilgrimage as metaphor for life itself."[25]

The first spiritual autobiography that we are aware of was the *Confessions of St. Augustine*, and only in the seventh century did these works become more common. To Bellaby the works of this period constitute the first life stories, strictly speaking. As mentioned above, however, the autobiography as such evolved as a specific form of expression much more recently, resulting from certain European cultural developments in the last quarter of the eighteenth century. The best examples of autobiography as a literary genre in that century were by Jean-Jacques Rousseau in *Four Letters to M. de Malesherbes*. It was in these self-portraits that Rousseau first manifested his need to explain and justify himself and his life.[26] As Rousseau said in his *Confessions*, "I want to show my fellow-men a man, in every sense of the word," a sensitive, vulnerable, irrational, and inhibited man, passionate about nature and solitude.[27]

Many varieties of biographies and autobiographies have been produced since the nineteenth century, frequently retaining none of the spiritual or subjective content that originally characterized the genre; and some forms of the life story are more typical of post-Enlightenment society, for example the curriculum vitae or résumé, personnel records kept by employers, and medical and criminal records. These documents are of only limited interest and are useful only for specific purposes, their authors having "routinised what originally had a religious impulse."[28]

Since the end of the nineteenth century, certain varieties of life stories have commonly been used for research purposes in history, psychiatry, medicine, sociology, anthropology, and psychology. Adam Kuper and Jessica Kuper propose a tripartite periodization of these modern uses beginning with a period from 1920 until World War II, when there was a growing interest in many kinds of personal documents, including a number of North American Indian autobiographies that were produced at this time.[29] During a second period lasting from the Second World War to the mid-1960s, more highly structured and quantitative methods gained favor and social scientists were less interested in life stories. However, their use grew significantly in a third period beginning in 1965 as they were taken up by sociologists doing life course studies, anthropologists analyzing life stories, and researchers in psychopathology, oral history, and psychobiography.

L. L. Langness also distinguishes three periods, the first of them before 1925 when the use of life stories and biographies by anthropologists was associated with an interest in certain indigenous personages.[30] According to Langness, they were seen at this time through a romantic and nostalgic lens as "good savages" doomed by an encroaching civilization. The autobiography of Geronimo and the biographies of Black Hawk, Pontiac, and Sitting Bull are only some of the well-known examples of this genre.[31]

Langness describes how Paul Radin broke new ground with *Crashing Thunder*, and many other anthropologists used life stories, biographies, and autobiographies between 1925 and 1944. Their use was further increased after 1945 due to a new emphasis on the individual and in keeping with the approach called "culture and personality." The increased use of life stories and the new interest in culture that coincided with it were particularly influenced by two closely related books: *The People of Alor* (1944) by Cora du Bois and *The Psychological Frontiers of Society* by Abraham Kardiner in 1945. Both of these works looked at life stories in their cultural context in order to discern distinctive personality types, and each had a profound influence on subsequent research.[32]

The use of personal documents in anthropology was less common after the mid-1950s, with the exception of the quasi-literary works of Oscar Lewis, who attempted to portray the subjective side of Latin American family dynamics and awakened a new interest in the field with his books *The Children of Sánchez* in 1961 and *Pedro Martínez* in 1964.

Anthropologists, historians, and sociologists have increasingly used life stories and autobiographies in the last twenty years.[33] Some anthropologists have taken up these stories in order to shed light on particular phenomena such as family, political, and intergenerational relations along with social change, the role of the state, work histories, and social categories such as women, immigrants, and others.

In Colombia, life stories have provided information for studies on the anthropology of the family, on work history, and on internal migration.[34] With the exception of sociologist Alfredo Molano, though, researchers have used them as only one of a series of research techniques in a given project. Molano on the other hand has systematically used life stories and presented them in narrative form.[35] Molano believes that people's language must be respected absolutely as one of the fundamental elements of their life stories. He argues that the language people use is a crucially important analytical instrument: "To me people's language and diversity of expression are better than any theoretical text.

They are richer in content and get much more directly to the core of problems, to the core of life and history, than any great concepts or the most profound of reflections."[36]

Life stories and testimonies have proliferated in Colombia in recent years as a form of narrative used to recount personal experiences of pain and violence. Since the 1996 publication of News of a Kidnapping by Gabriel García Márquez, many narratives have been produced in a struggle against forgetting, specifically against forgetting the violent events of recent history. This narrative wave has grown to include the narratives and autobiographies of released kidnapping victims, victims of organized violence, and former guerrillas and paramilitaries. The impact of these works on the collective memory and on social action is ongoing.[37]

In addition, several founders of the Colombian indigenous movement have recently published memoirs, for example Lorenzo Muelas with La fuerza de la gente: Juntando recuerdos sobre la terrajería in Guambía, Colombia [The Power of the People: Remembering the Days of Terrajería in Guambía, Colombia] and Trino Morales with ¡A mí no me manda nadie! Historia de la vida de Trino Morales [Nobody Tells Me What to Do! The Autobiography of Trino Morales]. These life stories are tales of resistance and struggle against the established powers and forms of self-representation, both personal on the part of their subjects and more generally of the particular cultural milieu to which they belong. Similar projects have been undertaken in other parts of Latin America as well, such as a text in Brazil by anthropologist Bruce Albert with Davi Kopenawa.[38] They are forms of recovering the subaltern vision that form part and parcel of broader conceptual and analytic efforts.

Recovering the Subaltern Vision

Ralph Samuel and Paul Thompson argue that historians are predisposed by their training to devalue images, legends, desires, unsupported beliefs, and individual experience. With the growth of oral history, say Samuel and Thompson, historians have come to fetishize domestic and daily life while ignoring myths, fears, and symbolic categories that are just as real and decisive as the social structure. The telling of life stories is significant both for what is said and for how it is expressed. They provide a platform for the appreciation of subjective and individual testimonies that reinject emotion into history as a constituent element of social life. Rather than being an impediment to generalization, the individuality of each story documents the construction of consciousness, emphasizing both the variability of experience within the group and the patterns of shared features within the culture.[39] Oral history in any of its modalities is equally shaped by reality and fantasy, by the conscious and the unconscious mind. It exposes omissions, reinterpretations, the displacement of events, the dramatization of some incidents, the condensation or elision of others, and the distortion of emotional elements. This does not mean that these narratives are false, though. Their value is in the light that they throw on the past and in the meaning that they attribute to it as interpreted from the perspective of the present.[40]

Biographical narratives expose the interaction between collective cultural traditions and the life of individual participants in those traditions. The role of tradition is particularly important with respect to the individual and collective memory of minorities and culturally oppressed groups. Traditions come alive in the context of autobiographical narratives like that of Juan Gregorio Palechor. In these narratives, traditions are shown to actively contribute to the consolidation and maintenance of a sense of belonging. To minority groups excluded from the collective mythology of the majority, strengthening their own sense of themselves is a survival strategy. Their group traditions validate the past and provide a source of strength for meeting the challenges of the present.[41]

This is true not only for the minority indigenous cultures of Colombia. It is also the case among groups who migrate to more industrialized countries and even among demographic majorities who have been politically and culturally marginalized, as in the case of South Africa. For example, Bill Nasson studied the death of Abraham Esau in that country at the hands of Boers. Esau was a pro-British black leader in the 1901 Anglo-Boer War.[42] His life story became part of a collective "myth" of resistance and patriotism in the Calvinia area, and his symbolic importance grew with the racist domination of the country by Afrikaners and Boers in the postwar period.

Influential works about autobiographies and life stories have criticized official and monumentalist metanarratives that give place of privilege to illustrious, exemplary, and heroic individuals while excluding everyday people.[43] They question traditional historiographic practices and favor a social history that makes more room for those human categories or groups insufficiently familiar to or previously ignored by those who produce our societies' historical narratives.[44]

Many of these critical authors are enthusiastic about studying social conflict and people who make up subaltern social groups, and they promote the use of newly available sources or ones not previously consulted.[45] They are inspired by the works of historians such as Le Roy Ladurie in his work on Montaillou, Natalie Davis on Martin Guerre, and Carlo Ginzburg on Menoccio. Thanks to what we learn about the lives of the marginal individuals explored in these works we are introduced to new facets of the mindset prevalent in different historical periods.[46] An essential aspect of these works is that in addition to factual events, the individual and collective oral sources of these histories discuss cultural representations and meanings.[47]

There is an important ideological element to the oral history presented in this book. From the very beginning of Palechor's narrative there is no doubt that he was addressing a broad and diverse public—both indigenous and nonindigenous—the latter being a group that constitutes an "other" with whom the indigenous have experienced ruptures and confrontations, and in relation to whom they have experienced dependency and subordination.

Reality, Experience, and Expression: The Authorship of Oral Histories

In studying narratives and oral histories, some anthropologists have stressed the distinction between reality and experience. Inspired by Wilhelm Dilthey and John Dewey, they propose that social scientists study the recounting of lived experience and they point to the distinctions between reality, subjective experience, and the recounting of that experience.

Multiple distinctions are exemplified in life stories, says Bruner: life as it is lived (reality); life as it is experienced (experience); and life as narrative (expression).[48] Expression—embodied in this case through narrative—is not equivalent to reality. The two phenomena diverge and there is even tension between them.[49] A narrative life story or autobiography is a symbolic expression of lived experience. The researcher and the reader must take into account that this expression is influenced by the circumstances within which it is produced. This includes the social and cultural context as well as the entirely personal circumstances and expectations of the person who generates the narration. In this sense, life stories are more than a simple reflection of the culture. As Bruner says, every narrative is an interpretive exercise comprised of units of meaning extracted for subjective reasons from the continuity of life and the stream of memory.[50]

Sarah Lamb, on the other hand, questions the distinction made by some academics between life as representation and as lived experience.[51] She considers the recounting of a life story to be part of lived experience since the act of retelling is itself lived, at least while it is taking place. On the other hand, she supports the distinction between reality and narrative. She says that a life story as it is related must not be interpreted as a direct and objective recounting of events occurring in the past: "A life story cannot be taken to be a direct, objective account of actual events that happened in the past: we cannot assume there is a transparent reality external to the story that the story simply mirrors."[52] Whereas history often implies a verifiable recounting of information about the past, life stories convey meaning through a creative retelling.[53]

Of course every memory is "inherently revisionist, an exercise in selective amnesia."[54] The important thing is to realize that memories are narrative constructions whose logic is similar to that of fables. Memories that can not be discounted as "false" may often glorify the past, illustrate cultural and personal values, and reveal archetypes. This is not to say that they obscure reality. On the contrary, they help us to understand "the symbolic categories through which reality is perceived."[55]

Interpreting this kind of autobiographical narrative poses conceptual and methodological problems, but recognizing these problems should not be confused with skepticism toward verifiable knowledge. They are problems inherent to any attempt to understand other individuals and social groups and must be confronted.

In this sense the autobiographer cedes the role of a faithful and reliable witness and sets out to establish an ultimately unattainable identity. The reader in turn is an interpreter rather than a verifier of the data that the author presents.[56] In other words, the author of an autobiography engages in an act of self-creation that entails the demand that someone play the role of reader. Elizabeth Bruss and Philippe Lejeune describe this creative act as requiring an "autobiographical pact" under the terms of which the identity of the author, the narrator, and the protagonist coincide.[57] Finally, Eakin refers to the cognitive capacity required to produce autobiography as an act of "self-invention" practiced first in life and subsequently formalized in writing.[58]

It is common for analysts to describe problems associated with researchers' influence over their subjects. This was mentioned above, but it is worth reiterating the difficulty implicit in the narrative autobiography given that it represents a simultaneous dialogue among different subjects.[59] The individuals actually engaged in conversation are accompanied by a broad spectrum of social, cultural, and individual conditions that are established in the exchange between them but that do not end there.[60] The words and expressions that make up the narrative transcend the exchange of the interviewer and the interviewee, the anthropologist and the indigene. The terrain defined by autobiographical expression is shared by the speaker and his or her interlocutor in a much broader sense than in the usual, simpler narrative framework.

Mikhail Bakhtin provides guidelines for exploring the limitations of autobiography without succumbing to the reductionism of simply distinguishing between the objective and the subjective.[61] First of all one must consider the distinction between the author as the producer of the narrative and the author as a person. A certain structural inadequacy of the genre does not permit the author as a person to fully establish his or her own image. This helps explain the complex cognitive nature of the autobiographical enterprise. There is never full correspondence between the active ego and the external signs that it generates. At the same time, consciousness of self is possible only by contrast, since polarity is an intrinsic characteristic of language itself, determined by the social and cultural context.

Georges Gusdorf argues that just as the past can not be reconstructed as it once was, neither can autobiography objectively re-create it. Nevertheless autobiography provides a truer reading of human experience than does a mere recollection of events, because in writing an autobiography one gives expression to the consciousness of that experience. Gusdorf maintains that autobiography is never a fixed image or the immortalization of an individual life because the human being is always under construction, always a work in progress.[62]

Debates on Technique in Life Stories

According to Richard Werbner, many authors of life stories tend to produce a kind of self-centered confessional literature focusing on the protagonist as antihero, fugitive, or "eternal other." Unfortunately, he says, many of these works lack social resonance due to their excessive focus on the individual. He calls for a new kind of biography that would illustrate how the lives of multiple people come to be intertwined, and proposes a social form of biography that would take contexts and social processes into account and establish a dialogue among several people in a "narrative of narratives." This approach would require attention not only to what is said but also to what is suppressed, what is implicit, what is taken for granted, and even to the most spontaneous expressions in routine discourse.[63]

But it is not enough to juxtapose perspectives and counterpose narrative voices. The interpretation and analysis by the biographer must take place in what Bakhtin calls the "micro-dialogue" that is produced as all the different voices constantly attend to, interrogate, and reflect off one another.[64]

There is a technical criticism to these kinds of narratives: causality can not be established because one can not generalize from individual cases. Thus verification, reliability, and generalization seem to be the critical issues in determining the usefulness of personal narratives. As case studies in which particular individuals define their relationships, conflicts, and interpretations of events, they do not follow schematic structures that allow for easy comparison. Nevertheless, it is possible to reach generalizations on the basis of these works by making the additional effort required to identify comparable variables and examine narrative structure to find common elements and correspondence among the juxtaposed perspectives and counterposed voices.

Although making statistical inferences based on life stories is as problematic as it is with all case studies, some researchers have noted that more scientific discoveries have in fact been made by intensely observing specific cases than by applying statistical analysis to larger groups.[65]

Many studies have demonstrated that the biographical approach is gaining adherents as a method that gives voice to subjects. It is "especially useful as a means to restructure the overall practice of sociology," whose primary objective is not to demonstrate that certain phenomena obey the physical laws of nature, but rather "to elucidate in a sustained and progressive fashion the historical process with respect to social relations."[66]

Autobiography and other self-reflective works have often been seen as threatening the ethnographic canon due to their explicit attack on positivism. As Judith Okely says, "The reflexive 'I' of the ethnographer subverts the idea of the observer as impersonal machine."[67] Along the same lines, Alfredo Molano upholds life stories and autobiographies as methods for establishing knowledge with emotional content, made possible by the connection between the interviewer and the interviewee.[68] "Something is created in this relationship, something invisible that isn't arrived at through a process of reflection. It's an emotional component, a relational channel between two people that permits one of them to say things to the other that can't be said with words alone."[69]

Life stories and autobiographies can not be evaluated for their effectiveness in establishing causal generalizations, but they can be valued for the help they provide in interpreting information regarding the lives of individuals. As stated above, autobiographies construct an internal reality whose correspondence with external facts is sometimes beside the point. Their interpretation of personal and cultural realities is a source of knowledge in and of itself.

In the case of Palechor, the narrative offers the advantage of establishing a special unity between indigenous and nonindigenous society in Colombia, given that these two social groups are not as separate from each other with respect to contemporary historical processes as is sometimes asserted. At the beginning of this work I pointed out that this is particularly evident in the case of Palechor's autobiography. For example, his vocabulary and his social analysis reflect the fact that in the 1960s and 1970s indigenous leaders adopted the analyses and the language of the political left to demand redress of cultural grievances, including long-standing territorial demands.

Palechor's narrative illustrates that the struggle for cultural recognition produces a political language used to enter into an inevitable dialogue with the broader Colombian society. The development of this language can not be attributed simply to acculturation or cultural loss. That would be a static view of cultures, ignoring their dynamism, their capacity to recognize and adapt to new historical circumstances. Ethnic and cultural continuity is not a timeless repetition of unchanging patterns. As Joanne Rappaport has clearly argued, the demand for recognition of cultural heritage is motivated and expressed in the context of present-day needs. That is why it gives rise to new forms of language, new leaders, and new political demands.[70]

Palechor's narrative reinforces the dynamic vision of culture reconstructed in the here and now, not a relic of its historical origins. A culture is not something fixed, handed down whole, and transmitted as though it were a replica of an older original, says Bruner. On the contrary, if it is alive it is sensitive to context and contains within it the seeds of both change and continuity.[71] In fact, the narrative form itself connects past, present, and future. As Sarah Lamb has said, "How we choose to talk about the past is connected to what we want to work out in the present."[72]

As for the limitations of life stories and autobiographies, it is often said that they present the subject from his or her own perspective, unlike case studies and biographies in which the subject is viewed from the point of view of an external observer. It is also said that the distinction between a life story and an autobiography is that the former is a response to someone else's request while the latter is written on the initiative of the subject himself or herself. But this distinction between life stories and autobiographies is superficial. Both genres are self-contained and fixed in time by language, and in both the individual experiences himself or herself indirectly.[73]

The choice was made to use the autobiographical form for this book, since it reflects the interest expressed by Palechor in retelling the story of his life with certain emphases established in the course of the dialogue between us. Life stories are often understood as serving more specific purposes, to help understand certain phenomena as opposed to others. While this narrative responds to an interest in Palechor's political participation, no attempt was made to limit it to that aspect of his life. The word "autobiography" may be more apt in this case in order to emphasize that Palechor's narrative has been recorded and presented in its entirety.

Another technical difficulty with this kind of narrative is that meaning is lost in the process of transcription, since oral expression conveys a broad set of meanings through contextual elements such as intonation, pausing, volume, voice quality, corporal gestures, positioning, and so forth. According to Paul Ricoeur, when discourse is transformed into text a meaning is established for it, it loses the flexibility of its original dialogic context, and it becomes impenetrable, taking on the form of an ordered, unchangeable, and limited set of component meanings. The text is then available to others only in the same form as it was for those who determined its features. In this sense the text is dissociated from the thoughts and intentions of the author.[74]

But despite these difficulties and limitations, autobiographical narratives and life stories offer us explicit documentary evidence of how in the process of changing their lives, individuals also change the world that others inhabit, making them agents of social change. As subjective documents they show us what the individual in question perceives his or her own impact on the social milieu to be.[75] These narratives are creative acts of self construction and cultural formation through the use of words. They constitute a unique kind of performative act through which a social actor contributes to the creation of meaning in the world he or she inhabits. A person who retells a life recovers some of the substance of his or her own experience in both the immediate and the less immediate past, and reformulates it as a meaningful history. In doing so, says Lamb, and in the process of attributing meaning to the narrative, these people often criticize the broader social and cultural systems that have molded and affected them.[76] The actor reproduces himself or herself in the image of and constrained by existing social forms, albeit redefining those forms in keeping with his or her individual particularities.[77]

The two-faceted nature of reading autobiographies as a way to understand cultural phenomena is evident. As individual and personal texts on one hand and testimonies to culture on the other, they are and remain open to new readings and interpretations.

PART 2

....

Juan Gregorio Palechor:
Between the Community
and the Nation

As with any text reflecting human experience and reflection, Palechor's narration of his life story can be interpreted on different levels and analyzed from different perspectives. In this section I will address only those aspects relating to ethnicity and its affirmation.

Some approaches to the belief systems and behaviors of campesinos and indigenous people reflect an underlying idea that rural ideologies are premodern, that they differ in fundamental ways from contemporary rational thought. From this perspective they are considered nativist or traditionalist. Those who take this approach identify rural ideologies or interpretive systems as obstacles or reactions to modernization or as obstacles to liberating forms of consciousness. They see campesino, ethnic, and religious movements as revivalist, primarily intended to restore tradition. These movements are interpreted as nativist to the extent that both their ideological underpinnings and the means that they adopt to achieve their goals depend to a great extent on the invocation of a cultural or religious heritage sometimes called *syncretic*.

Those who take these approaches are faced with the conceptual challenge of separating and excluding processes representing both cultural heritage and cultural transformation expressed simultaneously in social practice. In these phenomena, present and past may be linked by an internal logic not understood if practices are reduced to expressions of either traditionalism or syncretism. They also fail to take into account that in these cases the past is not revived. Rather, cultural elements are borrowed from the past and applied in keeping with present-day conditions. As Joanne Rappaport has shown, this is exactly the role played by indigenous intellectuals. Palechor's narrative illustrates that they contribute with their interpretations to creating a relationship between structure and event, between a changing world and a dynamic interpretation of the past.[1]

Kay Warren also explains that "given the Mayan use of history to understand the political-psychology of violence and domination, these flashes represent the reflection of present violence and racism in a past of which the present is a part."[2]

The researcher faces several problems in trying to understand the internal reasoning of the consciousness adopted by rural social movements. As Palechor shows, no clear dividing lines exist between what we call traditional systems of thinking and the more general influence of the national society. Campesinos and indigenous people in a given region share many characteristics, which blurs the line between them. What's more, it is precisely their position as observers and participants and their evaluation of the strengths and weaknesses of the dominant society that provide them with the grounding and the reasoning that inform their political action.[3] In this sense indigenous society is as contemporary as ours, despite the fact that indigenous people affirm their otherness in their relations with us.

In effect, while mestizo[4] campesinos and indigenous people use similar language, clothing, forms of production, and agricultural technology, the two groups differ with respect to their own self-consciousness and self-identification. It is the struggle for recognition of a distinctive indigenous social identity, rather than any specific cultural characteristic, that has brought together native people of different ethnicities (Paez, Guambiano, and Yanacona) in the Regional Indigenous Council of Cauca (Consejo Regional Indígena del Cauca — CRIC) since the beginning of the 1970s. This indigenous identity is a general and diffuse category but as has been noted, national categories have these characteristics, and this identity is no more abstract or diffuse than other identities that we are familiar with in our own society.

Colombia's many indigenous peoples constitute a diverse and heterogeneous minority. The 2005 census counts an indigenous population of 1,392,623 people belonging to eighty-seven different peoples, speaking sixty-four languages, and belonging to fourteen different language families. Cultural variety and geographical dispersion are a particular characteristic of the indigenous situation in Colombia.[5] According to the 2005 census conducted by Colombia's bureau of statistics (Departamento Administrativo Nacional de Estadística — DANE), the total

Colombian population is about forty-three million, so the indigenous population represents 3.43 percent of the total. A little more than half of the indigenous population lives in the country's west and southwest and on the Guajira Peninsula bordering Venezuela, while about a fourth of them live in tropical forests.[6] The largest indigenous group is the Paez, or the Nasa as they call themselves, with about 170,000 people. Most of the Nasa live on lands that have been recognized as indigenous *resguardos*[7] since colonial times. The next largest group is the Guajiros, who call themselves the Wayúu. The Wayúu are a group of decreasingly mobile pastoralists numbering some 150,000 people who occupy the semiarid lands of the Guajira Peninsula in the north of the country on the border with Venezuela. Another large indigenous group is the Emberá people (forty thousand), who live in the country's northwestern rain forests and in some areas near the westernmost range of the Andes. The Paez, the Wayúu, the Emberá and the indigenous population in the southwestern department (province) of Nariño on the Ecuadoran border constitute nearly half the indigenous population of the country, while the remainder is divided into seventy-eight different groups.[8]

The indigenous population is numerically much lower in the Amazon region, but sixty-two different ethnic groups live there in the departments of Amazonas, Vaupés, Guaviare, and Putumayo[9] and the indigenous population is a significant proportion of the regional total. For example, native people make up 67 percent of the population in the department of Vaupés and 65 percent in Guanía.[10] While these groups share many cultural characteristics, they speak multiple languages belonging to ten different language families and they relate to Colombian national society in many different ways. The linguistic and cultural diversity of the Amazon region is truly exceptional.

Other smaller groups with equally complex cultural systems and relationships with the natural environment also exist. These groups are concentrated in relatively small areas of the country and include peoples such as the Koguis, the Arhuacos (also known as Ijkas), and Kankuamos in the Sierra Nevada of Santa Marta, the Kuna on the Panamanian border, and the Barís on the Venezuelan border. About four thousand U'wa, or Tunebos as they were formerly known, have lived since pre-

Hispanic times at varying altitudes in the Sierra Nevada del Cocuy in the eastern range of the Andes near Venezuela. This group has long been the focus of Catholic missionaries and from 1992 until a few years ago they were at the center of a debate about the right to explore for oil. The state oil company signed a contract with the multinational Occidental Petroleum Company (OXY) to explore in the eastern part of the country, including part of the territory in this area legally recognized as an indigenous *resguardo*. This led to years of contentious negotiations and confrontations between the U'wa and the Colombian state as well as between different factions of the U'wa themselves.

The indigenous question in Colombia, where the indigenous population is a small minority distributed throughout the country, is not just a matter of confrontation between the national state and indigenous people. Above all it is an arena of negotiation, confrontation, and interchange among diverse social actors. It is not restricted to the status of indigenous organizations, which are relatively consolidated today, nor to institutional action, omission, or reaction to different matters, and it is not merely a legal question. In addition to being contested terrain where multiple social actors enter into conflict, the indigenous question is an active arena for cultural creation. It is best understood as a terrain of cultural production that can not be reduced to permanent structural tension between the interests and perspectives of the nation-state and indigenous peoples. In fact, reconceptualizing the indigenous question in Colombia as has been done with respect to other Latin American countries means casting doubt on the self-image to which countries with indigenous minorities often recur: the metaphor of three components, black, white, and indigenous, having been melded into one in a melting pot. This is the metaphorical basis for the ideology of *mestizaje*, the idea that the populations of countries such as Colombia, Brazil, and Venezuela have experienced a socioracial convergence where the great majority is now mestizo, of mixed race. Alcida Ramos has examined the Brazilian ideology of mestizaje in depth through the lens of indigenism.[11]

Challenging the "melting pot" approach in Colombia entails an arduous struggle against conventional wisdom. Those who demand re-

not just a confrontation between state + indigenous groups, but an arena among diverse social actors

this arena is an arena of cultural production

Respect of difference

spect for cultural difference or the particularity of indigenous identity may be called segregationists, isolationists, enemies of progress, or politically dangerous, and to the majority this is only common sense. This majority attitude is shared by the political right and left, by upper and lower social classes, by the highly educated, and by those with little schooling. To confront this approach successfully, those who defend difference must be strong and unrelenting in their organizational process and in the process of cultural production. The indigenous people of southwestern Colombia participating in organizations like CRIC and the Movement of Indigenous Authorities of Colombia (Movimiento de Autoridades Indígenas de Colombia—AICO) have been particularly active in this struggle as have nonindigenous intellectuals from other parts of the world.[12] They have had to reinvent symbolic markers of national identity to generate broad sympathy with their goals, and it has taken a great deal of audacity to struggle for equitable relations and respect between indigenous peoples and the broader Colombian society.

From the beginning of the 1970s, native people and a handful of activists and intellectuals who supported them—several anthropologists among them—were convinced that the struggle to deepen Colombian democracy required granting special rights to Amerindians.[13] But the struggle to improve the condition of indigenous peoples meant convincing many others that more was at stake than social justice. The interests and aspirations of a wide variety of social sectors converge in the debate over the role of indigenous peoples, requiring the construction of new representations and interpretations, the readaptation of language and expression, and the appropriation of political capital jealously guarded by the Marxist left, despite the strongly worded objections of this ideological sector. This is the terrain where struggles over cultural politics take place.

Thanks to the existence of this broad-based struggle over cultural politics, it was possible for just two indigenous representatives among the total of 72 representatives elected to the National Constituent Assembly that produced a new Colombian Constitution in 1991 to win the inclusion of a series of provisions that satisfied deeply felt wishes expressed over decades of struggle. And as important as these constitu-

confrontation w/ majority "melting pot" view ↓

to create respect for difference required

broad-based struggles/ appeals to many actors

tional provisions have been, their effects are conditioned by the existing social dynamics, which in turn give rise to new challenges.[13]

The first organization to fight for the indigenous cause in recent times came into being in the department of Cauca among the Paez, the Guambianos, and the Yanaconas. The Regional Indigenous Council of Cauca—CRIC was founded in 1971 with the slogan "Land and Culture." The existence and the activities of CRIC have been the principal inspiration for the repositioning of the ethnic question in Colombia, a complicated and often cruel process that has cost the lives of hundreds of social leaders.

The indigenous movement brought about changes to the national legal framework through decades of demands, debates, organizing, and mobilization in which indigenous people, political activists, and intellectuals worked together. These changes came into being in the context of increasing indigenous mobilization throughout Latin America at the beginning of the 1970s.[14] The movement's success was due to the work of local and regional organizations through which outstanding individuals like Juan Gregorio Palechor were able to formulate a general framework for struggle on the basis of local grievances. They gained national and even international visibility thanks to a process of active cultural production in which they constructed a political imaginary that made sense to nonindigenous population sectors. A sufficient number of nonindigenious people recognized in the language used to express ethnic aspirations a means to express their own wishes to deepen Colombian democracy and their own ideals of cultural resistance. This made it possible to place respect for cultural diversity on the political agenda. Beyond establishing a dialogue with state agencies and making specific demands, indigenous activists struggled for the representation of cultural difference and likewise over symbolic structures and forms of social classification, as Bourdieu called them.[15] This meant modifying the categories of indigenous self identification and influencing the understandings, perceptions, and attitudes of others. As Virginie Laurent put it, broader changes in the representations of power underlie struggles over identity.[16]

Colombia's 1991 Constitution recognizes the country's cultural diversity, and with its passage indigenous people were granted specific rights to land, education, health services, cultural practices, legal jurisdiction in their territories, and language use. Most important though, it established "collective rights" for "collective subjects" as described by Esther Sánchez.[17] As the body charged with enforcing these provisions, the Constitutional Court has repeatedly ruled that the requirement to respect these rights "overrides and takes precedence" over any legislation that may conflict with it.[18] Nevertheless, these special rights have been implemented unevenly due to indigenous groups' disparate levels of organizational capacity and capacity for action, differences in local situations, and the many interests at stake in different cases. Joanne Rappaport also points to the tension between two different orientations: the push for autonomy and the emphasis on cultural difference.[19] But, she says, actions favoring the two positions should complement each other when indigenous groups adopt a pragmatic approach that considers more than just tradition, taking into account the many conditions and influences that impact their local communities. Rappaport shows that the cultural constructs of intellectuals who emphasize cultural difference and those who focus on sovereignty or autonomy are operationalized in local politics when pragmatic leaders like Palechor act on the realization that they must find a balance between affirming cultural difference and recognizing the heterogeneous reality of their communities. Under these circumstances, they engage in complex negotiations in which they take on state functions while protecting difference. For example, they may be responsible for imparting justice or protecting territory, for overcoming differences between native people who practice Catholicism and those who practice other religions, or for finessing the relationship between the indigenous cosmovision and the presence of armed groups. These complexities illustrate the multiple circuits with which native peoples engage when they relate to the state and the dominant society, a circumstance that calls for the translation and strategic adaptation of concepts and strategies deriving from the dominant society.

Jean Jackson argues that the turn toward the discourse of rights in three senses—the right to have rights, the right to participation, and the right to difference—has made it possible to avoid a rhetoric of exclusion.[20] The demand for the right to difference allows for a heterogeneous, flexible, and expansive definition of rights, while at the same time bringing into focus the tense relation between certain "basic" human rights of the individual—such as the right not to be tortured—and the right to culture and to difference.

For all of the above reasons, the fact that the 1991 Constitution affirms Colombia's identity as a pluriethnic state and calls for the adoption of special rights does not imply that these issues are settled. On the contrary, the legal norms attest to the contested state of the current cultural struggle, including the absence of an unachievable all-round consistency. The multiplicity of convergent and divergent actors makes it difficult to sustain what is won at any given time without new conflicts emerging and requiring successive renegotiation.[21] Definitive advances in the field of ethnicity are intrinsically unobtainable due to the many actors involved and the political implications of new paradigms.

Ethnicity as a Social Relation

It has been said that the term "ethnicity," like other such terms referring to social identifiers, has a duality in that it speaks to both familiarity and otherness. The term can be seen from two relatively distinct perspectives: on the one hand as linking identity with characteristics or attributes of a human group; while on the other hand stemming from the notion of relative similarities and oppositions. But even though the term must be understood in a context of relative and dynamic identifications, analysts try to use ethnicities or ethnic categories both as attributes and as analytic concepts.[22]

If we take a relational approach to ethnic identity, the concept can not be explained in terms of cultural continuity since an identity may persist even after a group has lost most of its cultural traditions. Ethnic identity is then manifested in relation to economic, social, and political situations, particularly conditions of domination, marginalization, rejection, and exclusion. If ethnic identity is seen as a set of associated social ties rather than the continuity of cultural practices, it is not surprising that it is strengthened rather than weakened among populations experiencing cultural adaptation. The geopolitical position of the community and the nature of its internal and external social relations and interactions are decisive. Ethnic identity becomes relative and contextual, with unclear boundaries, and it is strengthened by particular social agents and under certain circumstances. For this reason Peter Burke has suggested using the plural term "identities," indicating that even conceptually it is not singular: While we may privilege one identity over others at any given moment, each of us has multiple, simultaneous, fluid, and negotiable identities.[23] Warren similarly proposes an understanding of ethnic identity as "a collage of collective meanings" characterized by internal differentiation and discontinuities.[24]

This understanding of ethnic identity allows the reader of Palechor's text to appreciate the significance of unceasing movement between national and indigenous institutions, the flow of ideas and concepts without regard for artificial barriers, and the considered use of indigenous ethnicity in the context of political struggles. These expressions of flexibility always cause problems for people with purist pretensions. As Warren has shown in the case of the Maya, intercultural strategies are employed by indigenous groups when engaging in social criticism and participating in social movements. In conforming these strategies, they borrow the discourse of human rights that is heard in the region and the nation, and by interweaving different political and cultural voices they transform what has been borrowed into something new of their own.[25] That's why there was room in the movements in which Palechor participated—and in his narrative—both for leftist discourses and the recognition of and participation in institutional politics.

But there are limits to the demands, actions, and discourses regarding ethnic rights. As we shall see, the most important contemporary limit is the unity of the nation-state.

Ethnicity as a "set of associated social ties"
⌐ Flexible, discontinuous, internal differentiation,
   adaptive, strategic

36 Part Two

└→ borrow national discourse + interweave diff. cultural +
   political voices. (subversive).

The Limits of Diversity and Ethnic Recognition

In her 2002 lecture "*Los dilemas del pluralismo en Brasil*" (The Dilemmas of Pluralism in Brazil), Ramos proposed indigenism as a concept that helps to explain the relationship between indigenous and national societies in Latin America.[26] Her approach is worth examining since in Colombia the term "indigenism" is understood in a much narrower sense. To Ramos, indigenism is that set of ideas and practices that relates to the incorporation of indigenous people into the national state.[27] In this sense, indigenism includes not only the actions of the state itself, but also the copious production of images and practices by the national population regarding indigenous people. These images can range from romantic imaginaries of pure and childlike natives to representations of threatening savages, each version with its related practices.

This use of the word describes a much more complex relation—one rife with contradictions—than the way it is used in Colombia to refer merely to institutional policy toward indigenous societies. In Colombian usage, indigenism is a result, an ideological construct in which indigenous and nonindigenous members of national society participate, including those who represent institutions and those who represent everyday people. In her view, this construct is characterized by the interplay of multiple and counterposed factors with respect to the breadth of relations affected by "interethnicity." It is a field of ethnically charged political struggle in which the participants, by definition, include the entire nation.

But not everyone participates in the same way. In her essay, Ramos says that Brazilians promoting the country's national character posit territorial and linguistic unity as markers of Brazilian nationality, and she adds a third marker: the supposed equality resulting from the combination of three "races": black, white, and indigenous. Thus, the first product of the Brazilian state's indigenism is the "fiction"—Ramos's word—of a happy outcome resulting from the fusion of the three races. This fiction has undergone transformations—as do all fictions that are maintained because people wish them to be true—and in order to be maintained it must continue to change with circumstances. But it has also been confronted, challenged, and resignified because it exists and functions not in a social vacuum but among social agents with contradictory visions and interests. And incessant struggle over those divergent visions and interests frequently lays bare the slippery ground on which the fiction stands.

Ramos gives examples of institutional and other actions in Brazil to maintain the fiction of racial homogeneity and to smooth over the many contradictions to which it gives rise. For example, throughout the twentieth century the Brazilian state formulated integrationist policies and promoted integrationist images that transparently posed racial "whitening"—the dissolving of separate ethnicities into a homogeneous national category—as the desired result of social fusion, as if to say that there could be pluriethnicity without any apparent ethnicities. But at the same time, the state was promoting and implementing strong segregationist policies in indigenous territory such as the long-standing policy of state tutelage and protection of indigenous people, held to be necessary due to their social deficiencies. While assimilation was promoted in the name of liberality and "emancipation," missionaries and other forces promoted confinement, vigilance, and control. This contradiction was evident on a popular level as evidenced by the use of an expression to the effect that one's (native) grandmother had been roped and brought in from the wild, a way to jokingly claim indigenous ancestry, but comfortably remote in time.

To further complicate the question of pluriethnicity, the challenge put forward by indigenous movements was strengthened by the support of other social sectors in the 1980s. Indigenous movements in Brazil—and I think this is true for most Latin American countries—took advantage of a new political situation in which their demands were heard to greater effect in local and international contexts. I have argued that the indigenous movement in Colombia had been able not only to translate its territorial demands into the focus of a new ethnic identity, but also to leverage those demands as a bridge between local and global politics.[28] The idea of territory allowed for the transformation of the practical subsistence needs of specific groups into symbols of struggle that were effectively communicated among different indigenous organizations and on the world stage. Palechor was particularly effective in this framework given his multicultural approach to indigenous struggles and his ability to move between his community and the nation. New indigenous leaders today are seeking their own symbolic means to reaffirm and expand indigenous rights. As we shall see, one way of doing this is to bear witness to acts of violence suffered by native people in recent years as a result of increasing confrontations between guerrillas, paramilitaries, and the state.

Ramos demonstrates that indigenous movements in Brazil successfully appealed to government concern—largely during the military dictatorship—for its international reputation with respect to protecting human rights. There as in Colombia, nongovernmental organizations served to link local demands with the interests of international actors at a given moment. In the past few decades, indigenous movements in different countries have gained constitutional recognition, which while important is only a first step toward the broader political and symbolic relocation of indigenous society within each national state. Having achieved this first step, indigenous movements continue their arduous work toward further political and cultural affirmation. But the question remains: Given this trajectory, why is pluralism still on such slippery ground, plagued with ambiguities and contradictions? Is the structure of interethnicity described by Ramos specifically Brazilian, a unique product of the relationship between Portuguese conquerors and the founders of the new Brazilian nation? Or notwithstanding the undeniable particularities of Luso-Brazilian history, are the dilemmas of pluralism intrinsic to the structure of the modern nation-state?

In his book *Culture as Praxis* Zygmund Bauman maintains that "the unyielding ambiguity of the concept of culture is notorious" and proposes that the fundamental ambiguity of the concept reflects the ambivalence of modern existence.[29] Specifically, he says, the idea of culture is a historical invention, driven by the necessity to assimilate a particular historical experience. Nevertheless, culture is proposed as a "universal feature of human beings."[30] It is supposed that while culture is a universal condition common to human beings at all times and in all places, it distinguishes individual groups from all other groups. According to Bauman, this conception born of European modernity is a historical trade-off. It increases the freedom of humankind as the creator of the world but also imposes the "necessary" restrictions, constraints, and limits implicit to belonging to a particular culture, as well as those that stem from social relations themselves.

This ambiguity extends to the question of whether to accept the freedom of others to be what they are. At the beginning of the twentieth century, H. G. Wells asserted that "those swarms of black, and brown, and dirty-white, and yellow people" who did not meet the modern need for efficiency "will have to go,"[31] and few would dare to go as far as Nietzsche in revealing an unambiguous double standard when he said that "the great majority of men have no right to existence, but are a misfortune to higher men."[32]

A less crude but no less revealing take on the paradoxical nature of culture is well known to anthropologists as a result of the long and ongoing debate over cultural relativism. To what extent should the cultural practices of human groups be relativized, and what limits to relativism should be recognized? I think that Norbert Elias has some useful ideas about these questions.

In "A Digression on Nationalism: 'History of Culture' and 'Political History,'" Elias describes how the humanist and universalist pretensions of the notion of culture corresponded to the self-image and ideals of the German elite and middle classes in the eighteenth century, and to the role that they attributed to themselves in their view of the development of humankind.[33] While middle-class French and British intellectuals shared the same optimism, they diverged on the concept of culture. These were the ascendant social sectors in Europe, undergoing consolidation under a new political form, the national state. "Culture" was the source and expression of their freedom and a reason to be proud, held up in opposition to the long-standing reign of autocracy. Elias says that when Friedrich Schiller, an important figure in propagating the concept of culture, gave a lecture in a German university in 1789, he indicated with complete confidence that "culture" had progressed.[34] He held up the culture of his time and place against the whole of human history and

Figure 2.1. Juan Gregorio Palechor with his wife and children.
Photo by Libio Palechor.

extolled its progress in comparison with the coarseness and cruelty of life in many simpler societies. With time, and as the new social classes consolidated their political positions, intellectuals no longer included political connotations in the concept of culture, and instead emphasized its nature as the element that particularizes nations. This approach only added to the ambivalence of the concept.

Elias contrasts Schiller's lecture with one given by Dietrich Schäfer on the occasion of his investiture in Jena in 1884, almost one hundred years later, at the same university where Schiller had spoken about the course of human history.[35] Schäfer asserted that in the 19th century, "nationality took the place of humanity" and "the striving for universal human culture was followed by that for national culture."[36] This "nationalization of culture" had many implications, including a new intellectual orientation. Where intellectuals had previously looked to a promising future, they instead turned back toward origins and a heroic past. Culture was now seen as coextensive with the borders of the national state, and like the national state it had pretensions of perma-

Culture changed from a process + progression into the "essence" of a nation.

nence. It no longer referred to a process as it had for Schiller, but to the "unchanging and eternal attributes of a nation."[37] "Culture" was reduced to "national culture" and conceptualized as homogeneous within the nation.

The historical outline provided by Elias helps us to understand the difficulty associated with ethnic recognition in modern Latin American states. It is interesting to note that this reorientation of the concept of culture coincides with the increased importance given to the interests of nation-states, for which nationalist ideologies are fundamental. The assimilation of cultural plurality is intrinsically difficult in the context of nationalist ideology. Managing multi- or pluriethnicity is difficult in a context where universalist or relativist connotations are subordinated to national interests and the state may see cultural diversity as a danger to national unity. This is clear from the resistance that has arisen to every recognition of ethnic plurality in Colombia, whether in relation to indigenous or Afro-Colombian social groups or gypsy communities.

To some authors, such as Francisco Colom, recognizing cultural diversity or multiculturalism is valuable as a rejection of one culture's dominance over others.[38] But if this idea is accepted one has to ask just how far the value of diversity may go: Does it include linguistic pluralism? Gender equity? The political equality of multiple ethnicities? Legal pluralism? Colom maintains that the term "multiculturalism" no longer designates a concrete analytical or ideological corpus, despite the fact that it alludes to cultural pluralism. Perhaps, Bauman proposes, the term is an ambiguous and paradoxical offspring of its parent, the equally ambiguous and paradoxical term "culture."

So struggles for the recognition of cultural and ethnic diversity seem by necessity to be long term. In fact they can be expected to last just as long as the ambivalence of national states toward these goals. This also suggests that the dilemmas of pluralism are the dilemmas of national states, colored in each case by the characteristics of the society in question. Concepts such as indigenism help us to understand these dilemmas, which entail concrete struggles of human groups including people like Palechor, and are much more than abstractions.

Figure 2.2. Juan Gregorio Palechor. Photo from CRIC Archives.

Juan Gregorio Palechor:
Between the Community and the Nation

··

Toward the end of my conversations with Palechor, I asked him why he considered himself indigenous when his group no longer had most of the characteristics that people consider indigenous.[39] He responded: "We fight for our rights as indigenous people because even though we've lost our language we are still protected by our indigenous structures. We're governed by the *cabildo*[40] and we live on *resguardos* . . . Despite having lost customs, we believe that if we don't get organized [as indigenous people] they'll wipe us out. But we want to survive."[41]

The Colombian indigenous movements that arose at the beginning of the 1970s have striven for indigenous groups to form part of the nation while maintaining their cultural distinctiveness. The same approach was taken by Palechor as an organizing principle in his political activism and in his role as a pioneer in the new indigenous organizations. In fact, Palechor's narrative is structured by references to the affirmation and reaffirmation of indigenous identity and to identification with this differentiated group. But ethnic reaffirmation didn't come naturally to Palechor. He underwent a process of struggle to reach this perspective, and his narrative provides a window on his transition from a resident of a remote resguardo, first into a campesino activist and then into an indigenous leader. This meant coming to see his own community in perspective and in relation to regional and national forces and authorities.

The cabildo discussed by Palechor is a body made up of members of indigenous communities that manages the use of land and other resources, resolves internal conflicts, and represents the community in its relations with the nonindigenous world. Its members are designated annually by the people of the community. The origin of the cabildos lies with Spanish colonial authorities who imposed them on indigenous societies as a control mechanism. Despite their exogenous and colonial origins, however, the cabildos have been thoroughly assimilated by indigenous societies, especially in the department of Cauca, which now consider them very much their own. Like the cabildo, the resguardo was an Iberian institution and legal entity that was important in the process of colonization. The resguardo was made up of lands assigned to a community for its use in common and was an important feature of Spanish colonial legislation that sought to protect the supply of indigenous labor threatened with extinction by abuses and expropriations perpetrated by the Spanish colonizers themselves. In fact, the resguardos allowed for the regrouping of the indigenous population and made survival possible for many pre-Hispanic societies. Lands for the resguardo were donated or distributed by the colonial administration, and indigenous groups could also purchase lands that they wished to include. The organizational expression of the resguardo was the *cabildo de indios*.[42] The resguardos and cabildos established by the Spanish were appropriated by native peoples and provided an institutional framework for the recovery of cultural practices and indigenous forms of leadership and the establishment of new forms as they adapted the institutions to changing sociopolitical conditions. CRIC is a good example of this process.

Palechor begins his life story telling us that one of the reasons that he dedicated his life to the indigenous movement was his wish to be true to a family obligation: "I was born in 1923 on the resguardo of Guachicono in the *municipio*[43] of La Vega on the Macizo Colombiano.[44] I don't want to be some guy who likes to brag about himself or his family and the indigenous people of the Guachicono resguardo. I want to tell the truth. And the truth is that I belong to a family, and at this time I belong to the fifth generation on the family tree, what we call the old line of Valerio Palechor."

He goes on to tell us that his ancestor Valerio Palechor was a general in the civil war at the end of the nineteenth and the beginning of the twentieth century (1899–1902) called the War of a Thousand Days, and from that time on the family took a leadership role and was "visible in the community," with a responsibility to their ancestors, and that this "visibility" must be maintained in the present.[45]

According to the historical archives of Cauca, Valerio Palechor could hardly have participated in the 1899–1902 war due to his advanced age at the time. The same sources, however, show him to have been an important leader in the 1830 struggle against the dissolution of the indigenous resguardos of the Macizo Colombiano, the Colombian Massif, and a member of the indigenous cabildo that opposed measures to reduce the size of the Guachicono resguardo (see documents 1–8 in the appendix).

At that time laws had been issued requiring the dissolution of the indigenous resguardos throughout the new republic. The name Valerio Palechor appears on several petitions issued in 1833 and 1834 by the indigenous cabildo opposing the dissolution of the resguardo of Guachicono.[46] These petitions succeeded in postponing the distribution of communally held lands.

As a child, Palechor witnessed a confrontation with mestizos who invaded resguardo lands in a series of boundary disputes that languished in the courts for many years before a final indigenous victory. Perhaps this impressed him with the value of submitting written complaints to legal authorities. In my judgment, several of Palechor's personal experiences contributed in particular ways to him becoming a leader. He often recounted these experiences in our conversations, but his own interpretation of their importance may differ from mine. The first of these experiences was his attendance at a rural school for several years. Throughout his life he lamented his limited education and the inability of his father to keep him in school. Even after he had concluded his narrative, he said half in jest but with a degree of seriousness, "Just so you understand, being denied an education: that's Palechor's anger." But it was also his schooling that opened doors to a broader nonindigenous world, and with time made it possible for him to incorporate his community into a vastly larger political project. I will come back to this point below as an element of his leadership in the indigenous movement.

Military service was another experience that was a rupture with everyday indigenous life and gave Palechor access to the nonindigenous world. Theoretically, service was obligatory for all; but young rural men without material or social resources had no means to avoid it as more privileged Colombians did and continue to do to this day, so that young rural men were and are disproportionately represented in the ranks of the military. Palechor's military service awakened his political consciousness and opened his eyes to many aspects of Colombian national life, but it was a bitter experience full of the humiliation and rejection reserved for those who were pejoratively called *indios*. Many generations of young indigenous men, boys really, had experienced in their military service a sudden, involuntary, and intense initiation into the national culture and its ethnoracial prejudices. The pain of these experiences led to the recent struggle, ultimately successful, to make military service voluntary for indigenous men.

After his experience with obligatory military service and his exposure to life outside the resguardo, Palechor became an active participant in political movements. In the 1940s, he participated in a number of different ways, but always in dissident factions of the Liberal Party, one of the traditional parties in Colombia's two-party system.

Once he finished his military service, Palechor returned to his community and found that due to the limited availability of land within the resguardo of Guachicono, his father had bought a small piece of land in a nearby town as a way out of poverty. Palechor started farming there, and soon married a young mestiza farm girl. He also acquired his own piece of land in La Sierra, a municipio bordering Guachicono. It is common for indigenous families to seek outside land because resguardos are usually located in the steepest and least fertile areas and are too small to meet the needs of their expanding populations. Despite the indigenous population's image of stability and local attachment, they have a long history of mobility that takes them off the resguardos and even to relatively distant areas to settle new lands.

Shortly after returning home, Palechor became an enthusiastic follower of Liberal Party leader Jorge Eliécer Gaitán. In the 1940s Gaitán became a national political phenomenon and wielded tremendous influence. For more than ten years he galvanized millions of Colombians with fiery speeches against the oligarchy and the traditional party leaders, mobilizing and inspiring deep-seated loyalty among the urban and rural middle class and among artisans, small merchants, and campesinos in a country that was then predominantly rural.

Gaitán denounced inequality and called for a society of "small urban and rural property owners who controlled their own labor and the fruits of their endeavors."[47] Gaitán's "impassioned egalitarianism" and his defense of small property rights made a huge impression on Palechor. Although the resguardo is collectively owned, each member family earned its living by farming a piece of land assigned to it by the cabildo, and use rights to that land were generally passed down to the next generation or at least to one member of the next generation given the limited amount of land available within the resguardo and the need to avoid successive fragmentation of family plots.

Gaitán's vision of a society of upright and self-reliant individuals was a good match for Palechor's own ideal, which stemmed from a demanding and austere upbringing at the hands of his father.[48] In Gaitán, Palechor found a leader who vociferously denounced existing social conditions including rural poverty, and who held up the ideal of a society of small producers. Perhaps it was meaningful to Palechor that Gaitán's nickname was el indio, "the Indian," in reference to his lower class origin. Gaitán's influence reached its peak in the 1940s and culminated with his unsolved assassination on April 9, 1948, when he was a presidential candidate thought to have a very good chance of being elected. His murder led to a spontaneous insurrection with particularly grave consequences in the capital city of Bogotá.[49]

The persecution of Gaitán's followers and bloody confrontations between members of the two parties continued for almost ten years, a period known in Colombia as La Violencia, "the Violence." In this difficult environment, Palechor left political activity and dedicated himself to farming his small piece of land and to his craftsmanship, in particular working as a carpenter in La Sierra. But above all, he developed his ability to interpret Colombian law and work as a de facto attorney, an occupation known locally as tinterillo.[50] He litigated small lawsuits and local disputes, some of them regarding sporadic land disputes between indigenous and nonindigenous people, but mostly resolving many small problems that arose among rural inhabitants. To a great extent, this was the source of his prestige in the community.

Palechor began his work as a local political activist with Gaitán. Years later, at the beginning of the 1960s, the violence that had shaken rural Andean zones in Colombia since several years before the assassination of Gaitán finally began to let up, and he became involved in another dissident movement, the Liberal Revolutionary Movement (*Movimiento Revolucionario Liberal*—MRL). He won a seat on the municipal council as an MRL candidate and soon became the MRL leader in Cauca. At this time he made no particular reference to the indigenous problem, focusing his political activity on the problem of rural poverty and the rural population as a whole. "El indio Palechor," as he called himself, was proud to have the ear of political leaders such as Alfonso López Michelsen, who years later would become the president of Colombia. Palechor's affiliation with the MRL is an example of his search for organizational vehicles through which to express his discontent with conditions in rural communities.

The MRL was a dissident movement within the Liberal Party that was formed in 1957 around the figure of López Michelsen, the son of a distinguished Liberal and former president. The MRL survived until 1967, when it dissolved into the Liberal Party during the government of President Carlos Lleras Restrepo. The movement "was mostly composed of young people who were anxious to get started in politics and who agreed with its legal objections to some of the changes that the Conservatives had imposed in the agreements establishing the National Front."[51] The National Front was the name given to a political agreement signed in 1957 between the leaders of the two traditional parties, the Liberals and the Conservatives. The goal of this political pact was to end the bloodletting of the interparty confrontation that had led to thousands of deaths between 1946 and 1957 and that had devastating consequences for the country, particularly in rural areas east and west of Bogotá.[52] According to the agreement, the two parties would share all political positions equally and would alternate in the presidency for sixteen years. López Michelsen objected to this last provision on the basis that the enforced alternation in power was a denial of the people's democratic right to freely elect the president. The movement gained strength and eventually took up the call to fight against social inequality.

Many popular leaders, including Palechor, felt betrayed in 1967 when López Michelsen dissolved the MRL, merged his followers into the Liberal Party, and entered into a bipartisan government. For Palechor and some of the others this was the moment when they would distance themselves once and for all from the traditional parties. But the defense of ethnic identity would only gain force with the growth of indigenous movements in the beginning of the 1970s. That's when Palechor enthusiastically embraced ethnic identity as an organizing principle in defense of the resguardos, which were threatened by modernizing tendencies within the central state.

The late 1960s and early 1970s were turbulent times. Irregular armed groups that had formed during the interparty conflict known as La Violencia were still not completely suppressed, and new Marxist guerrilla groups were established. Campesinos mobilized to demand land and occupy rural properties, defying a timid and limited agrarian reform program.[53] Though discouraged by the failure of the MRL, Palechor joined the organized campesino movement and was soon part of the departmental (Cauca) leadership of the National Association of Campesinos (*Asociación National de Usuarios Campesinos*—ANUC). Soon a group of ANUC leaders, supported by intellectual activists, recognized the need for an autonomous indigenous voice, and the independent indigenous organization known as the *Consejo Regional Indígena del Cauca* or CRIC was established as a union of cabildos from different areas and ethnicities in Cauca.[54] According to the booklet "Spreading the Word of the Congresses of the Regional Indigenous Council of Cauca, February 1971– March 2009" [*Caminando la palabra de los Congresos del Consejo Regional Indígena del Cauca CRIC, febrero de 1971 a marzo de 2009*], CRIC was established in Toribío, in northern Cauca, in February 1971 at a congress of more than two thousand indigenous Paeces and Guambianos meeting to defend their rights. "The tasks of the new organization," they declared, "are to reclaim land and strengthen the culture. . . . Soon thereafter," said the booklet, "the *terrajeros*[55] of Jambaló and Toribío decided to stop paying *terraje*,"[56] which elicited an immediate reaction from local authorities and led to the jailing of two of the indigenous leaders and of Gustavo Mejía, the peasant leader behind the strategy.

The *terraje* was the obligation of landless indigenous people to pay the landowner for the right to live on and work the land by providing labor and turning over a portion of the harvest. This payment was the greatest source of anger for those who formed the new organization and the call for its nonpayment was one of the first steps undertaken to counter the power of hacienda owners. Indigenous leader Lorenzo Muelas dedicated the first two chapters of his memoirs to this humiliating, servile institution and held it up as a symbol of the usurpation of indigenous lands.[57] In the chapter "How the Whites Appropriated the Land for Themselves and Made You into Terrajeros," Muelas speaks directly to the indigenous population, recounting the process that began in the nineteenth century: "[The whites] expanded their pastures and increased their livestock; they seemed to own the land; it was like the land then belonged to the whites and not to you; they didn't let indigenous people farm; then they couldn't have cattle; then they couldn't have poultry; then they couldn't have sheep. Then the situation got really bad . . . our life was over."[58]

Palechor joined CRIC at its Second Congress in late 1971 held in the rural settlement of Susana in the municipio of Toribío. The cabildos that met at this congress reformulated the seven-point program and established an executive committee as the highest decision-making body of the organization, a structure that continues to the present. Palechor was named secretary of the organization due to his reading and writing ability and his prestige as a leader in the Guachicono region in southern Cauca. He continued to be a member of the executive committee, serving as treasurer or secretary until the Fifth Congress in 1981.

Beginning with the 1971 Congress, CRIC began to consolidate its position as a coordinating body of indigenous authorities from each of the resguardos and cabildos. Activists from CRIC also established new cabildos or reestablished ones that had been dissolved where resguardos had been abolished over the years for various legal reasons. The organization increasingly stressed explicit, organic indigenous identity as its reason for being and crystallized its demands under the generic slogan "Land and Culture." According to the CRIC Handbook, its points of struggle were land, economy, culture, education, governance, and autonomy. With this orientation, CRIC organized the recovery of former resguardo lands in Cauca held by hacienda owners and the Catholic

Church. It called for changes to indigenous education, and demanded respect for native languages and the end of humiliating and unjust obligations that tied indigenous people to haciendas in the region.[59]

In 1972, Palechor had an opportunity to advance in the organization when the central government's statistical agency DANE set out to conduct the country's first indigenous census. This project offered an opportunity to travel around indigenous areas throughout Cauca to organize gatherings and discussions. A short while later, an ombudsperson charged with overseeing agrarian issues (*procurador agrario*) reported on inadequate access to land in northern and eastern Cauca and the Ministry of Government along with INCORA (*Instituto Colombiano de la Reforma Agraria*), the government agency in charge of agrarian issues, made a commitment to resolve land conflicts in various resguardos in the northern part of the department.[60] Soon after it was established, CRIC initiated a movement to organize indigenous communities beyond the department of Cauca and throughout the country. In 1982, CRIC and several other regional indigenous organizations established the National Indigenous Organization of Colombia (*Organización Nacional Indígena de Colombia*—ONIC).

The largest indigenous ethnicities of the Andean region of Cauca participated in CRIC from its founding, including the Paeces, the Guambianos, and the Yanaconas, as did other peoples such as the Coconucos.[61] The organization was not identified with any of these groups in particular but with a generic indigenous identity. Ethnic identity was assumed not to stem from any differentiated cultural characteristics in particular but from the consciousness of political and social domination shared by all indigenous groups. The dividing line between indigenous and nonindigenous was not the retention or loss of territory or language, nor the adoption of Catholicism. As Guillermo Bonfil Batalla has written, indigeneity reflected the re-creation of a distinctive group identity rooted in a cultural tradition—albeit modified by contact with the colonial system—and incorporated questioning this group's subordination.[62]

The modern indigenous mobilization is not a romantic effort to revive an extinguished past, nor is it traditionalist in the strict sense of the term. This may be what distinguishes today's indigenous movements like CRIC and ONIC from prophetic millenarianists, individuals or groups who see themselves as divine instruments embodying the voice of tradition and a coming restoration of indigenous culture.

The contemporary orientation of the movement led to an indigenous presence at the national constituent assembly of 1991 and in the Colombian Congress after that year's adoption of the new constitution, and in general to participation in national politics. Palechor's life experience gave him privilege of place in the new movement, constructed as it was over socially contested terrain with the participation of a multiplicity of agents and voices that could not be reduced to the formula "indigenous tradition" versus "modernity," a distinction discussed by Terence Turner with respect to the representation of indigenous people in videos.[63]

The regional organization gradually gave way to more complex national organizations and leadership structures. Its demands became more political and less local, and the first generation of leaders composed of people like Palechor was replaced with new figures. National and international nongovernmental organizations played an important role in this process. They provided fairly substantial resources and an incentive to supplant older leaders with younger ones who were even more skilled at building relationships with nonindigenous people.[64] Like other indigenous leaders, Palechor was a transitional figure for the movement between the rural, isolated base from which he emerged and the national political arena.

To many within CRIC, the beliefs and leadership style of first-generation figures came into conflict with other figures in the broader indigenous movement, and there was disagreement with their interpretation and implementation of tradition and their style of indigenous politics. Nonetheless, Palechor stayed in CRIC and eschewed factionalism up to his death. He exemplified the transition of rural Colombian society and was in this sense a liminal figure moving between separation and incorporation as defined by Victor Turner.[65] He stood on the threshold between two political eras and their corresponding cultural styles of doing politics.

Cauca, the Resguardo of Guachicono, and Indigenous Movements

Palechor was from southwestern Cauca in southwestern Colombia, home to several thousand indigenous people who call themselves Yanacona. Most Yanacona live in areas held in common called resguardos (see map 2.1).

The native language in this region fell into disuse more than a century ago, and as I have noted, the indigenous population is similar in many ways to the mestizo campesinos in the area. Nevertheless, the community actively and explicitly identifies itself as indigenous and the primary characteristic by which they distinguish themselves from mestizos is that they live on collectively owned land under an organizational form historically associated with indigeneity.

Palechor was born on the resguardo of Guachicono, located on a large massif in the Central Range of the Andes known as the Macizo Colombiano. The first contact between the indigenous people and Spanish colonizers in this area was in the sixteenth century. By the seventeenth century, the population had declined so dramatically that the area was repopulated with the offspring of the few surviving natives and indigenous people imported from other provinces by the colonial administration.[66]

The Cauca region grew in prosperity and influence during the second half of the eighteenth century thanks to gold mining. This expansion coincided with the decline of other gold mining areas, particularly around Mariquita and Pamplona, which allowed for the rise of the western region more generally, dominated by the city of Popayán; and with the economic resources generated by mining, Popayán acquired a significant degree of influence in the colonial world.[67] By the end of the eighteenth century, mining was gaining favor over livestock production as an economic activity and mine operators had invested in slaves and expanded into the department of Chocó. Since that time, social and political power and prestige have been closely guarded by those who claim

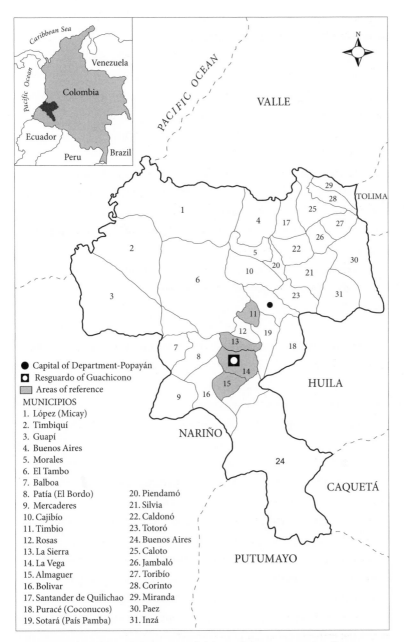

Map 2.1. The political-administrative divisions of the Department of Cauca.

Within the map image:

Caribbean Sea

Venezuela

Colombia

Pacific Ocean

Ecuador

Peru   Brazil

PACIFIC OCEAN

VALLE

N

TOLIMA

HUILA

NARIÑO

CAQUETÁ

PUTUMAYO

● Capital of Department-Popayán
◻ Resguardo of Guachicono
▨ Areas of reference

MUNICIPIOS
1. López (Micay)
2. Timbiquí
3. Guapí
4. Buenos Aires
5. Morales
6. El Tambo
7. Balboa
8. Patía (El Bordo)
9. Mercaderes
10. Cajibío
11. Timbio
12. Rosas
13. La Sierra
14. La Vega
15. Almaguer
16. Bolivar
17. Santander de Quilichao
18. Puracé (Coconucos)
19. Sotará (País Pamba)
20. Piendamó
21. Silvia
22. Caldonó
23. Totoró
24. Buenos Aires
25. Caloto
26. Jambaló
27. Toribío
28. Corinto
29. Miranda
30. Paez
31. Inzá

nobleza de sangre, "purity of (Spanish) blood" in contrast to the indigenous and black population.[68]

Vestiges of these social relations with aristocratic pretensions persist throughout the department of Cauca in rural areas and even in Popayán. Relations are tense between hacienda owners and rural inhabitants who own little or no land, some 150,000 of whom belong to indigenous groups including the Paeces, Guambianos, Coconucos, and the so-called Yanaconas.

The resguardo of Guachicono is located in the municipio of Almaguer, where gold was first discovered in 1551. Just thirty-one years later Fray Jerónimo de Escobar wrote about the importance of the gold deposits in Almaguer, where he estimated that thirty thousand pesos worth of gold were mined each year, and said that at just one mine in the region there were "ordinarily two thousand Indians and Negroes working in the mines, for which reason work crews arrive from other towns."[69] He also noted that gold was being extracted from rich alluvial deposits in the Guachicono River valley (probably the lower valley).

Beginning in the second half of the sixteenth century resguardos were established in the area of the Macizo from donated, distributed, and purchased land. A leader called a *cacique* was assigned to govern each resguardo with authority recognized under colonial law, and he would designate a group of officials whose responsibilities included assigning a piece of land to each indigenous family and the oversight of collectively worked lands.[70] Assigning resguardo lands to the indigenous population kept them tied to agricultural production. Many resguardos did not survive, however, due to the pressure of neighboring hacienda owners or the inability of resguardo properties to provide sufficient support to their growing populations. As a result, many landless natives were forced to enter into exploitative relationships with nonindigenous landowners, the terraje system being one example.

Juan Friede argues that by the time of the mining boom, the resguardos on the Macizo Colombiano were no longer natural concentrations of people native to the area, but of people who lived there as a result of displacement and forced resettlement.[71] In fact, the native population of the area decreased rapidly beginning in the sixteenth century.

17 de julio. POPAYAN

Por primera vez, en la Universidad del Cauca, se oyen nuestras palabras.

Figure 2.3. Closing ceremony of the Third Indigenous Gathering of Cauca held in Popayán. An indigenous organization occupies the main auditorium at the University of Cauca for the first time on July 17, 1973. Photo from CRIC Archives.

Figure 2.4. Poster of Quintín Lame on a school wall in Tierradentro, Cauca, 1976. Photo by author.

Kathleen Romoli points out that while there is little documentation about the conquest of this territory and its original inhabitants, available documents suggest an estimated native population in the midsixteenth century of some forty thousand.[72] There is a record of forty *encomiendas*[73] at that time, six of which had a total of 2,200 adult males.

Documents of the day describe the inhabitants of the Macizo as peaceful, and its conquest did not rise to the level of a war, but the Spanish conducted what were known as "pacification and population" operations beginning in 1551 that led an unknown number of inhabitants to flee, although some contemporaneous sources considered that number to be high. In addition, smallpox epidemics in 1566 and 1588 dramatically decreased the indigenous population in the zone and were decisive in its demographic transformation.[74]

Under the colonial administration, the province had three principal divisions, the most important of them being Guachiconu, which included the Guachiconu, Pansitará, and San Jorge river basins.[75] According to documents examined by Romoli, the inhabitants of the lower Guachiconu and San Jorge basins were of different ethnicities, while the population of the upper Guachiconu and Pansitará areas was homogeneous. The conquistadors brought indigenous people known as Anaconas or Yanaconas to the area of the Macizo from further south. Romoli believed that the number was fewer than is usually reported, while Friede alluded to documents saying that their number was in the thousands. Also contributing to the repopulation of the area were migrations of indigenous people ascending the Andes from the east. One such migration included "1,300 Indians" who settled in Pancitará.[76] In addition, all indications are that there was a long tradition of movement between the Macizo and the Amazon basin.

According to Romoli, all available documentation tells us that the area where the resguardo of Guachicono is located today was populated at the time of the conquest by sedentary, agricultural, semistratified native societies.[77] The conquest led to massive displacements, the relocation of the population, depopulation resulting from epidemics, and the entry of Yanaconas and other indigenous groups. The presence of black slaves in the mines of Almaguer was another demographic change.

This agglomeration of peoples produced an "ethnogenesis," says Franz Faust.[78] The population of people native to the area decreased and merged with migrants of other indigenous ethnicities, adopting cultural elements including the Spanish language, and this newly integrated population came to consider itself Yanacona. This self-designation demonstrates the dynamic nature of ethnic identity, since at the time of the conquest there was no Yanacona ethnicity. The term referred instead to a social category that encompassed landless people of different indigenous origins who worked for the Inca Empire. Many of these people were forcibly recruited to serve the Spanish conquerors as porters and in other capacities.

Like other inhabitants of the Macizo Colombiano, Palechor considered himself Yanacona, but it is not unusual for people in the area to simply call themselves indigenous with no need for further ethnic iden-

Figure 2.5. Palechor addressing a crowd. Photo from Palechor Family Archive.

tification. In his work on the ethnogeography of the region, Faust notes that anyone who lives in an indigenous community where land is held in common is considered indigenous. And the ascription of indigenous identity has played a central role in social mobilization in the defense of the resguardo. The social movement to defend the resguardos entails the mobilization of multiple political resources both practical and symbolic, including legal actions and appeals to ancestral memory. All of these resources operate as means of cohesion and common identification. In Palechor's narrative, it is clear that his interest in public affairs both before joining CRIC and then within the organization revolved around the defense of the resguardo. In this sense he followed the traditional and long-standing form of social action described below.

Identity and the Struggle for the Resguardo

Palechor stresses the importance to indigenous people in the zone of persisting in the struggle to protect the resguardo as a legal form and a protective community, to maintain the indigenous cabildo, and to defend the safeguards provided for in Law 89 of 1890. Faust also points out that since indigenous people do not differ substantially from other campesinos in physical or cultural characteristics, belonging to the resguardo is what sets them apart.[79]

The struggle to maintain special lands for indigenous communities is reiterated time and again in Palechor's narrative and has been documented as a ubiquitous refrain in local history since the eighteenth century. Indigenous resistance coming out of the resguardos of the Macizo Colombiano began as a reaction to laws passed by a newly independent Colombia in the nineteenth century aiming to expropriate indigenous land. The resguardos of La Cruz, Los Milagros, and El Carmen were dissolved and their lands distributed to individual families under these "anti-communitarian" laws in the middle of the nineteenth century (see documents 1–3 in the appendix). In the twentieth century as well, the collectively owned lands of El Rosal and Santiago del Pongo were distributed after Santiago del Pongo had resisted for a full century. Friede's research indicates that sixteen years after the 1927 dissolution of the resguardo, more than half of its resident families had migrated out of the area and lost the land that they had received as individual property.[80]

A delegation of officials visited the resguardo of Guachicono in 1833 to distribute its land to private owners. They counted 437 communal owners and in compliance with a March 1832 law on the distribution of resguardo land, they evaluated its quality and marked off boundaries to divide it into twelve parts. The residents submitted a petition asking for authorities to protect their possession of the land "so that no person may interfere with it" (see document 5 in the appendix). The mayor acceded to the petition but gave each communal owner the possession of his own parcel. Nevertheless, the resguardo was not dissolved. As the mayor of the indigenous cabildo, Valerio Palechor was one of the signatories of the petition (see G9 in appendix). He also signed the 1833 "Petition submitted by the authorities of the San Sebastián, Caquiona, Pancitará and Guachicono indigenous communities to the provincial governor, requesting his intervention to suspend the laws on the distribution of lands" (see document 3 in the appendix). The five generations mentioned by Palechor in his autobiography must have descended from this forebear. Other Palechors also appear in different cabildo documents over the last two hundred years (see documents 1–3 in the appendix).[81]

In the middle of the nineteenth century, Guachicono was part of the canton of Almaguer. The Guachicono River was the northern boundary between this canton and Popayán, and it also bordered on Pasto to the south and Caquetá and Neiva to the east. According to Agustín Codazzi, the regional hub at this time was the "small city" of Almaguer with a total of 21,477 inhabitants who produced wheat, maize, rice, potatoes, sweet potatoes, indigo, flax, coca, cacao, coffee, cotton, and livestock, and manufactured the poncho-like garments known as *ruanas*, as well as rugs, sombreros, saddles, cloaks known as *capisayos*, everyday crockery, and hides.[82]

At that time there were narrow vein gold mines at higher altitudes in Almaguer and an abundance of cinchona trees used to produce quinine. The presence of these trees attracted many bark gatherers, particularly in the Guachi area, who later tried to wrest land away from the resguardo (see documents 9–10 in the appendix).

Between 1850 and 1882, there was a boom in harvesting cinchona bark to produce quinine when external demand for the chemical increased sharply due to the spread of malaria in the United States as well as in Europe and its colonies.[83]

In 1853 and 1855, the resguardo rented to Mr. Manuel Muñoz "the woodlands or cinchona groves on our resguardo within the boundaries attested on our deeds," corresponding to the western boundary of the resguardo (transcribed in the decision of the first instance, First Circuit Court, Bolívar, 1934; see document 8 in the appendix). The resguardo filed lawsuits regarding this boundary in several courts between 1929 and 1937, a history mentioned by Palechor in the section of his memoirs that deal with his childhood (see documents 7–10 in the appendix). The rental of cinchona groves, and particularly their rental to José María and Pedro Parra in 1857, led the cabildo to file a lawsuit in 1867 (see document 4 in the appendix). When the cabildo declined to continue the rental agreement due to what they considered unfavorable terms, José

Figure 2.6. Juan Gregorio Palechor at a CRIC conference with
indigenous representatives from the Sierra Nevada de Santa Marta.
Photo from CRIC Archives.

María and Pedro Parra seized the land by force. The results of this lawsuit were mixed. The cabildo was awarded control over part of the land,
but the quinine extractors were able to continue their operations on
another section of the property. Some of them left the area once the quinine boom abated, but their abandonment of the property was exploited
by third parties who took control of the land. As mentioned above, the
cabildo initiated legal action to recover this land in 1929 and expended
significant resources in airing its complaint before every possible judicial body. As Palechor says in his narrative, the resguardo mobilized its
collective forces in an organized and persistent fashion, going beyond
a purely legalistic approach. Although every court ruled against it, the
resguardo maintained physical possession of the property until their
challengers finally decided to leave the region.[84]

The cabildo's 1929 petition to recover these lands was signed by
Juan A. Palechor (see documents 3–4 in the appendix).

In 1942 Juan Friede found 2,342 indigenous people on the resguardo
of Guachicono and recorded their complaints about the scarcity of land.

Figure 2.7. Palechor and his wife. Photo from Palechor Family Archive.

At that time the Catholic Church was growing wheat on resguardo land and even had two grain mills there. Referring to the indigenous population, Friede noted that "the desperate struggle goes on to hold onto what is left to them of the past: collective property rights on the land that they inhabit."[85] Most of the land was rugged and infertile, sometimes reaching heights of more than 11,500 feet. The continued struggle of the indigenous population to hold on to this land can only be explained, according to Friede, by their extraordinary willingness to work at whatever was necessary to survive in such a difficult environment. Romoli describes the topography as dominated by the huge and imposing hulk of the massif, "from which the jagged mountains multiplied and set themselves apart in frayed lines like some kind of gigantic tassel twisted into stark relief; these enormous peaks and mountainsides seemed to reject the hand of man."[86]

The resguardo is now part of the municipio of La Vega, whose seat is about ninety-five miles from Popayán. Travel from the resguardo to La Vega is difficult and trails within the resguardo are suitable only for travel by animal. The resguardo is comprised of approximately 13,605 hectares of mountainous terrain with a variety of climates due to the altitude ranging from 6,500 to more than 11,500 feet above sea level. Cultivation of coca for commercial purposes began on the resguardo in the early 1980s, seriously affecting structures of authority and consumption habits among the population. The cultivation of certain other crops declined, armed groups entered the zone, and local violence increased. Official action taken against growing coca immersed the region in waves of vengeance and retaliation. But the profitability of illegal crops diminished in the 1980s and a certain amount of aid became available for crop substitution. These factors along with the population's general fatigue brought several years of relative calm.[87] However, this calm came to an end in the first decade of the twenty-first century with a new expansion of coca processing.

The existence of the resguardo as a legal form still provides protections to the indigenous community and its population, but tensions and confrontations between illegal armed groups, state forces, and drug traffickers continue to affect the life of the population.[88]

A Politics of Our Own and the Reinvention of Identity

Before concluding I should say a few words about the reinvention of ethnic identity so well illustrated by Palechor's life story. For a good part of his political life his only focus on indigenous identity was the defense of resguardo lands, although the resguardo itself was being weakened over the course of many years. Indeed, the lack of sufficient land on the resguardo led him to acquire his own parcel elsewhere and he engaged in activities that resembled those of many other campesinos who were local leaders.

At the height of the political movement led by Jorge Eliécer Gaitán, Palechor was a "Gaitanista," a follower of Gaitán. He adopted Gaitán's discourse as his own and incorporated it into his ideal of an egalitarian society where campesinos, indigenous people among them, would be able to live a decent life. Later he affiliated with the MRL, a dissident faction of the Liberal Party, hoping to consolidate a vehicle for political expression outside the National Front, the bipartisan alliance that governed the country between 1958 and 1974.

When the indigenous movement bloomed in the 1970s, Palechor became a full-time activist, finally emphasizing the importance of building, as he would often say, "a politics of our own." The defense of indigenous territory was the core of this politics, whether the immediate goal was to reclaim lost land, expand existing land, or acquire new land. It was the central focus of the movement in both a practical and a symbolic sense. But the idea of defending territory slowly evolved from actions around specific demands to become the core component of a politicocultural ideology. The idea of indigenous territory bridged immediate and global demands, encompassing multiple discourses and traditions, and ethnicity transcended the narrow field of culture to become an expression of a renewed cultural politics.

Palechor's narrative describes the road he took to reassert his indigenous identity, which had been diluted in more generic social demands, and to make it his political identity. We see how local demands were integrated into a new ethnic discourse where the category "indigenous" subsumed the particularities of different native ethnicities. Using Benedict Anderson's expression, indigenous people as a group conformed a new imagined community in opposition to the imagined community of the nation. And this imagined community sought to engage the nation and the state as its interlocutors.[89]

In this sense, Palechor's life story shows how indigenous societies construct contemporary identities incorporating multiple political discourses with varying cultural origins, including the discourse of leftist activists and intellectuals and of the campesino movement. It shows how this new discourse is directed at a national and nonindigenous audience (see document 10 in the appendix), and it illustrates the weaknesses, dilemmas, and contradictions of the new indigenous ethnicity. The new ethnic discourse with its national, global, and integrative approach has appealed to significant numbers of nonindigenous people who have rejected traditional politics and are searching for new political options and ideals, but experience has shown that it is difficult to maintain contact with the needs and aspirations of local indigenous groups. It is hard to find a balance between the national discourse and political participation on the national stage and the participation of local communities and organizations. While indigenous ethnic discourse has had significant national success and many articles of the 1991 Constitution reflect the accumulated demands of the indigenous movement, it is not unusual for local demands to be filtered and mediated by national indigenous organizations and leaders.

But it's important to remember that the indigenous question is addressed in the 1991 Constitution as a result of the indigenous struggle and mobilizations initiated by CRIC in 1971. Thanks to this history, indigenous people had gained organizational strength and presence in the national political imagination and were engaged in ongoing dialogue with state agencies. Special bilingual education programs had been established in indigenous languages several years previously, new laws had been passed for health-care programs specifically addressing the indigenous population, and indigenous people were the recognized owners of almost 72,000,000 acres in the country. By the beginning of the 1990s the demands of the Colombian indigenous movement had produced positive results with respect to the right to cultural difference as a symbolic underpinning for the concept of special rights.

By that time, the new political discourse had found followers among certain sectors of nonindigenous Colombians. Legal structures originating in the colonial period such as resguardos and cabildos still existed in the southwest and had proved to be effective tools that could be extended to all the indigenous communities in the country. In 1991, certain laws were elevated to constitutional principles. At the same time, legal recognition meant taking on commitments to fulfill unfamiliar responsibilities for resource management and developing capacities for negotiation.[90] To some extent it also weakened ties to local communities and compromised capacities for local action. The future of the indigenous movement will depend on how the internal contradictions and tensions of the indigenous ethnicity are resolved and how local and national actors are able to interact.

Palechor's life also illustrates how individuals continually reinvent their individual identities based on their interests and perspectives. There is no intracommunal homogeneity that excludes the individual motivations of social subjects. Ethnicity and ethnic identities are points where individual identities and aspirations converge, where groups and individuals interact to project a continually reinvented "politics of their own."

This approach breaks with a tendency that privileges cultural aspects said to be traditional and underestimates interactions with external forces. From this perspective such interactions are seen as overpowering tradition and indigenous people are schematized as passive victims. This point of view makes it difficult to understand individuals like Palechor, who for different reasons but based on their personal experiences come to know two worlds and manage their lives within both of them. But the historical condition of indigenous societies immersed in national societies as minority groups motivates leaders with multicultural inclinations and characteristics.

As a leader in the south of Cauca, Palechor was decisive in organizing CRIC. His penetrating and lofty rhetoric was reassuring and his experience with the nitty gritty of politics was important for the movement's expansion and consolidation. Throughout CRIC's first decade, he was a central organizer thanks to skills that were highly valued in rural societies: he read and wrote Spanish fluently, he was good with words, he spoke well in public, and he was knowledgeable about national legislation.[91] In his work at CRIC he could not only interpret written documents but also write letters, petitions, complaints, and legal pleadings in support of indigenous petitions. With time, however, nonindigenous "collaborators" came on the scene, usually intellectuals, as did other leaders who were even more skilled in the same areas.

Palechor enjoyed great prestige in the indigenous communities of the south of Cauca, which like many other rural communities operate on the frontier between the worlds of oral and written language. Most residents attend the state school but not many achieve high levels of passive or active literacy. Most important knowledge is transmitted orally and social reproduction is dependent on oral sources and oral communication. While residents have to deal with property titles and other written documents in their dealings with the Colombian world, only a minority have the knowledge necessary to do so independently; most depend on intermediaries. Thus the power to manipulate legal and written language is the power to control social groups.

Writing about the Peruvian Andes, C. I. Degregori says that breaking the monopoly on knowledge is comparable to Prometheus's theft of fire, since a monopoly on the use of Spanish, on reading and writing, allows for the exercise of "total domination."[92] Thus it is not unusual to find the demand for education as a source of liberation or to find that sacred figures choose the written word as the medium by which to declare rights or prescribe behavior. Among the Paeces of Cauca, many indigenous leaders, and most notably Quintín Lame in the early twentieth century, have used the written word as a form of interethnic communication and a vehicle to express their demands and defend their lands.[93]

As Joanne Rappaport has pointed out, several written documents have been central to the political life of the resguardos and to the assertion of resguardo territorial rights.[94] Some groups such as the Paeces have even fetishized the written word, ascribing supernatural origins to their resguardos' written land titles.

The organizations that arose in the 1970s focused on local problems and demands such as respect for indigenous culture in rural schools, against the payment of the terraje to hacienda owners, recovering resguardo lands, and opposing and confronting the power of Catholic missionaries. Palechor highly valued rural schools, even though he attended for a very short time. These schools were highly authoritarian with an emphasis on religion, and they instilled contempt for indigenous beliefs and the indigenous way of life. Nonetheless, Palechor's schooling opened the door to a form of expression that brought him great respect in his community, and with time allowed him to crack open the coded world of nonindigenous society by using the law, one of its own salient elements. In rural Colombian communities there was a long tradition of the self-taught lawyer called a tinterillo, a kind of campesino intellectual who provided a means of official communication between the community and the outside, law-based society, performing functions beyond the ability of the majority. Tinterillos often allied themselves with the power of hacienda owners, merchants, and local political bosses, but in some cases they became dissident political leaders who resisted the established order. Palechor became a tinterillo at an early age and slowly constructed and consolidated his image as an indigenous intellectual and political actor able to move between two worlds. He moved beyond the technical expertise of the tinterillo and beyond his role in local politics to become an activist in defense of ethnic rights when this issue was projected into the national arena.

With time, however, it was just this transitional figure of a storied local political figure prominent among the ranks of the new indigenous leadership that discomfited some within CRIC. For years he was highly respected for his ability to move an audience with long, elaborate, and humorous speeches, to produce needed documents, and to engage in sharp polemics. His ability to express himself helped to consolidate CRIC and to put it on the national stage. Thanks to these abilities, he had the opportunity to represent the indigenous movement on many important occasions. He was particularly proud of a speech he gave to a large crowd in the Plaza de Bolívar in downtown Bogotá in the 1970s at a time when the movement led by ANUC was growing rapidly. Addresses to other campesino organizations, unionists, university students, cabinet ministers, and President López Michelsen added to his fame (see figure 2.5).

Palechor was primarily self-taught. He expanded his knowledge of national issues and developed his own political discourse by reading newspapers and magazines. He was also familiar with Marxist literature and more generally with the leftist discourse of the 1960s and 1970s, but he never affiliated with any overtly political current or group. Over time, his failure to join any one sector of the left attracted a certain amount of hostility from some CRIC leaders and nonindigenous advisers.

During the period of CRIC's consolidation between 1973 and 1979, Palechor displayed decisive qualities including a capacity for hard work and long hours traveling from community to community in the mountains of Cauca, unfazed by threats of violence.

Land occupations were the most common form of indigenous action in those years. This outraged the closed society of hacienda owners in the region, and killings of indigenous leaders were not long in coming. People like sociologists Teresa Suárez and Pedro Cortés who walked the trails of Cauca with Palechor remember that despite the tension generated by frequent threats and by the hostility of local political leaders, and after grueling workdays under conditions that made relaxation difficult, he was able to lift the spirits of exhausted activists with a few humorous comments.

CRIC also had to confront skepticism and even hostility from orthodox Marxist groups who promoted class struggle and belittled the indigenous movement as a backward and nativist approach to social change. But while Palechor flirted with leftist activists and their ideas, he also ridiculed them at times. He got along better with less orthodox intellectuals, who were also welcomed to collaborate with CRIC and who played roles like that described by Ramos in relation to the Yanomami: they stimulated the indigenous imagination, emphasizing an imagined indigenous unity in pursuit of a common consciousness not only within the region but also in the entire country.[95]

CRIC initially directed its demands to local authorities and established itself as a regional body. Once it was consolidated, it sought to expand its influence on the national level (see G11). Indigenous people around the country were contacted and encouraged to establish their own local and regional organizations, which many of them did and which flourished in the 1980s. Despite some internal differences that gave rise to alternative organizations such as AICO, CRIC and its allies successfully established ONIC. ONIC went on to articulate an ethnocultural politics in defense of indigenous rights and was recognized by the state as a voice of the indigenous population.[96]

As a result of this process of national expansion and consolidation, CRIC went beyond Palechor's vision as a self-taught tinterillo to engage in professional legal activities conducted by specialists. Palechor did not live to see a time when the mass media would make indigenous individuals known to Colombians, people such as Lorenzo Muelas at the time of the 1991 Constitution and later Jesús Piñacué as a national senator.[97]

In fact, Piñacué of the Paez indigenous group was a candidate for the Colombian vice presidency in 1994, representing a political movement that resulted from the peace agreement between the government and the former M-19 guerrillas.

Palechor's point of view on indigenous people and his wider political perspective reflected his transition from the context of remote resguardos to that of ethnic politics on the national level. He left his community and took on an ethnically conditioned political identity but was ultimately left behind. As Warren says, ethnicity is by nature contradictory and unstable. The qualities that define it are susceptible to erosion and loss, and it exists in a permanent state of tension, with temporal reorganizations and multiple authorship but little historical continuity.[98]

The strengthening of indigenous land rights in Colombia since the days of Palechor is notable. The Colombian Institute for Rural Development (*Instituto Colombiano para el Desarrollo Rural*—INCODER) indicates that 639 new resguardos have been registered in addition to the fifty-five that were established during the colonial period, and they include a total of 76,600,000 acres. Despite the immensity of this area, it must be said that the vast majority of it is in the Amazon region and outside productive agricultural areas, and that it was legally carved out of *terra nullius* under state jurisdiction rather than from private property. Nevertheless, the cry of the 1970s for "Land and Culture," a goal for which Palechor worked for more than twenty years, has to some extent been realized.

In conclusion, it seems to me that since the contemporary Colombian indigenous movement began in the 1970s, indigenous people have successfully enshrined their image in the portrait of the Colombian people. In order to achieve this they have had to engage in an intense effort at cultural production that allowed, among other things, for a discourse that would speak to Colombians and others of ideals reflecting integrity, spirituality, a connection with the natural world, and participatory democracy. The indigenous organizations that came into being since the early 1970s focused first on local demands: the nonpayment of the terraje to hacienda owners, reclaiming resguardo lands, opposition to the cultural impositions of Catholic missionaries, and respect for indigenous languages in school. But little by little they evolved from local organizations to national organizations with complex leadership structures and international relationships. Their demands became more political and less specific to local conditions, while the work that they did and the goals that they set became progressively broader.

The indigenous question is a vast one in which multiple forces converge and come into contradiction, and in which there are no definitive victories. Nevertheless, indigenous people in Colombia have been catalysts for the creation of new categories of positive identification that strengthen the country's democracy, and they have contributed to a more inclusive understanding of the country's national history. For these reasons the words of CRIC activists Avelina Pancho and Elizabeth Castillo marking the death of Palechor bear repeating: "He constructed a great house . . . open to many inhabitants . . . which is why as his friends we now thank him for his life."[99]

PART 3

....

Juan Gregorio Palechor:

The Story of My Life

Where I Come From: Five Generations
of the Macizo Colombiano and Guachicono

I was born in 1923 on the *resguardo* of Guachicono[1] in the *municipio*[2] of La Vega, right on the Macizo Colombiano (Colombian Massif).[3] It's not like I want to brag about myself or my family and the indigenous people of Guachicono, I just want to tell the truth. And the truth is I belong to the fifth generation on the family tree, on the main line, what we call the old line of Valerio Palechor. All of us Palechors in Guachicono come from this line. Men from this family have been very active as members of the *cabildo*,[4] very reputable and very visible all this time in the progress of the community. Then came their descendants, five generations of them. Very reputable and showing a lot of initiative; progressive and visible in the community.

In the third generation, which was our grandparents' generation, it was important to distinguish yourself in the War of a Thousand Days. As indigenous people we served as colonels, captains, lieutenants, and in many other positions in active service. For those of the fourth generation, when the War of a Thousand Days was over, they filled important positions such as members and governors of the cabildo, and we guarded against the enemy, against mestizos,[5] adamant that they or other people who had nothing to do with the community wouldn't find a way in. And that's why even today there haven't been mestizos slipping into the resguardo of Guachicono, because they acted. And later, in our generation, contemporaries of my own, people from the same generation and the same race hold public office as *inspectores de policía*[6] and mayors. The last one was a mayor who just served the interests of some *politiqueros*.[7] He was completely taken in, docile, but he thought very highly of himself for being mayor. Out of pure ambition, or maybe it was politics, and maybe because of his race, they started to attack him and eventually they drove him out of the mayor's office.

Also there's my friend Moisés Chicangana of Guachicono, an intellectual from the same generation, my race, indigenous. There's been a group of people that've been very active, dedicated to serving the community and very honest.

The Macizo includes a lot of peaks: Narigón, Pelado, the inactive and snowy Sotará volcano, snowcapped Sucubún, and there's a small valley among this cluster of mountains, the valley of the Cajibío River. It's about 20 kilometers long and 5 kilometers wide. This is within the resguardo of Guachicono.

The vegetation in this valley is *frailejón*.[8] Beyond the high point of Pelado, looking from east to west, is the Laguna de la Magdalena, the lake where the Magdalena River is born. One kilometer from there is a rock formation. To the right of this rock formation and the *laguna* is the source of the Caquetá River. Following Pelado off to the right is the *páramo*[9] of Barbillas and a peak called Vellones, the highest point on the resguardo. From there you can see the city of Popayán. After Pelado you come to the Valley of Las Papas, right next to the Laguna de la Magdalena. There used to be frailejón and woody shrubs there, but now it's pasture and livestock.

In the Valley of Las Papas the resguardo of Guachicono borders on the other resguardos: San Sebastián, Pancitará, and Caquiona. To the left of the lake are the mountain range and the Laguna de Santiago (Santiago Lake). Then the Laguna Cusiyaco, and farther on is the Laguna Curvaco. Finally, you reach the Bota Caucana,[10] which borders on the departments of Putumayo, Huila, Nariño, and part of it on Caquetá.

I come from a humble family, an indigenous family dedicated exclusively to farming and to raising animals such as horses, cattle, and sheep, and also pigs, chickens, and guinea pigs. But it was a very isolated life. There was hardly any contact with neighbors or with other indigenous *compañeros*[11] because in those days there was still a lot of land to work. So my dad lived on a pretty big piece of land not close to any other people. He grew a lot of potatoes and corn and raised the kinds of animals I mentioned. But that life was totally, well, let's say very ignorant. My dad never learned any more than just to sign his name; that's all. My mom never attended school at all, not even for a single day. But what stands out about that time is they were upstanding in their dealings with neighbors, very honest and very respectful. And as I say, they were totally dedicated to their work. They never talked about other people or other things.

To me life was very happy in those days, even though I knew absolutely nothing about what they call civilization. There were seven of us with my brothers and my sister, two of them older than myself and four of them younger. We spoke only Spanish, because nobody in the resguardo remembered the indigenous language. Sometimes the neighbors came around when there was farm produce like potatoes. They came to harvest potatoes, to help in the harvest or sometimes to buy potatoes or trade for something. For example, they liked to trade corn for potatoes and since my dad had lots of potatoes, he would trade them. Just talking about this, I can easily remember from my young childhood how my dad grew so many potatoes; he produced so many potatoes that there were two large wooden bins of potatoes and one of them was completely full, and those potatoes lasted nine months in some wooden cribs we called *tabucos*, and sometimes the pressure of so many potatoes, the weight of so many potatoes, damaged or broke those tabucos.

Back at that time there were *mingas*,[12] communal work days. There were mingas of twenty, thirty, forty, up to eighty people. But the way I see it, what's taken over now is the kind of work that's to have money. On those work days, in any case, the landowner had to provide food and pay a small amount for the day's work. Still, people were accustomed to working at mingas, and in that sense it was a paid day of work.

Recognizing the Way of the World and Observing the Weather

I think at the age of two I awoke as if from a dream. One morning, and this will always be a happy morning for me, because I remember that sunlight was coming in through the cracks in the house and I began to wonder about things and study them. That's when I began to be aware of people and things in the world, and I began to think I would have to see a lot more things.

From then on you can say I began to look around, to realize how things were, to see. I saw there were animals. As I said, cattle and horses. I saw there were hens and there were guinea pigs, and this was really interesting. I remember that after five in the morning they would leave us alone, all alone. My mom and dad did physical work, farming that is, turning mountains into farmland, so to speak. My mom would grab the axe, the shovel, or the machete and they went to their daily work to make the land produce. Most of the time my mom and dad did all the work on the farm without anyone working for them. In the meantime we were alone in the house, but as I said I was mostly concerned about seeing the sun.

First I observed the weather very closely. For instance, I liked to find signs to guide me in what kind of weather was coming. As a boy I figured out how to tell in the morning if it was going to be sunny that day or if it was going to rain. I could tell partly from how my body felt and partly, the other thing was by how the first rays of the sun would shine in the morning sky, I mean toward the ground, and I saw that the sun would show if it was going to rain or not that day.

Among the other things I was starting to analyze was that people, that human beings had to concern themselves with work, and I started to realize that people needed something to live on. Then my brothers and sister and I began to imitate how people traveled. We got to pretending we had a caravan of pack animals and we had to arrange their loads. For loads we took some small sacks and filled them with sand. These were the things that helped us to realize, that helped us focus on the need to work if you want to have something to sustain life. But that wasn't enough. We also began to work at small projects. For example I started a garden and planted potatoes. I pretended it was a big garden, but it was only four plants. But I enjoyed it and I began to get interested in growing food and that was useful, even if it was just to roast a few potatoes or eat them in a soup or whatever. That would have been when I was about five years old, before I went to school.

Life on the Resguardo

My grandfather fought in the War of a Thousand Days.[13] He talked about what happened in the war, how the different people acted. One group would attack another one and steal cows and sheep, but there wasn't the kind of bloody violence that there is now. When the peace treaty was signed everybody respected each other and got busy farming. The scarcity and hunger brought on by the war was a thing of the past. But people were still uncivilized. They had no schooling. School was only in town, in the *cabecera*.[14]

I went to school for two years starting in 1930. Before 1930 there were only two schools in the cabecera, the administrative seat of the *corregimiento*.[15] Children were unlettered, ignorant but respectful. Our dads and moms taught us to respect them and to respect our neighbors, our relatives, and their *compadres*.[16] There were thirty-five of us families on the *vereda*[17] of Cajibío in Guachicono right on the Macizo Colombiano. Each family had ten or fifteen people. There was only one thief. Once in a while maybe a chicken got stolen, but not often; or he would go into a field and grab a few ears of corn or strip a few plants.

People didn't use firearms against each other. If *chicha*[18] got the best of some people there was a fistfight, and the strongest person won. If there was a thief the constable would take him to town and put him to work for a few days, depending on the crime. Some regular people would see that misdeeds got punished so others wouldn't follow suit.

The way to show respect was to be obedient, but you were told what to do depending on your ability. They gave you time, repeating several times what you were supposed to do. If you still didn't do it you got punished with a belt. Mothers made sure that their children did their chores and everyone had to obey. Boys had to learn to do what their fathers did.

My mom got up at four in the morning and made lunch. By five it was light and we went out to work with her as she cleared land with her little machete. We didn't do much but that's how we learned to follow orders and see how things were done. They taught the girls to do women's work. They gave them wool to work, but not the best wool.

One big thing they taught us was that people shouldn't be dishonest with each other. We shouldn't lie or try to deceive anybody.

It was a happy time and people showed respect, so there weren't any fights. The kid who stayed behind watched out for things. There were minor frictions with my brothers and sisters, of course. I was the third. I greatly respected my older brother. He's four years older than me.

I had another brother who was between my oldest brother and me. He died of typhus when he was twenty-one. This left me with an empty feeling because he was the closest to me, and nobody else could help me like he did to deal with problems of being a man. My oldest brother went out a lot to work and he didn't have time.

A man and a woman didn't have sex until they knew how to set up a household, to be responsible, and what needed to be done.

I had three brothers and one sister. After the age of ten we went to work in the fields and we saw less of each other.

My mom knew the dates when she was going to give birth. When she felt the pains she set up a comfortable space but she didn't sit or lie down. She kept moving so her body would feel like it was in normal life and the baby wouldn't get stuck; because for us, life is hard right from the womb. She would cut the umbilical cord and set it out to dry. If my dad was there he would help, but since he followed his regular routine on those occasions, sometimes he was out in the fields. There was no special diet for childbirth.

They began to prepare children for life right from the womb. Our daily routine was rigorous, not like today when kids are so spoiled. They prepared us for life. My youngest brother only went to school for six months. Then he went out to look for work. He learned construction, but not just the physical part. He learned to draw up plans for a building up to four stories high. And he didn't just work on buildings. He learned to lay sewers and water lines in Popayán, and then in Cali, in Calarcá, and he worked in Huila and Ibagué. Now he's come back to Cauca.

My oldest brother kept farming. The one after me went to La Sierra, where my dad had bought a piece of property. He was with mestizos there. The teachers valued everyone's learning ability, and my brother made a big impression on them. My dad decided to send him to school

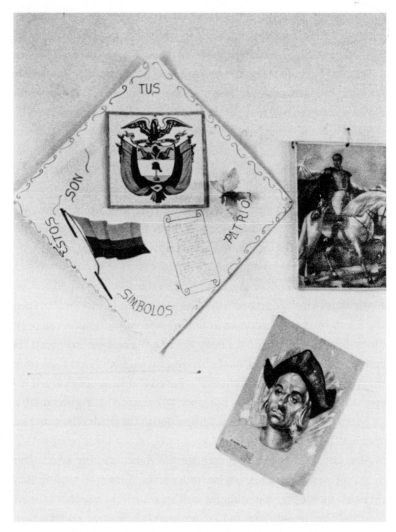

Figure 3.1. Patriotic symbols on the school wall in Corinto, Cauca, 1980, include images of Columbus and Bolívar. Photo by author.

in Almaguer where he could also learn tailoring and dressmaking, and he finished the fourth grade. He got out and started teaching. He worked as a teacher for twenty-eight years; then he took some other courses to learn more. The next one after him is a sister. She had a family and then she got typhus and died at the age of twenty-five. She had four children. Two of them are still alive; they're teachers.

As for my dad, what he never forgot was responsibility. "If you don't do your homework," he would say, "I'll take a belt to you." If you were at work you had to keep at it and keep at it, because if you stopped he would lash you with a switch. He taught us that our responsibility was also to society. He worked every day but Sunday, and a lot. Relations between my parents were very serious and both of them worked hard. They had animals such as sheep to take care of and he would reprimand my mother if she didn't do what needed doing.

He was very proper with others. If he agreed to sell a cow, for example, and he made a promise, his word was as good as a contract. Even if someone else offered him more money, he wouldn't sell it except to the person he had an agreement with. He was strong willed and could be severe. He criticized us harshly. For example if one of us was friends with someone who didn't behave correctly, we had to end that friendship. He died at the age of sixty-eight.

I had stayed home alone with my dad. He felt sick and sent me to a doctor in Popayán to analyze his urine and depending on what he saw send some herbal remedies.[19] But the doctor said "Your father is going to die. I'll send him this medicine, but he's going to die." My dad took the medicine and felt a little bit better. That was a Sunday. He got up and went to the vegetable garden and said, "It's all right now. Let's make a little something to eat. But tomorrow bring me another infusion; it made me feel better. I got up early to catch the car to Popayán that left at four in the morning, but he said, "Don't go. I'm still really bad."

I went out to work and I was really jumpy. A dragonfly startled me. I was nervous. I called my brother. It was three thirty in the afternoon when my dad called me inside. "I'm going to die," he said. If I made mistakes with you all, please forgive me."

"Rest easy," I replied, "you can make amends with Eternity." He died like that, with me by his side. It was hard, but life is like that.

I can't talk about death, but there are some illnesses that are even more distressing than death. Who knows if what you fear is to die or to be sick? There's more fear of sickness than of death.

My mom was from Guachicono, also poor. Her last name was Papamija, but a priest gave them the name Beltrán. Her life wasn't easy, but she was very organized and consistent in her work. We didn't have candles or kerosene, so when she when got up at four in the morning she had to make the afternoon meal by the light of the fire. She had it rough. Before going out to work in the fields with my dad she milked and came back with firewood. She would make corn soup (*mazamorra*) or cream of pumpkin soup. She would serve supper at seven in the evening and then stir up the coals to get enough light to work some wool. She was illiterate and very humble. She wasn't one to make a lot of friends. The neighbors were far off and didn't come around much. Everybody had their own work to do. My mother was quiet but my father was outgoing and talkative like me.

My dad fell for the *politiquería*[20] of the Liberal Party. My grandfather had fought in the War of a Thousand Days to defend the party and my dad liked that a lot. He was very excited about the 1930 elections. I was only a boy but I heard they changed clothes during the day so they could vote more than once. He didn't participate except for voting, but he talked about how our grandfather had fought in the war. My grandfather was a fearless man who defended the Liberal cause. Some leaders had convinced him to be a Liberal. Being a Liberal meant being a free man. You had freedom to speak and to travel. Now though, I think being a Liberal is a dead end. To be free means you can ask the state to meet your needs; but openly, not through manipulations.

Once, for example, I drew up a truly outstanding petition for a new school. I talked about independence. They gave me three thousand pesos for that. I became a *tinterillo*[21] to defend people. That's how I got started in CRIC. But some intellectuals who were CRIC supporters criticized my writing and marginalized me in the organization. So I stopped writing. What I wanted was to keep learning, relating to different kinds of people. I had to live up to that heroic image of my grandfather; we had to be worthy of him.

My dad told me that Valerio Palechor was a great indigenous leader who helped the indigenous people in 1840, and we were descended from him.[22] I observed that there were individuals who related to society by representing their own people. I dreamed of being like him and I was drawn to work for my people. It was like I had no choice. Valerio Palechor was the root of our family tree. He had three sons: Juan Gregorio, who was a general in the War of a Thousand Days, and Silvestre, and Matías. My grandfather Miguel Palechor was the son of Silvestre, and he was a lieutenant in that war.[23]

My mom breastfed her children until they were two years old. Of course when the breast is taken away, the child misses it. That's why Palechor is an angry man, because the government took away the breast, which was my education.

I left school because it wasn't economically feasible. The economic crisis was upon us. It was in the years '31 and '32, and it was a private school. The war with Peru came along.[24] Those were two very difficult years. But the teacher in that school taught a lot of submissiveness to the Catholic religion. She said that the purpose of religion was to pray and send souls to heaven. I don't understand this because religion is to help a group of people.[25]

As a boy I didn't like to play. I would read. I don't know what it is to play. I didn't like it because there were fights and disagreements. I've never fought with my hands; with my head, yes. I fought when there was something to be gained.

From the time I was young I cut wood to make spoons and bowls. When I was twelve we didn't have stairs to get up to the loft, so I built a ladder. I traded spoons with the neighbors for guinea pigs or chickens. Just barter, no money. When I was fifteen my dad gave us a piece of land to plant our own potatoes.

It was forbidden to talk about sex at our house. It was a sin to talk about it. There was a lot of religious influence. Having sex was considered sinful and a man could only do it when he was fully mature. They taught us that there was no right to have sex until you could take full responsibility for your actions.

When I was young I was also very interested in the night sky, especially the moon. You can't plant during the new moon. Planting is from the fifth to the seventh day, when the moon is waxing. You mustn't work the land on the eighth day, nor when the moon is waning. Plantain is set out when the moon is waning but it doesn't grow much, it just thickens around; the same for wood, too. The best wood is high on the tree. Cutting wood is done in the afternoon, and never during the new moon because it gets wormy. Cutting is done in the afternoon because that's when the sap is in the roots and it'll be more durable. I thought there was a connection between the earth, the heavenly bodies, and the plants. I would get up early and look at the sky and I could tell the weather for the day. Depending on the rays of the early sun, on how they looked!

I remembered what the teachers said in school when I was younger: that I had ability. As I grew up, I got a reputation in the family for being responsible—I stood out that way. When I started to work as a tinterillo in La Vega, I discovered that people were illiterate. So I wrote a petition for money [to build] a school. They gave it to me.

When I was a boy, the parties were on saint days. That meant bringing in some musicians to play flutes and drums. Saint Anthony was our family's patron saint. This came down from my grandparents and we had a wooden saint, a statue that is, and another one made of leather. We still have it. Saint Anthony protected the family with his miracles. The party was on June 13. We invited the family and prepared sheep, chickens, corn, and sacks of potatoes. We cooked sweet potatoes with mutton, and also potatoes and coffee.

My dad and mom chewed coca leaf, but we don't do that any more. At that time we lived in a colder place so they always had to buy their coca. They bought it once a week and sometimes they had to sacrifice buying something else in order to pay for it. People who chewed coca could tolerate a long day of work without eating, and that's what everybody did.

There wasn't a lot of open affection in the family. When I was a boy our lives were completely dedicated to work, so there was no time. Get-togethers were rare. Sometimes there were baptisms or weddings, but not often.

The resguardo had its festival on the Feast of the Immaculate Conception though. People went to the little town of Guachicono in December. The priest came and people drank and danced. They bought fireworks, and we really liked that. In those days the fiesta lasted three days, but not any more. There was a short procession with flute and drum music. Later, some people learned to play the *tiple*,[26] guitar, and *bandolín*.[27] These instruments are still played here. People didn't sing to the music, but they did dance. It was decent dancing, not like now, when it's shameful.

[handwritten: Changing Customs]

There were always problems among indigenous compañeros. Sometimes they were foolish and superficial and sometimes they were more serious, but never with landowners because we in the resguardo and in the cabildos were very careful. They were very strict in enforcing Law 89 of 1890, so they never let in any mestizos. But of course there were conflicts.

Sometime around 1932 there was a conflict with the mestizos of the corregimiento of San Miguel in the same municipio, La Vega. The conflict was because the mestizos of San Miguel tried to take control of a piece of land where the corregimiento bordered on the resguardo. It was because this land was very good for crops and livestock. That struggle lasted ten years and it presented the community with many problems. In the official investigations, the lawsuits that were being contested, for instance, first in the municipal government and then in the first on-site inspections, they were all decided in favor of the mestizos, whom we called *calentanos*.[28] In the San Miguel corregimiento where this struggle between mestizos and indigenous people was taking place, there was a certain man who was ruthless, very clever and very aggressive. He was helping the mestizos of San Miguel, egging them on, and that's why the dispute took a long time; that's why it lasted ten years. But according to the cabildo, my dad contributed a lot during that time, during those ten years.

My dad wasn't an official of the cabildo at that time, but he knew it was up to the resguardo to show that it should be respected. So when the cabildo ordered people to go work in the disputed area, my dad took me there with him to participate. I was very little, but he took me with him to do whatever I could, even if it was just watch the tools: the shovels, the machetes, you know. The indigenous people were very astute. There were some very strong and brave women, and they knew there was going to be a confrontation during the on-site inspection of the disputed land. So they gathered a bunch of rocks, of stones and things, because they knew that the mestizos were very aggressive and they would provoke a confrontation to win the dispute by force.

The case was heard in the municipal court, then it went to a circuit judge in Bolívar, and then to Popayán. The cabildo fought on all these fronts with the support of the whole community. Then it went to the Supreme Court in Bogotá, and the members of the cabildo had to go there. In the end the cabildo, with the support of the whole community, won a complete victory. They didn't allow a single millimeter of resguardo land to be lost.

Our Nervousness about School and What We Were Taught

When we were six years old, they told us that we had to go to a school. We didn't know what a school was, so Dad told us that it was a place where children got together and they were led by other people called teachers. In our case we were very nervous about this. We didn't have any social contact with neighbors or anyone else, and we were afraid to go to a place where we would meet other people. Also, we would have to deal with a big problem—our own inadequacy. But that's what happened. At the age of six they sent three of us to school, among them myself, the youngest. It was about an hour and a half's walk away on very bad paths and trails. An uneventful walk to school was out of the question because it was very muddy, with a lot of downed trees and a lot of big roots to get around or climb over. It was very hard for us because it's a cold place and there were a lot of really muddy stretches. But we were all trained by my dad to be very obedient and that's what we had to do, to obey to the letter everything we were told in school.

The school was run by a teacher, a woman who had attended primary school for two years. Looking back it seems that if she went to primary school for two years she must have had zero learning capacity. So with absolutely no chance to learn our letters, we barely learned to sign our names, and poorly at that. The school was completely indigenous, right on the resguardo of Guachicono. The teacher wasn't indigenous, though, she was from outside. I don't even know where she was from, but she showed every sign of belonging to the Conservative Party.

My dad was able to keep us in school for three years, but for those three years one of the teachers was unqualified, and the only thing I learned of any use was first-grade material. But despite this, school was where we began to learn, to be part of something outside the family, to have a social life together with our indigenous schoolmates.

During those years at school, the main thing the teacher impressed on us was that we had to learn how to pray; we had to learn to pray. Yes, first the "Divine Praises," then the sign of the cross, then the "Angelic Salutation," the "Hail Mary," and so on and so forth. Then we had to learn the "Rosary," and I was kind of good at this so I learned. The teacher told us if we learned to pray, it was so we could save our souls. She said there was a book they called the *Catechism* that taught about the Catholic religion and another book they called *Bible History*.

Then she told us about the creation of the world, how the creation of the world took place. That the world was created and a man called Adam was created in an earthly paradise at that time. But there was also a tree in that paradise they called the "Tree of Knowledge of Good and Evil." They said that the errors that were made in this earthly paradise, for instance the error of Adam and Eve at that time, would be an original sin and it would last forever, for all time. If we continued committing that, then humanity would continue committing it. They said there was a "Tree of Knowledge of Good and Evil," and anyone who picked the fruit of that tree and ate it would be condemned, you see? So for us, those things kept us frightened for a long time and maybe I'm still frightened.[29]

Since the house was far away, we didn't go to mass. It was only when the school brought a priest to celebrate mass. One thing I remember very well is there was a group of people from Spain—their last mission was in 1933. One day the priest asked us what we thought was the worst, most horrible and unspeakable sin. But what were we kids going to know about unspeakable sins? Also we didn't want to say, so we got really nervous. We just kind of trembled while he waited; but finally he said that the worst, most heinous and unspeakable sin was the sin of impurity, but then he never explained what it was. He talked about impurity, but what did we know about impurity? We didn't know anything about impurity because our social structure wouldn't have us learn all that kind of thing.

A little more about conforming to religious teachings. In the talks and the sermons that the priests gave us, they would say that you had to be a Conservative, because if you were a Liberal, then the devil would get you, right? That there was a hell and that all the Liberals were communists, and that there was eternal hellfire, and it was scorching and the devil never got tired of feeding the flames. That's why you had to be a Conservative because if you were a Liberal you were a communist, and therefore you were Satan. They said you were committing a lot of sins, and that's how they convinced people.

They told us other things when we were children, both in school and what the priests said. They told us that we had to buy books that dealt only and exclusively with the Catholic religion. There was a book called *The Guide to Heaven*, and by studying and practicing that book we would go right to heaven. My dad bought it and we had it at home. We read it after we knew how to read. But the woman teacher also told us that we had to pray, because people who prayed plenary indulgences would be able to save their souls. But what did we know about plenary indulgences? Even today we don't know what they are, but since at that time we didn't know anything about life, about what it means to be a human being on the earth, we believed that this prayer could save our souls.

She said that when people died their souls were burdened with a certain amount of sin, you see. But by praying they would go straight to heaven, and the teacher even showed us with her finger like this, pointing straight up above to where heaven was, but she never said where hell was, never ever. So that's how they fooled us. That's how they made us submit.

Then the priest said we had to buy some prayer cards with images of Our Lady of Perpetual Help, the Virgin Mary, Saint Peter, Saint Joseph, all that kind of stuff, and then you had to use them; because if you wore a cross or an image of the Virgin around your neck, then the Virgin would look kindly on you. If a person was already perverted, that is if they were really sinful, then Our Lady of Perpetual Help would defend him when he got to the place where he had to cross from earth into hell, where they would be roasting him every day. The Virgin would be the one to intercede. The devil already had a list of those he was going to carry off to hell, written in the blood of the person, they said. He had a list on a piece of paper and he was ready to carry them off into hell. He was happy because he was going to roast them, but Our Lady of Perpetual Help would intercede because you had prayed to her. And your prayer cards worked against the devil's list. Our Lady of Perpetual Help was there to defend you—she defended you.

The other things they taught us in school were we should get used to being very respectful of the law. I mean you had to respect the police chief, for example, because he was an authority; the inspector, because he was an authority; the mayor, the governor, all of them. We should be very respectful of these authorities because if we weren't the punishment was they would take you to jail and tie you up. Well, in any case, we had to be very respectful.

The teacher was the same. She said that we had to respect the priest because he was a saint, because he was the only human being who would go to heaven because he was very pure; he was innocent of all sin. He was a person who was worthy of honor, of respect. That there was also another more senior person called the bishop and this bishop was even closer to heaven, and above him there was an archbishop but you couldn't just call these people "bishop" or "archbishop," you had to say "Your Excellency Señor Archbishop." Then there was a cardinal and you also had to call the cardinal "Your Excellency Señor Cardinal, Your Eminence." Well I don't remember much about this, but all of these words were the same when it came to government officials, too. You had to say "Your Excellency Señor President" and "Your Excellency Señor Minister."

I think the people you should really say "Your Excellency" to are the working people, those who produce the agricultural goods that sustain human life, and who do so with the sweat of their brow. They make it possible for all human beings to survive, including those who work in offices or in administrative positions, because not everybody has to work in agriculture. Other people work in the government, in the oligarchy, or in capitalism.

The Harshness of Family Life and the Art of Agriculture

From that point on I began to have relationships with other people, what people today call relationships, to have contact with more people, but mostly during my years at school. Then we went back to our completely private lives. Since my dad was a very serious man, very severe and rigid, we had to do exactly what he said, to follow whatever order he gave. We could never so much as look at him the wrong way, because if you looked at him the wrong way after he gave you an order, you would get punished and punished severely. I mean with a strap for example, a belt or a whip.

Anyway, that's the way we lived, under very harsh discipline. We considered our situation very difficult because we would get back home to family life and it was pure physical labor again. They gave us work to do from the time we got out of school such as "Well, today you're all going to weed the garden." I mean as soon as we got out of school we had to start work. If there was no firewood, for example, we had to go bring firewood. But on top of that they controlled our time. They would tell us "You have so much time to go bring back a bundle of firewood and if anyone is late, well you know what happens; the strap will be flying."

So we had no choice but to endure this situation. We absolutely couldn't go anywhere at all because if any of us went somewhere they'd be severely punished. All this time we lived in this situation, showing complete respect for the rule of my dad's absolute authority with no chance to go anyplace where we could keep having social relationships with other people.

After we got out of school they sent us to pick up food items such as panela[30] or salt, or things they used at work, like sometimes coca leaf for example, which they liked to chew and would send us to get. Still, when they sent us like that they also limited the time we had to bring it back: "Okay, you're going at such and such a time so at such and such a time you have to be back here because there's nothing to do at the market." That's how they ordered us and that's how we had to obey. So there was no way we could interact with any other kind of people because there was no time for that.

This lasted for a period of about twelve years because we were under my dad's control, under his authority until we were twenty-one years old. No one could go off anywhere else and no one could, say, engage in any work or any activity other than the work they told us to do. But sometimes we needed a few cents to buy necessary foodstuffs or other goods that I talked about from the market, such as panela, coca, salt, or something else, so they sent us to do day labor. But we couldn't use any of our pay. When we got home in the evening we had to hand it over— my dad collected the money for household expenses.

As we discussed at the beginning, there were some people who needed the help of community mingas, you know; and when the time came for the work they would say "Well, on such and such a day I'm going to have such and such a minga, or sometimes they needed day laborers. And ever since we were children people considered us obedient, honest, and very hard working people, so we spent a lot of time doing day labor for our neighbors, who were also indigenous.

In those days people used coca to help them work. They said that chewing coca gave them more staying power—they didn't get tired, hungry, or thirsty, so the custom was to work all day without eating. They went to work at five in the morning after breakfast and they went home at seven in the evening. They were also accustomed to using coca medicinally for problems such as chills and upset stomachs, and they rubbed it onto where they had rheumatism. Some people there still use coca. You can buy it in town, at the market in Almaguer or Guachicono. They grew it in Almaguer because of the mild climate, and they brought it into Guachicono from there. Mestizos sold it by the pound, dry and toasted leaves. People had a lot of faith in coca and used it for strength, for endurance, to keep working all day long; but we young people didn't chew it any more—none of us in my family used it. I think maybe [we were] fooled by modern chemical medicine and there was publicity saying that coca gives you cancer.

After I was ten, as I looked at the things going on around me, what I had learned from my dad was to respect people, to respect the rights of others, the work of others, but I wanted to learn some other things besides our daily work, like certain kinds of craftsmanship that I'd seen, for instance. I saw that there were wooden spoons and wooden bowls for making bread dough out of wheat or corn. So I took up this art, but only when I had some extra time off of work, or sometimes on Sundays. I started making spoons, bowls, ladders, things that other people weren't doing, and I started to have sort of a little business. I sold things. I sold spoons and I traded large and small spoons for chickens, for guinea pigs, for hens, and I made ladders and they gave me a few hens. Things like that, you know? With all this I saw that it was work that got you things, no? So I worked at it even more because I believed I should work more than just what was expected of me in order to acquire the economic resources that in my opinion were necessary, that a man should have.

As far as working the land goes, well my dad was very dedicated to his farming and he had the technical knowledge for it, so whatever he planted produced a good crop, whether it was potatoes or corn. We never lost a crop, and I learned all these things from a very young age, from boyhood. You can say that from early on we had technical knowledge in the field of agriculture.

My dad told us that fertile soil for growing potatoes, onions, or corn was black; they should be grown in black soil. In those days farming was organic; there weren't any chemicals. He taught us to judge the soil by its color. The most fertile was black, and then there was the yellow.

Certain crops such as wheat, linseed, and onions could be planted in yellow soil, in sterile soil.

Wheat and barley stalks fertilize the earth. Pretty soon we'd learned a lot and we knew about the different kinds of soil. We were told that it was important to use chemical fertilizer because that's the way things were done and there had been a lot of experiments about it. And you could plant and cultivate like that, but after the second harvest the yield decreased and the third crop produced very little. We've seen the evidence: chemical fertilizer is a complete sham and a rip-off because it burns and sterilizes the soil, and it's exploitative because when the *Caja Agraria*, the Agricultural Bank,[31] INCORA[32] gives you credit, they require you to buy chemical fertilizer. If possible, that you buy it before they lend you the money, so we can see that chemical fertilizer does the grower no good.

One year we would plant corn and beans, and the next year we would plant barley or wheat on the same land. That way the more the soil was worked the more it got fertilized; barley stalks are very good for the soil. Then we went back to corn. After the wheat was harvested it was dried and taken to one of the water-powered stone mills that belonged to the community. Almost everything was consumed within the family.

For the kind of farming I'm talking about you had to be very familiar with the seasons, particularly the short dry season, the time of year when it doesn't rain much. That's when we planted, in September. Then we planted again in February and March. For the weather throughout the year, we paid close attention to the *cabañuelas*[33] in January, the long cabañuelas and the short cabañuelas. Each day of the long cabañuelas for a month and the short cabañuelas one day for each two months. It worked like this: The long cabañuelas were January 1 to January 12, and the short cabañuelas were January 12 to January 18. We paid close attention to the weather on those days because if it rained during the day, that meant it would rain the whole month that it represented. The same if it was dry. To work with this custom you had to keep in mind that the short cabañuelas were more accurate.

As for the heavenly bodies, the moon was the most important. Planting was done when the moon was waxing, between five and fifteen days after the moon changed, the time when it wasn't visible during the day or the night. The day it didn't appear was the day it changed, when it began to wax. Planting was five days later. Fifteen days after the change was the full moon, when it was largest and lasted all night. Starting on this day and from then on the moon was waning. You don't plant at this time, and if you do plant it doesn't produce food.

We generally fell trees after the full moon, too, because they're considered mature and the wood doesn't rot. If they're cut on the new moon or when the moon is waxing the wood rots. You also harvest according to the moon. You don't harvest on the days when the moon is changing or when it's new. You don't harvest on the first day of the new moon, or when the moon is full, when it's starting to wane. After the day of the full moon you can harvest. Long experience tells us that the moon definitely has an influence on the crops in the ground. Up in these cold regions the heat of the sun has very little influence.

During all this time none of us left home, not at all. We didn't leave home and we didn't leave the resguardo. What we really did was submit to my dad, to his orders, and to his ruling over us. Now I realize that this was very important because that experience gave us a model to follow, a way to be responsible men, not just in private life but in society, too. Nobody left home, nobody, not until each of us reached the age of twenty-one.

When I Was Conscripted

As I said, we lived under the strictest of discipline and we'd never left home, never left the house. But one day we got a message from the municipio that I should report to the municipal offices. I didn't know anything at all about this kind of thing, like what was an "order from higher authorities," and I got scared. Who knew what this could be? Anyway, I was very frightened, but since I was instructed to comply, I immediately left for town to ask the mayor why my presence had been requested, you know?

So he said to me "Well, we need you here because of La Sierra," — see I forgot to tell you that when we were almost grown up my dad bought a small farm, private property, in the municipio of La Sierra — and that's how the military recruitment caught up with me. The mayor said the order had arrived from La Sierra, that the time had come for conscription there and that's why they'd called on me. So I said to him, I answered the mayor, "So what should I do now?" The mayor said I had to provide a stand-in so the person who was the stand-in would appear on the day when they were going to draw lots to choose who would have to serve in the military.

Well, I was very worried about this problem and I went to the house of a man whose economic situation was not too good. He was an individual who didn't know anything about such matters and said he didn't know what it meant to serve as a stand-in. But I'd heard people saying a few things about it, and I explained to him that "a stand-in means you'll respond if they call my name and I'm not there. Then if that happens you can find me and I'll report for the medical exam." Anyway, the lots were drawn just two weeks later. A military doctor arrived along with a recruitment officer, who was a lieutenant. They had to conscript ten young men from that municipio, but as it turned out they'd examined about a hundred. They had about thirty more exams to do, and they still hadn't found more than a very few who were "fit for service." They started to call on the rest of us, including me. So they told me to take off my clothes and to walk, to walk normally. So I walked normally and they said I was fit for service. I'm going to tell you, I was paralyzed with fright because I had no idea what military service was going to be like. I'd been told that serving in the military meant using rifles and things like that. I didn't know what was going to happen and I was scared stiff, but they put me in the line of guys who were fit for service. I'd heard, though, that they were going to put the guys they found fit for service in a car so I asked, "So, aren't they going to send a car?" The lieutenant, the recruiter replied, "No you have to go by foot." Well, it turned out there was a car, and we had to walk to the municipio of Rosas and wait there for the car to Popayán. But anyway I'd been chosen to serve in the military.

When I was caught up in the draft I didn't know anything about cars. When they started approaching us there in Rosas they looked small, from far away that is, but they seemed to get bigger as they got closer. I started moving off to one side thinking that by the time they got there they'd be getting huge and they'd run me over. Well as it happens, we had to ride in a truck and we were terrified. Since the teacher and the priest had taught us to pray for salvation, that's what we did. I prayed and prayed all the way to Popayán; and it helped me remember everything the teacher had told us.

To me that was a great experience in the sense that it was a school for me. I knew nothing. I knew absolutely nothing about those things, so I learned. I saw people carrying firearms, and they ordered them to load them, and they ordered them to do different exercises. All of this was really hard for me, because I didn't know anything at all about these things. I mean I knew nothing, but luckily I paid a lot of attention and took advantage of every minute of those thirteen months when I was serving. I didn't get distracted or waste any time fooling around, not at all. I took care to observe every aspect of whatever they were doing so I'd be able to do it too. I especially watched the ones who were most experienced, observing even how they pronounced their words, the ones that people said were high school graduates or people who were lance corporals, corporals, sergeants, and all kinds of officers and noncommissioned officers, all of them. I was very attentive when those who were called "civilized," when they talked among themselves. I would stop to listen because of wanting to find out what things were called and in general how they talked about the things there in the army, in the battalion.

I say the army was my school, because I learned things that I didn't know at that time. Above all I learned about military life. Basically I was a person who took a strong interest in things and I excelled as a soldier. I was a model soldier and I wasn't punished even once during the whole year. And since I was a model soldier I managed to handle military life so well that I was given the opportunity to reenlist to continue doing the same work, to continue doing what I was doing. That's why I was serving in the military in 1944 when they imprisoned Alfonso López Pumarejo[34] in Pasto.

I was stationed in the department of Cauca, in Popayán. When the reserves were called up in the general mobilization, the commissioned and noncommissioned officers who knew me were sent to other companies and their interest in having me reenlist went along with them.

Before 1944 I knew only our private life, the daily customs we lived by. But then I started seeing new things. I was there when they took López Pumarejo prisoner. I realized that I was blind—I mean I didn't know why I was a Liberal. My dad had told us very little. Who benefitted from the political struggles around us? While I was in the military I thought I should keep my eyes open, that I shouldn't sleep. I wanted to remember everything. After six months I had a chance at a promotion, and since I was a good soldier they gave me a leave to go home. But one morning when I'd been in the service for eight months, I heard a new voice, not the voice of the officer who usually roused the company. I heard other voices as I quickly got dressed. It had been raining a lot and there were mud puddles on parade ground number 4 and they had the cows and mules there. Before we had time to get dressed the lance corporal who had ordered the company to get up shouted "Forward march!" Some of us left without pants, others with their pants in their hands, and others were stark naked.

Anyway, he marched us out to parade ground number 4 and had us lie face down in the mud. Then he went around kicking people so they would put their actual faces right down into the mud. We had no choice. He forced us to do it. Right then and there I swore to myself that I'd get out of the army as soon as possible and from that day on I wanted no part of military life, whether in the police or the army. As far as I was concerned no man should have to suffer that kind of humiliation. No man should be humiliated by another man, and I wouldn't stay in the military to be humiliated or to humiliate others. To me that went against human respect and that's why I left the army even though I was an outstanding soldier.

I left the army and took up the political life, trying to help the Liberal

Figure 3.2. Jorge Eliécer Gaitán.

Party recover lost ground in the legislative elections of 1948. The political situation was volatile: Turbay, Gaitán, and Ospina.[35] I was a Liberal, so I considered the alternatives, but I liked Gaitán's ideas a lot more. I was proud that they called him "*el indio* Gaitán" (the Indian Gaitán), because to me it's an honor if I'm called that.

That's where I learned a lot of things, that a man can be subordinate to another man but be treated honorably, not the kind of conditions you find in the army, based on kicking, on being kicked. What they do in the army is humiliate you. The officer humiliates his subordinate the soldier, and I didn't like that kind of thing. Based on the way I was brought up, I believed there was another way, and I thought they should use this other way of treating people a little more equally as if they were like another father, that they should treat people with dignity—decently and respectfully. But that's not the way it was. It was very degrading and unseemly how they hit people with their rifle butts, beat them, and kicked them around. That was one of the things I didn't like when I learned something about military life from the inside.

But what I saw also helped me. It helped me a lot and it still helps me, because I learned there were different classes. I mean a country like

Colombia was made up of different social classes, there was the middle class and the upper class, and the upper class was the powerful one. I didn't like that because according to the way I was raised by my dad, as people all of us should have rights to things. There was also racial discrimination in the sense that as indigenous people we couldn't, or the compañeros couldn't pronounce Spanish the way it should sound so others would imitate how they spoke, those who couldn't speak Spanish right. Anyway, those people were seen as different and they would make fun of them for their own amusement.

But in the army I liked seeing how they built houses. Since I was an outstanding soldier they sent me to the air field in Popayán, where they were building a new house. The construction boss was black and the workers were very downtrodden. I saw that the afternoon meal was brought in for them and one day when I saw it arrive I called one of the workers over to eat, but it wasn't time yet. The boss grabbed him roughly and gave him a kick, yelling "You Indian son of a bitch." It was very humiliating and of course that was the idea. I spoke up to defend the worker and I decided I wanted to become a construction boss and treat people well.

I also realized that the officers and the military were at the service of the government and the president, the commander-in-chief, but serving a capitalist caste that engaged in politiquería, a caste of political parties. Anyway, the military had to obey the orders of the capitalists, such as sending soldiers to defend the house of some captain or guard the house of some major or colonel, so in this sense I saw that the common soldier whether or not he even had enough to eat was just at the service of those with more money.

The thing is they told us we had to defend the interests of private property, which was the property of the rich, so for example, if someone came along and wanted to take it away from them, to impose order and protect those things.

When I saw all these complications we had to put up with as common soldiers I decided not to stay on, not to reenlist, not to continue serving in the army, because it seemed to me that staying in the army meant men who had to humiliate other men. And for me to be humiliated by other men who were my superiors and were going to give me orders, well I decided to go home and see if I could go back to my private life, even if it was difficult or disagreeable. Even if it meant suffering, because when I was young there had also been short periods of crisis. Not long ones, but even so. Anyway, I went home and I didn't have to beg the government or the system for anything. I would be able to make a living just from my work.

Learning New Things

When I went home I went to La Sierra, not to the resguardo but to the municipio, which was then and still is made up of people called mestizos. I didn't like it because in any case they rejected us as indigenous people. We were rejected—there was racial discrimination. They rejected us and spoke to us using offensive words, calling us Indian savages, stupid Indians, stupid onion farmers, all that kind of thing. So I stayed just a few days and then I went back to the resguardo, to Guachicono.

I was there for many days, but I never stopped going back to the house in La Sierra to visit, even if it was for a short time, because those lessons or that school that I had in the army showed me many more things that a man should know, like what ways you can use to learn what you don't know. For instance, I liked woodworking and architecture, so I tried to learn carpentry and the art of architecture, and I succeeded, but without anybody—nobody taught me. Instead I learned by going to where men were building to ask for work. They paid me for the day's work or they didn't pay me at all, but the thing I liked was that they gave me work so I [would] learn, and that I accomplished [things]. When I went home, I went home as a master builder. I went to woodworking shops for instance, and imitated. I saw what construction drawings looked like and how they did things. I also succeeded in becoming a carpenter, but I wasn't satisfied because then I went to, supposedly to help out with what they do on road construction, and before long I was working on the roads. I learned something about masonry, how to build walls, all that stuff. But that doesn't mean I gave up the habit of farming; no way.

Indigenous people sold onions in the town market, and I was farming on my dad's lot because I hadn't gotten any land of my own. That's because I was going around looking for chances to work, so I didn't have any money, I didn't have economic resources. In any case the cabildo distributed land to people who were legally of age and who submitted the official documents. So as for the cabildo there were no obstacles, but the thing was I felt totally alone because my family didn't live in Guachicono any more. They lived in the municipio of La Sierra, my brothers and my sister and my dad. All of them had gone to the municipio of La Sierra and I was left there alone, feeling alone, so I left.

As for my brothers, one of them farmed and the other one did up to fourth grade in the municipio of Almaguer, where he got hired as a teacher. He was a great worker, very dedicated. He handled everything very well, everything having to do with education. He fulfilled his responsibilities, so they kept him working and it seems like now he's going to retire. My other brother only went to school for six months, so he went to work in the same circumstances that I faced. I mean going to look for work and learning things, and he also specialized in woodworking. He's a great carpenter; he's a cabinetmaker now and has also worked in the field of architecture—a great builder—and has also worked with water mains and sewers, and now he's working with the National Federation of Coffee Growers. My dad went to La Sierra simply because the climate seemed a little better to him, because it's not as cold there.

Then I went out looking to learn something and I came and went for ten years. Those ten years were my schooling with respect to work skills. Then a certain damsel hoodwinked me into marrying her. I was a hard worker, but since I was still single, my mom had died, my dad had died, and we didn't have anybody to take care of us at all, I recognized that for me to keep working there was a need for someone even if it was just to make something to eat. So even though I [was] really reluctant, even though I was dubious about marriage due to the great responsibility that I thought one takes on—I mean two kinds of responsibility. There is the responsibility to keep a home the way a home should be and to be responsible for your family if you end up having one. But nevertheless, in 1955 this female hoodwinked me and I married her. From then on the children began to come; but I provided for them, because she took charge of the family and I provided by farming, with my knowledge of architecture, woodworking, all that kind of thing. So I was very busy with that. She isn't indigenous. She was sixteen when we got married in La Sierra, because that's where she's from.

To find my wife I looked [off the resguardo] on private property in La Sierra. She was an orphan and very poor. I wanted a woman who was empty-handed like me and with the same schooling. The other thing is I turned over every leaf and found that she was a very respectable person. We had six children. The oldest died in 1955, fifteen days after he was born. The next one is studying law at the University of Cauca. Antonio, the next, is at *Radio Super*,[36] and then there was a girl, who is thirty.[37] Then Chucho, who's in high school, and another boy died. We treat them with respect and solidarity.

Public Life and Political Violence

Let's move on to what I consider to be politiquería, okay? Well, at that time people talked about the Liberal Party and the Conservative Party. As far as politics, in our house my dad had started by telling us about our granddad, who as I mentioned had been a captain in the War of a Thousand Days. He told us about that from the time we were very small, before we even went to school. So I already had that in my thinking, and he told us how there had been atrocities, perpetrated for example by the governments and the Conservatives. That is, he had already been telling us that the Conservatives, in the War of a Thousand Days, would arrive and eat the cows, they'd eat the sheep, they'd eat the chickens, they'd eat the guinea pigs, and they made the Liberal women prepare their meals. The Liberals, on the other hand, were defending their right not to be persecuted like that. All these things were done to the Liberals, my father said, and that's what started the War of a Thousand Days, and that's why my granddad had done his part, because the Conservatives and the governments persecuted [Liberals] so harshly at that time, and that's why the Liberal Party had to be defended. So despite all my ignorance, I began to be affected emotionally, you know? To be moved emotionally because you had to defend a political position, the position of the Liberal Party. I developed that psychosis all that time, that you had to defend the Liberal Party. Up to a certain period of time, I was totally committed to that idea.

In the army they told us that as a soldier you couldn't belong to any political party; but as I said, I was very happy belonging to the Liberal Party from the time I was little because my granddad had fought in the War of a Thousand Days. All this influenced me so I would do the same, defend the Liberal Party. So at the time of the 1946 presidential elections, which were hotly contested, within the Liberal Party there was Gabriel Turbay, Jorge Eliécer Gaitán, and another one was Mariano Ospina Pérez, all of them candidates for the presidency. I really liked the political ideas of Jorge Eliécer Gaitán, and from then on I fought for his positions.

I liked him because he talked about the rights that man has no matter what, you see? At least in some speeches that I managed to hear about, because at that time it was very hard to learn more about a candidate's opinions. Still, sometimes I saw things in the newspapers and I observed that Gaitán's politics were completely different from the politics of Gabriel Turbay or some other Liberals. At first I liked, I got involved in activities helping convince people to vote for Gaitán. I wasn't very committed but I liked his politics and I stayed with him. Then the Conservative Party won, which was Mariano Ospina Pérez. When we lost, people like me were demoralized and we didn't know what to do. For us Doctor Gaitán's[38] loss was terribly hard. But I thought about it a lot, and by then I knew more about other factors like procedures, about a lot of administrative and political things. I was also very concerned with how personal hatreds were channeled and even hardened through politics, very worried, you know? So as I said, I left [politics].

I was also working hauling foodstuffs from the municipio of San Sebastián to the municipio of San Agustín in the department of Huila. I could sell potatoes as far away as San Agustín because there was a road over the Alto de las Papas pass and I rented animals to haul the potatoes across. As it happened, I was working there on April 9 when we found out by means of a radio broadcast about the death of Doctor Gaitán, about his assassination. Anyway, that was a big surprise for us and then we heard that Doctor Darío Echandía[39] would assume responsibility [to lead the Liberal Party] and in any case people would organize to see what would be done about all this.

Since I had been working to spread Gaitán's ideas in Popayán and San Agustín, I was persecuted. The day I went to San Agustín to sell potatoes, a Conservative politician, Silvio Villegas spoke, saying "Those Reds must be eliminated." People responded saying, "Wherever there's a Red we'll skin him." I grabbed my animals and got out of there.

The Liberals were thinking about getting organized to do something, but about three days later Darío Echandía said again that he wouldn't get involved in that kind of thing. I too had been thinking about participating in something, because after all I was a Liberal, but since Echandía had declined to take that path, we didn't act. And what happened was since there was already a lot of political discrimination against Liberals, and since the government was Conservative, they started to see us as enemies, all that kind of thing. If it was possible, they would want to be removing Liberals from their public positions, from administrative positions in the government. After Gaitán's death, violence was declared against the Liberal Party, and that was one of the most horrible things that happened in my time.

In 1950 they said they would force us to vote for Laureano Gómez.[40] Since I was visible as an organizer they called me to a meeting but I backed away; I preferred not to go to town. The elections came and went, but the violence only got worse. Mosquera Chaux[41] and the national leadership had left the country. I went to La Sierra because my dad had a piece of land where I could stay.

I advised everyone not to be confrontational. They came for me three times but I got away each time. I was working by applying the law. You had to work like that to defend people from the outrages taking place, to defend their land, and to defend them from the unjust decisions and orders by judges and mayors. And since I could get paid I went to work as a tinterillo.

We were hearing from other places on the Paez resguardos that people were being killed; they were being grabbed and thrown in cars, then taken down to the rivers and drowned. To us that was a degrading thing, very painful. They were also going to towns not on the resguardos and murdering Liberals, murdering women and children of all ages, and that was shocking. On the resguardo of Río Blanco, it was different because at least there weren't any killings. But still they were sending government workers acting as inspectores de policía to administer their so-called justice, which in fact was a lot of persecution and humiliation.

After a few years we got news that in the resguardos, in the resguardo of Caldono, for example, outsiders were using politiquería to appropriate the lands of indigenous compañeros, taking advantage of all the power in the hands of the Conservatives. It was said that a national senator by the name of Mario S. Vivas was appropriating lands that belonged to Indians and terrorizing them by hauling them off to jail and giving them the water torture for three days, forcing them to say that the resguardo should be abolished or the land should be divided up and distributed, just wearing them down, forcing them to say that, even if it was out of pure fright. Other compañeros left the area; they migrated and dispersed. That's how outsiders were able to grab land and get large properties. That's why there are large landowners in Caldono.

The Church did nothing to protect indigenous people during the violence. It did nothing, for instance, in the case of the Paez people in Tierradentro. There was a certain Monsignor Enrique Vallejo there, and it was whatever Monsignor Vallejo ordered. And it seems that in his time there was a disaster for the lives of our indigenous compañeros. As far as protecting them, nothing. I don't think Monsignor Vallejo adhered to any aspect of this invention they call the Catholic religion, because if he'd adhered to any part of it, even one part of the mission they claim to be dedicated to, to practice what Christ preached, like equality and respect, then they just didn't fulfill that role. Monsignor Vallejo, as a minister of Christ, as a minister of the Church, played no role. Instead he collaborated against indigenous people, even collaborated against them with landlords.

When he was alive compañero Benjamín Dindicué[42] described what happened:

> The Violence of 1948 was very bad when April 9 happened because before that the cabildo made very few individual land allotments. Everything was in common; everything was done as a community. Animals were raised all together. One person's animal and another person's animal were herded together. All around here there were mules or burros, cattle, sheep, and everything here together, all of them communally. But the violence came and most of the indigenous people's mules and livestock were stolen by the people who at that time we called *chulavitas* or *policía*.[43] They killed compañeros and burned their houses. In order to buy a pound of salt you had to get a permit at the military post and if you were found carrying more than that it was all of it confiscated. They searched you just like they're doing over there in the Middle Magdalena. Anyone considered suspicious was brought in and investigated. They could do anything to them, and they did. Even to buy clothes they bought pants and a shirt and then they had to go report to the military commander. A lot of indigenous people died.
>
> There was a Corporal Henao on the resguardo of Belalcázar, a [man named] Corredor, and a Lieutenant Bustamente. They carried out the massacre on the resguardo of San José. They killed thirty-nine people there. People say it was Monsignor Vallejo who told them the guerrillas were there in San José. Of course guerrillas had passed through the area, but not through town. They crossed the páramo near there, just passing through. But they seized those indigenous people who were working there; they called them together, they took the saints out of the church and put them in another house. They took the indigenous people to the bridge and killed them with bayonets. Just one of them survived.

A lot of people tell the same story about the San José massacre. Compañera Maximina Cuene, from Moras,[44] tells how people lived at that time:

> During the violence we couldn't sleep at home because the soldiers persecuted us as "people from the mountains."[45] But we didn't have contact with them, only with the army. The soldiers said they were going to do away with the people of Moras. In fact they wounded my father Rubén Cuene all because he didn't listen when people told him "Here come the troops, don't go out there. Let's go up the mountain to hide." "I have nothing to hide," he said.
>
> The troops came upon him on the road and they shot him once in the hip and threw him in a ditch. Later he died from that. He never recovered because the wound didn't heal. As for the women, the soldiers used them. If they didn't want to be seen by the soldiers they had to go off into the bush. They seized my husband Adelmo, saying he was giving food to "people from the mountains." But that was a complete lie. They kept him for a month, demanding that he tell them where they (the guerrillas) were. After a month they took him up the mountain at San José but all they found up there were some rams. They brought the rams to Mosoco and ate them. They let him go and gave him papers so he could get to Balalcázar and Silvia.
>
> In San José the soldiers told the cabildo to gather and wait for them, and the people believed them. There were men, women, and children. They told them they had to get all the saints [from the church] and take them to Mosoco. Then they burned all the houses. They left the women and the saints at Rancho del Molino. The men they brought to the bridge on the way to Mosoco and there they shot and killed them. The troops in Mosoco tricked the people of Cabuyo. At about 7:00 in the evening they entered a house and told seven men that they were compañeros; they should accompany them to Mosoco. They killed them right in the plaza in Mosoco after accusing them of being "people from the mountains." But that was a lie.
>
> In Moras they used a woman who was pretty old because they

couldn't find her daughters. She wasn't young, and the soldiers left saying "that old coca-chewing lady was pretty good."

Some indigenous people were arrested, too. They arrested Samuel Cuene and beat him, saying he was a leader of "the people from the mountains." When he asked the captain politely for a glass of water, all he got was a kick. Later when he was settling down to sleep a policeman said, "Step outside Samuel, someone needs to see you." When he got out the door they opened up on him with a machine gun and he was torn to shreds. They did the same thing to Ismael Casas, from Pitayó. The next day they said they were killed in an escape attempt but that was a lie. They killed them in cold blood and threw their bodies on a milk wagon so they could lie and say they were escaping. When they killed them they were happy and celebrated. One soldier they call *Cariculebra* (Snakeface) said he pulled out the others to kill them too but the sergeant said no. They had ten prisoners, almost all old men. These things happened in 1955 and 1956.

When we were at home we knew if troops were approaching because some women warned us. One day a woman with a child came running and said "Soldiers are coming! Get out of here!" One woman ran to hide in a cornfield. She was pretty old but they found her and made use of her too. That was the kind of thing that scared us so if people warned us they were coming we would head for the woods with the children. We would sleep in a thicket of trees.

During the Violence, I Was Forced by Necessity to Work as a Tinterillo

Since I had picked up some knowledge starting in school as well as on my own and in the army, I had an idea about what kind of rights a man should have, and that people shouldn't be humiliated by others. So I would say that you had to be very respectful of the needs of your neighbors. And I played a role, let's say helping my neighbors, above all the weakest among them, the poorest who were victimized when dishonest people took advantage of the fact that there were administrative conflicts, in order to help themselves, that is to win legal decisions. For instance, there were lawsuits over boundaries, over small pieces of land, or over slanders, all those kinds of things. So I started to become a tinterillo, but I knew absolutely nothing about how to do that. I racked my brains until I figured out how to focus on the issues in a written argument to present it to the appropriate authorities who were hearing the cases. That's how I was able to help the people with the least economic resources and with scant understanding of these things.

In my youth I treated the sick. I analyzed urine and made home remedies, but due to the persecution going on the most immediate need was to defend the people. My reason for working as a tinterillo was there was nobody to defend them. The enemy stole from them and ran roughshod over them and there was nobody to say anything about it. Everyone had to keep quiet. But that had to change.

I was already married in 1955 when a Conservative tried to take the land away from a relative of my wife. He had no idea that I knew something about the law. The mayor of La Sierra got involved and I accompanied them to conduct an on-site inspection. Several of them were conspiring against this relative of my wife and the mayor was going to unjustly hand over the land to the Conservative. I knew there were requirements to legally represent a person and I didn't meet them, but I decided to speak up anyway. I said to the mayor: "Since the gentleman doesn't have any representation I ask that you accept me." He looked at me funny and accepted, almost just to mock me. As the man's representative, I asked to see the documents before any decision was made. I also presented the deed. This made the Conservative mad. "You . . . you Indian," he said, "you don't even look like a human being." But I responded, "Let's talk about the law, not about personal matters." I argued and argued. My wife's relative was very poor; all he had was his small dwelling. At midday I went home with them for lunch and they boiled a small chicken because that was all they had to eat. While we were there the mayor arrived with some police and said he was going to transfer the land. I couldn't accept that and I refused to go with them. They went back to the disputed land and we followed. I kept arguing:

"Do whatever you want," I said, "because I've made valid arguments. Besides, there are more senior people and there are laws about private property." The mayor came over to me on his horse. I said "If you don't settle this problem there are people above you and there are laws to resolve it." The mayor got scared and I won my first lawsuit. From then on whenever there was a legal dispute I was there as a tinterillo. People trusted me and sought me out.

Before that, when I was in Guachicono in 1933, the mestizos were trying to take some land from the resguardo. My dad went to the meetings and got involved in the case and he took me with him. I helped by bringing people their mambe[46] or their machetes, and I heard everything that went on. But nobody knew me when I started out on my own. First I went to make oral arguments with a mayor, or rather whoever was in charge of the case, to a site inspection for example, and I asked questions. I understood that the only people they ever put in as local officials were partisan, hateful, spiteful types. So I asked questions about legal requirements when I knew the answers and I could tell they didn't know as much as me. Before long I was winning a lot of cases for the most downtrodden class and gaining a certain amount of renown.

To pick up this knowledge, the thing was that I didn't know anything about the law so I went to the Caicedo bookstore in Cali where I bought books on the different legal codes and some other books to guide me. That was a big help.

Between 1950 and 1960 I was defending people and they were very happy with me even though I belonged to an indigenous race, to a dispossessed class, because let me tell you I didn't even have clothes to wear. Well, I mean my clothes were all patched and I didn't have any underwear. I didn't have any shoes, not even alpargatas.[47] I mean nothing. People kept me busy though, and I provided my services.

But that wasn't all I was doing. Seeing that there were a lot of illiterate people, I began to look into this situation. People had started to ask me to draw up purchase and sale agreements and when I was putting them together I needed to find witnesses. But when I would ask a gentleman to sign a document he would often decline, saying "No, because I can't read. I can't be of any help." So I looked into this situation and I found there were a lot of illiterate people. I went around to peoples' houses asking if they were going to send their children to school. "No!" they all said, "Absolutely not!" So I tried to enlighten people with the message that their children needed to get educated, to learn something, because one day they would want to defend themselves; they should remember that the people who perpetrate violence, I would tell them, they take advantage of people who are helpless, who have no support and no money to hire a tinterillo or a lawyer to speak for them, so they always lose out.

I said that they had to educate themselves; they needed to prepare themselves for life. So at that time, which was 1954 or maybe 1953, we started by organizing a primary school in the area where my dad had bought property, in the municipio of La Sierra. I participated a lot in this effort and a school was established.

The school board was organized first and since I was indigenous nobody thought of sending me. They sent another man who had shoes, clothes made of nice fabric, and a strip of cloth around his neck that they call, what do they call it? Oh yeah, a necktie. They didn't consider me at all. But that school board was a lot of neckties and not much else. A year passed and they hadn't done a thing.

In 1954 I went back to organizing. I called the mayor and the priest so they would celebrate a mass and save a few souls. Then the new school board was organized and I was called on to be president. The school was started and the first thing we did was organize a system where we parents would pay to run the school. But that only lasted two weeks. In the course of those two weeks I organized the people and a petition was drawn up. At that time there was a municipal council (concejo) and a finance council (junta de hacienda) that authorized the municipio to make payments. Well, the municipio started to pay the school expenses. We accomplished this, and under my leadership. Then I worked hard on making sure that any teacher named to the school would be an able and responsible person because our eyes had been opened somewhat. We understood some things that teachers should do, that they did do, obligatorily. I helped them out a lot. As a person I wasn't prejudiced or spiteful, I didn't have it out for anybody. On the contrary I liked a peace-ful, relaxed kind of life, but only if people fulfilled their responsibilities. If they didn't then you had to say something to them, right?

As I've said, from the beginning I began to see, to realize that a man has a right to live. But the problem was in those days we had an inferiority complex. Up to the age of twenty-one, I didn't acquire any knowledge at all in my private life. But then as I said, military service was my school. What I am is more because of that. I saw that the population of this country is really composed of different social classes, and one of them was dominant while the majority of people were dominated. From then on I gained knowledge bit by bit, purely by necessity. I saw the need to resolve this mess, and I mean however I could do it. And that meant a lot of sacrifices for me to get that knowledge, because as I've said before, I had only three years of schooling and only the first year was useful because I more or less learned to read and sign my name. That was the only useful part.

At that time it seemed to me that I wasn't at all civilized. After I left the army I took up a lot of reading, a lot of writing. I used up a lot of paper trying to write correctly no matter what it took. I was writing things down and even if they were short I was getting them down little by little, correcting them, and eventually I saw they were coming out well. I thought that even if a man was ignorant he should play some kind of role in confronting the problems that existed, because I could see that we belonged to an exploited class.

I had seen that the policies of governments didn't work; they were good for nothing. I could tell that some people who spoke in public said a lot of things, but they said a lot and did very little. They had this idea of fooling people with a lot of empty talk, and because of this I thought I should talk to the people. At first I was a little scared to talk, but I did it. It was just necessity that made me start to speak in public, necessary because I saw that things should be stated more clearly within the family or the household. It was important to speak seriously and respect the public, like it was when the school was organized.

Being on the municipal council I learned a lot of things about the dirty tricks played by manipulative politiqueros and the National

Front.[48] That whole problem made me keep speaking out even though at first some intellectuals and ideologues began to make fun of me. They made fun of me; they laughed at me, but I didn't care. I knew I had the right as a man and a citizen to speak my mind.

Later I put my children in school. I was so poor that one time I had to go to the farm to get something to eat. One Saturday I came from the farm to Timbío, where I had my family, but my wife wasn't there. So I asked, "My wife, do you know where she is?" "At the school," was the reply. I didn't think my wife would be able to express the things that to me were important for the school to go well. So without even changing my clothes I went directly to the school, just the way I was. I went in and found a crowd of people at the school and one of the big shots in town was criticizing the teachers, the parents, and the children, the students. He was basically badmouthing the entire human race. The woman who was chairing the meeting was one of the teachers, and she was intimidated by this guy's harsh criticisms but she asked the people, the parents, if anyone wanted the floor. "Speak up," she implored them, "Say something," but no one responded. So I asked for the floor and people turned around to see who I was. Well, there were a lot of very well-dressed people at the meeting, decked out in their fancy shoes, fine dresses, and elegant suits, bowties, and so on. When they saw it was me asking to speak they laughed out loud; they made like it was some kind of comedy. But the teacher was more polite, saying "Let's find out what this parent wants to say," even though she didn't know if I could actually speak or if I wouldn't really be able to, you see?

So anyway, I went right up in front of where the school board was sitting and I expressed my defense, first of the teachers, because the previous speaker had been making unconstructive criticisms that the teachers didn't really deserve. His criticisms of us the parents were equally unfair, as were his criticisms of the children. So I answered for everyone. I contradicted everything the *cacique*[49] said.

Then the people understood. They saw that it wasn't the patched-up work clothes that were talking. It was a person. Then they told me the purpose of the meeting that day was to organize a parents' committee. The cacique was completely marginalized; he couldn't understand what had happened to him. It was outlandish for a person in mended old clothes to even enter a school and express his own point of view, let alone to have pushed him out of the picture.

The school board said they were going to put together a parents' committee, and see who would be the president, and well, the people at that meeting were very happy with what I said but very few of them even knew my name; so they started to point at me saying, "the one who talked, the one who talked," and others started to applaud. Well, I couldn't disappoint the other parents and I knew it was something that meant taking a lot of responsibility, so I turned them down. But then they wanted me for vice president and I accepted the vice presidency. So I went to town, right to the cabecera of the municipio, and those people realized that things weren't exactly the way they thought, they weren't the way people said, that Indians were savages, that campesinos were ignorant, and that no campesino was capable of speaking up for them. All of this was actually helpful to me and I went on to bring up a lot of issues. In fact I solved a lot of problems in the municipio of Timbío, in the schools that is, problems between students, teachers, and administrators.

All these responsibilities that I've undertaken personally and in organizations have helped me become a little more active, even if I don't have the words, even if I don't express my ideas very clearly. They may have considered me narrow, but I have something to tell them because it's my way of thinking. I understand that a person has rights because he's a human being. And he's a human being whose work helps produce revenue for the state because I'm a person who lives by my own work. I work and produce not just to support my family; but because the very process of work produces what serves to defend the people as a class, including all those students who need to prepare for life. I understood and still understand that the person who studies, who improves himself, that person will be the one who in time is going to represent this country. So all these things have been what led me to become what I am.

Also at another level, the university level, I also found out that some people at that level are a little narrow, including when I was working politically with the MRL.[50] When I was defending the positions of some person, some students would say things like, "You stupid Indian, do you think you have something to say here, you moron?" I understood that those people too were ill-mannered and foolish.

You can say there's a complex they give you, an idea they drill into you that the people who talk are those who are educated. The people who talk have gone to school, have gone to the university. They're the ones who can solve things and those of us who haven't gone to primary school, secondary school, and university, well we just don't have any ability. We pretty much don't have any right to talk because we're ignorant.

Like I said before, since we're not educated and all that, since they call us savages, this is what we've been subjected to and the feeling of inadequacy, we've accepted as real. It's a complex: The campesino is scared and ashamed, ashamed to speak, or as I said they make them ashamed the way they laugh at them and the way they ridicule them. This is how they've put them in their place.

I've had the great advantage of never wanting to disavow my heritage; I've never felt proud to deny being indigenous. To me it was an honor to be indigenous. I could be with whites or sometimes with mestiza women, and sometimes I liked the mestiza women, but [some people] never stopped being bigoted and calling me indio,[51] and actually a lot of other things.

I was happy to say "Okay, so I'm an Indian. And what's it to you if I'm an Indian? Because that's what I am." And then I felt very indigenous and never wanted to forget where I was from, you know? I wanted to go back there, to put down new roots, at least to try.[52] Sometimes I went back, and when I was talking with my indigenous neighbors they would say "Don't leave, man. Stay here with us and keep doing what you do. You're a good person and you're picking up skills. That helps us." I felt very good being with them, but I had another problem, you know? The problem was I go back without a penny to my name and who would help me in the house? No way would anybody respect me. So now I can't go back.

Nevertheless, I felt better as an indigenous person because anyway I was a different person now, you know? Whether they insulted me or treated me wrong, whether they discriminated against me, wherever I was I still felt very indigenous, and why not? I was proud of it. They continued to consider me indigenous because I made them respect my race, respect my being indigenous. So they could call me indio everywhere I went, including in the military. But if I'm an Indian, what did I care if they called me indio when to me it was a source of pride? That was my way of thinking and it wasn't changing.

When I had to do things in the legal system, the judges or the mayor, all those kind of people, they knew this ugly little indio was going to be appearing, so they had to scare him a little. The police would arrive and make a scene, but they didn't scare me anymore because I would think to myself, "If I have to die then let me die because what else can we do?" Because the important thing was to defend the people, to defend their rights, don't you think?

Little by little, because I continued to defend [people] despite all these threats, well anyway they made a lot of problems for me, because by then I was a different person, defending a class; I had a lot of problems. As time went on, though, the people in the cabecera of the municipio, the people on the veredas, the people themselves were coming to see that I was right there on the front lines defending them. That's how I started to acquire a lot of social prestige, political you could say, because people started to respect me and that was encouraging. So at that time I was feeling good about all these things.

During the struggle to get building materials for the school and other petitions submitted to the authorities, the municipal authorities laughed at me and ridiculed me. No matter how you look at it this is a form of discrimination, isn't it? What worked to draw attention to the petitions was to stand right up in front of them, to explain what was needed, why education mattered, what life was like for an ignorant person, and what it was like for a person who began to educate himself. So all these things worked for me.

Also when you went into Popayán, there were these women who worked in the departmental government, in the Education Department, and they noticed right away that your clothes were patched. These women with their mouths and eyes painted with who knows what, but they laughed and said, "Well the governor isn't in," and laughed some more. They made fun of me; they tried to make fun of me however they could, you know? And me just standing there seeing and hearing this, but I was actually trying to understand why they were prejudiced against me. I thought it was because I belonged to a certain class, but in any case I was there out of necessity; I had to be heard. They knew I was pained when they subjected me to all that ridicule, but what can you do when you have no choice but to forget about shame? I had to be strong and submit the petitions. Sometimes they made me come back two or three times until I realized they were using some techniques to avoid dealing with me.

So I had to persist and I got what I needed, including in 1957 after Gustavo Rojas Pinilla was overthrown when there was the military junta with five members and a different governor,[53] I filed a successful petition to get some help building the school. I succeeded and they responded. I had gotten more serious and more determined, and I was better able to do these things, to demand a response in these situations, but there was still that discrimination.

And that discrimination has not gone away. When compañeros come from the different regions [of Cauca], for example from the north, the center, the east, or Tierradentro, and they see you with these people, they never stop making fun of you. But what can you do? We think it's a right you have as a person, as a human being, so much so that we have to do it. I really think so. But the discrimination is the same as ever.

The Formation of Community Action Committees: The Liberal Revolutionary Movement and the National Front

At that time the petitions I was writing were for the school, but soon I saw that it wasn't just the school; other services were needed. Then this body called "Community Action"[54] started up, and I was named president of the committee in my community because I worked for the common good and I was progressive.

I started to write petitions and asked for a passable road from La

Gaining more Power
than small land
owner

using system
to get material
resources

Sierra to Río Blanco. This was difficult because some politicians were small property owners, and they considered themselves big shots. They thought they were untouchable, and they didn't want to let the road go through. But I defied them. I talked to the secretary of public works, and as president of the Community Action Committee I was able to get work started on the road, which as I said started in the municipio of La Sierra and went in the direction of the corregimiento of Río Blanco.

I realized that the Community Action Committee was originally established so some opportunistic politiqueros could manipulate it, since it was started by the government at that time. I saw that even if the material benefits were small, though, or the services they provided were limited, they could do some good, right? Knowing that the state was providing money that actually belonged to the working people.

At that time we were still in that period around 1957, and none of those scheming politiqueros, above all the Liberals but also from the Conservative Party, even though they had their government, none of them understood the Community Action Committees. But we thought they did this at the higher levels of the Conservative Party in order to politicize people in the rural areas. The political parties controlled the CACs through their departmental leadership or they controlled how they were managed at the level of the municipio or the vereda.

But at that time they weren't using them politically yet, at least not a lot. Politicizing all that . . . they politicized them more when they established the National Front. That's when Liberal and Conservative politicians inserted themselves into the Community Action Committees, and for a committee to get any help they had to serve the interests of these mendacious politiqueros, whether they were permanent functionaries or just during a certain time in office.

At that time I still believed in the Liberals. Whatever the issue I was determined to defend them even though I knew that some of them were sectarian and even hateful and vengeful with other people. I defended those of them who were fair-minded and just, but there wasn't any other organization, no option but the Liberal Party.

I didn't get involved in campaigns because it was the time of la Violencia[55] under the government of Mariano Ospina Pérez. That's when the national leaders of the Liberal Party started to lose sight of their principles. Then came the government of Laureano Gómez and then in '53 Rojas Pinilla overthrew the government of Laureano Gómez, but there was no Liberal Party organization. I defended Liberals but just as an individual, people who were Liberals from way back.

How did I change my way of thinking about politics? When the election of '46 was lost and then Gaitán was assassinated, that's when the persecution started. Then there was the coup by Rojas Pinilla, and he didn't do anything for the people either. Laureano Gómez did nothing and Rojas Pinilla did nothing. When they came out for the National Front, I was against it. How did two people, Laureano Gómez and Alberto Lleras Camargo, make us believe that we should forget all the bloodshed and put the deaths of three hundred thousand Liberals[56] behind us? The purpose of the National Front was just to divide up the spoils. By that time I had analyzed the way the parties worked, how they governed; I had studied the question of López Pumarejo.

In 1960 I fell for the MRL. Lots of pretty words; they talked about changing the Colombian state. Alfonso López Michelsen opposed the National Front and that's the way we thought, too. I was interested in the politics of change in order to set right the damage done by Conservative policies, to turn things around politically. I was in it from '60 to '66. I agreed to serve in the municipal leadership [of the MRL] and I was a municipal councilor in La Sierra for four years.

In Cauca we had Aníbal Prado, who I thought was great. He was a leftist from the time he was a student. We also had Omar Henry Velasco, also from the time he was a student. As councilor I fought for the proposals of the MRL. Prado talked about changing the country through social policy, making it an industrialized country. He was an honest person. Later he died.

In 1966 López Michelsen entered the government. That's why I left party politics. López Michelsen left the movement stranded without consulting anyone. We were worth nothing to him; he decided all by himself to join the government, without any discussion.

At the Third Campesino Congress[57] López Michelsen was sitting there as president, but I spoke up about the betrayal of the MRL. The compañeros from the department of Nariño were shocked that I had treated the president so badly. López Michelsen had been a personal acquaintance of mine. He had come to La Sierra and I had made public speeches there in his presence. One day I made a speech and said that we didn't want a revolution like the one in Cuba; we shouldn't be fooled by that kind of revolution.

Then, in 1966, I decided to step back from politics. That's when they instituted the new policies for campesinos. I didn't want to hear anything about it. Carlos Lleras Restrepo talked to us about a national transformation, but at the same time they raised the salaries of all members of Congress and all the rest. The campesino movement got busy because they said that with a card identifying you as an active campesino they would give you everything: land, credit, and everything.

There was a seminar in Popayán in 1970 and the people from La Sierra took me there because I had spoken out. I went as a delegate to this seminar for campesinos in Popayán and it was worthwhile because I helped get some things clear for people. They had me address the attendees of a short course, and I gave a good talk. It was on July 20.[58] I said we needed to find another policy, not that of Carlos Lleras Restrepo. We needed to define our own policy, which coincided with the position of the people following the so-called Sincelejo line.[59] Some indigenous people from Cauca also attended the course and after that they wanted me to work with CRIC.

But the National Front emerged suddenly in 1957. I heard about a delegation including Alberto Lleras Camargo to go to where Laureano Gómez was in Spain. The story was that coming out of that meeting they formed a National Front. That's when that arrangement was formed and they overthrew the government of Rojas Pinilla on May 10. I found out about that in the newspaper.

Since my education hasn't been just by reading books, my education has been reading a lot of newspapers, because I didn't have any framework and I wanted to know a lot of things; so reading a lot of journalism was very useful. I also read a lot of books, and I even became a scribe.

I wrote letters for people to their friends, also love letters, that kind of thing. I wrote for all those people and with my help they won over wives, girlfriends, and such.

When I heard people talk about the National Front policy, I didn't like it at all in the sense that this policy meant impunity for the death of three hundred thousand Liberals. Once the policy was established, that was that. That's how they covered up the murder of all those people that as I said, included people from the Liberal Party and the Conservative Party. And I was coming to realize that it wasn't the Liberal leaders prodding the Liberal Party or the Conservative leaders prodding the Conservative Party to do this. The motive was how to divide up the spoils produced by the state; I mean, what's produced by all working people.

I saw that by forming the National Front they took advantage of people who had experienced tragedies, problems, a lot of things that had happened, above all the murder of Liberals by the Conservative Party government. They fooled people into thinking that after they formed the National Front, life would be different and people would have access to all kinds of rights to get everything they needed, and by democratic means that is, in order to bring about a democratic politics, that the dictatorship would end, and since we people didn't understand what dictatorship was or what democracy was, people were fooled.

Under those circumstances, you had to vote for the National Front. In order to support the National Front policy, party leaders decided to organize an election called a *plebiscite* where the people would vote as to whether they agreed or didn't agree with it. It was understood that this plebiscite was a program devised by the two political parties, and the people were totally confused, because it seemed you had to vote in favor of this plebiscite for democracy and so the people voted that way.[60]

After the National Front policy was established, that's where they began to organize women, youth, and even children who had to support the policies of the plebiscite and of the National Front. I saw that more than anything the National Front depended on the support of the people who knew the least about politics. They brought these people in as supporters, as a pillar of support for the National Front, so then they

could live off it, dividing up the spoils such as monopolizing government positions like seats in Congress and alternating presidents from
the two parties. I understood that they were fooling the people badly
and that's why I didn't get involved in it.

So I became disillusioned with those Liberal leaders. I compared
them to the policies of Enrique Olaya Herrera and his government in
1930–1934. I realized he had done a great thing, which was reclaiming that land, that is he pursued the conflict over land the godos[61] had
sold off at the port of Leticia,[62] so I still held out some hope. Then I remembered the policies developed by Alfonso López Pumarejo and his
government, under which he always defended the rights of workers
and campesinos. For instance, workers and campesinos had a right to
their jobs, and they started to give the workers things like work clothes,
shoes, and so on. I thought these measures did some good and I still
felt connected to the so-called leaders of the Liberal Party. But I also remembered that Alberto Lleras Camargo was well known as the man responsible for thinking up the National Front, and I remembered he was
also the one who handed over the Liberal Party government to the Conservative Party in 1946. So I was utterly disenchanted with the leadership of those politicians.

Religion, Money, and Politics

At that time we didn't know anything or I didn't know anything about
what it was all about. I considered myself very much in the dark, like
someone feeling his way around, completely blind. Anyway I was frightened because I thought if I went against the way the priests taught religion, above all when they said that there's heaven, earth, and glory, then
I would be committing a sin. I was a little afraid on this particular question because then I might go to hell and the demons there would be
shoving fire up my butt.[63]

As for now, I think that religion has been a fraud and continues to
be a fraud because what's preached by the so-called ministers of the

church, who are the priests, the clerics, well they themselves don't practice what they preached back then nor what they preach now. To me, if the so-called minister doesn't observe these teachings, then none of the faithful are going to live that way either, no matter what they say.

To me it's a kind of submission, a ruse, and a way of keeping people completely subjugated to a way of thinking that they want to maintain for a long time as a way to exploit people. To me it's clear what a lot of priests have done is go into indigenous communities and into campesino areas to exploit them and live off them.

Some of the priests have gotten rich and become landowners, with fine homes and beautiful gardens in the cities. So what they're doing isn't about penitence. No, what they're doing is exploiting the ignorant to live off them.

And the way the Catholic religion works, or let's say the Church, it has to change. By all means, a change of some kind is needed. Not continuing to do things like the way it's been and the way it still is in some places, you know? If they don't change, I don't know how long it will be until that business has to be brought to an end, you know?

With the National Front I saw things had changed a lot. The social and political situation before that was totally different. At least there was more respect between one person and another. In business, for example, your word was a contract, a commitment, and people kept their word when they gave it, even more than any document. Nobody needed contracts or deeds because they knew a person had given his word of commitment and that's what would be done.

But after that things began to start, let's say, going down hill little by little. Very terrible things started to happen. There began to be thieves and murderers, that kind of unpleasantness. And every day it's been getting worse. I think this deterioration of social life we've been seeing in indigenous communities, among campesinos and among the workers, can be attributed to bad government policies. We can say it's a system adopted by politiqueros, those holding certain government positions just right now as well as the permanent ones, the fixtures. They get something to live off while they set us to fighting among ourselves. We

Liberals against the Conservatives, for example, or campesino against campesino, so they can appropriate what's produced, or the value of what the campesinos produce, and live off that.

I think there are two things: one thing is the political part, or let's say the capitalism of the landowners, business owners, and some middlemen. In my opinion there are also bad government policies completely run according to so-called constitutional law. But we know this supposed constitutional law is organized and defined by politiqueros who get into Congress, into the Senate and the House of Representatives. They're people who have a certain amount of capital to begin with, and once they get set up there they forget that the people have needs. They just remember to pass laws that hurt the poor and help themselves along with other capitalists and the government. So it's an organized and entrenched group, well situated to take advantage of the poor.

But getting back to their policies, what they're interested in is to defend wealth, to defend capital. They never take an interest in the needs of the workers. Anyway, since their goal is to enrich themselves, all they're interested in is to compound their own wealth, their money and many other kinds of property. To me this is a terrible thing, good only for these opportunistic politicos and government administrators, for landowners, and for all kinds of middlemen who facilitate exploitation, you could say, but very unfavorable for us.

The fact of subjugation tells us that the thing to do is get hold of some capital. You have to have enough money to have things, to live, so sometimes people want to have more, right? But we can say that really, indigenous unity, the majority thinks more along the lines of winning respect by achieving unity and as a result being able to enjoy the benefits of the things they produce.

Seeing how things were going in the National Front, the MRL came together in 1960 under the leadership of Alfonso López Michelsen. I thought that this was what was needed, a true Liberal, a defender of the Liberal Party, so there would be some leadership and above all that this leadership would defend its philosophy.

And López Michelsen launched his campaign in 1960. From the beginning he said that Colombia needed a social and economic revolution. So those of us who didn't agree with the National Front policy, we thought he would be a leader who would really take up the banner of the Liberal Party, not be concerned with dividing up the spoils of the state but defend the Liberal Party cause. Many of us believed that and many of us were fooled, but we threw ourselves into the cause of López Michelsen, which was the MRL.

For me to enter into MRL politics was a little unexpected because I was politically marginalized, completely so. I didn't know where to start, how to launch the movement in the municipio, because nobody was talking about Liberal Party policies. All the other Liberals had surrendered to the bureaucracy run by the Liberal and Conservative parties. So it seemed to me there were no leaders any more, you know?

Elections were coming up at that time for the municipal council, and there was a movement made up of young people who were not connected to any local politiqueros. We were opposed to some of the caciques and this youth movement grew. I became more visible at this time because I worked together with the youth movement and we had some successes.

One time we had a meeting where forty-five of us young people attended. I told them if they were going to take a stand as men, they had to be firm; they had to stay strong in their opposition to the National Front system. And they agreed. They liked what I said very much. Then, however, they let themselves be dissuaded because they were related one way or another to the cacique, to his compadre, or to his comadre, and those relationships won out.

Two weeks before the election this political movement, the youth movement, fell apart. At that time Dr. Aníbal Prado was the leader of the MRL's left wing in Cauca, and he went to the town of La Sierra two weeks before the election to coordinate with the youth movement; but by that time it had fallen apart because people had defected to the opportunists of the National Front. That was the end of it.

I wasn't even at the market the day that Dr. Prado arrived. He was very active, very antisectarian and appalled by the hatred some people had for the [working] class. He was interested in a life among the people, a life dedicated to the rights of man, or social rights in this country. He was very intelligent, very capable. He was even a poet, a great writer. He worked a lot in the area of criminal law. At that time he organized a provisional leadership group for the municipio, and the position of secretary fell to a brother of mine who barely knew how to sign his name. I had to laugh, it was so ridiculous that my brother was secretary of this committee and he didn't know what he was saying or doing, you know? Well, the people came together and they wanted me to participate, to help out. I didn't accept the offer; I just said I would think about it.

Then I saw that some people were starting to move, so I joined up and became an active participant. A week later we presented a slate [of candidates] for the municipal council, even though we had done no campaigning and there was no time to do so. But we had to present a slate in order to establish our values as people of the left, as people, let's say, who wanted to exercise their rights, the right to political access. Unfortunately it fell upon me to head up the list, but since we had only two weeks to campaign I got only ninety-six votes, which meant I didn't win a seat.

And, well, the caciques as usual were offering a lot of things like schools, jobs, and health services, the usual. What we were offering was to break those ties, to go off without them and the Liberal Party would end up being stronger. We had to follow the MRL because it was the group that was defending the political ideals of the Liberal Party. The others were sellouts. So some very honest people who had been persecuted, who had been harshly persecuted at the time of the violence, they came over into our sector. We didn't offer a single thing. Not a single thing. They were volunteers who thought the MRL position would be productive in the long and short term. We thought the great leader López Michelsen would keep his word.

Here in Cauca, Dr. Prado founded the weekly *Orientación Liberal*. Nationally, López Michelsen founded the weekly *La Calle*. A lot of leftist politicians were writers in these periodicals, and they wrote a lot; they wrote and spoke very well. Sometimes they talked about the Left and about the Right and about social and political change in the country. They were also taken in, most of them, and we, well, we too swallowed the story because it was something new.

The conflict between the MRL and the National Front sharpened in '62. The working and lower classes again wanted me to head up the local MRL and to be on the electoral list for the council. I accepted again in order to oppose the caciques and the politiqueros of the National Front. Despite all their dirty tricks, we got 777 votes in the election for municipal council, and those of the National Front got 787 votes; so in the end they beat us by ten votes, despite all the trickery that's built into the system, as you well know. We elected the first two people on the MRL list, two councilors, and two Liberal councilors were elected from the National Front, and the other four were Conservatives.

So on that occasion we were very visible and we won a lot of political prestige on the municipal level. The MRL also grew at the departmental level. We who were the MRL councilors, which was another compañero and myself, we were very strong in upholding and defending the cause. You can say we were defeating the cacique system and all the problems the National Front people were causing at the municipal level. We were gaining ground. We got the municipio to pay off some of the debts that had burdened it and the right to jobs for some of the youth who needed them. They had to state that they were able to provide a service and they would be named as employees.

Before long it was 1964 and we faced another set of elections. This time I didn't want to head the list as a candidate for office. Instead I ran as a substitute to be called on only if needed. But my line came out a winner and the main candidate resigned. That's how I came to prevail over the caciques, because we had a municipal agreement to rotate the leadership between the Liberals for six months and the Conservatives for six months. So for the first six months a Conservative presided over the leadership and then it was time to rotate. The responsibility fell to me and I headed up the leadership for eighteen months. I ended up presiding over the municipal council not for six months, but for eighteen months.

In 1964 there were elections for representative bodies at all levels. Our leader López Michelsen had us believe he would keep on working. By this time the president was Guillermo León Valencia.

Then in '66 there were presidential elections and López Michelsen was a candidate but not so strong any more. In any case, Carlos Lleras Restrepo won the election. Until the election, López Michelsen was having us believe he was a man of the MRL and he'd uphold the ideal of a clean Liberal Party. But the dust had hardly settled after Lleras Restrepo's victory when just three months later López Michelsen defected to the government of Lleras Restrepo and left all us MRL followers out in the cold with no idea how to start over.

People here in Cauca went in a lot of different directions. Some people went with the National Front, and others backed off politics entirely. The whole movement split up and the people who had been in the struggle were completely disillusioned, determined to never again let themselves be fooled by that kind of charlatan, because after what he did we considered him absolutely shameless and a complete sellout, not worth a damn for anything having to do with politics.

I think what happened to me also happened to a lot of other people, you know what I mean? That's what I think. Politics made me so mad that I completely separated myself. It made me mad just to hear anything about politics. It was something I hated to talk about or even to hear about, to hear anyone talk about the Liberal Party, because he was a . . . a . . . At that time I considered that man to be vile and corrupt, a miserable turncoat who left us out in the cold, so what was the point?

I didn't even want to think about all the politiquería; it was just useless. I considered at that time, and I would still say that the National Front was really just a cover for the enemy's misdeeds, I mean the enemy at the time of the worst violence, the time of La Violencia, which was the Conservative Party. Then there were the patronage positions controlled by both the Liberal and Conservative parties, so the Liberal Party was completely discredited as a bunch of conservatized, unprincipled sellouts. I can't explain all this perfectly, but it meant the end of the faith, the fervor, the thirst for change that existed in the Liberal Party. There had been a kind of excitement in the party, hope for the future, but not after that.

Being in the MRL, the political struggles I went through were tragic, because we were also persecuted. The people in the National Front called us crooks, thieves. It was popular then to talk about the rabble, bandits, hooligans, all that kind of thing. So that's what they called us. And they fingered people. They persecuted and jailed MRL people all over the place. In some places they kicked and beat people in the process, clubbed people. It was a terrible situation for us.

When López Michelsen betrayed the movement in favor of Lleras Restrepo, I felt like such a bonehead that I ought to get someone to whip my bare ass once a day every day. I'd been getting a lot of work and making good money in architecture, farming, carpentry, and building, and most of what I made was going right to the MRL. I'm not going to lie; I lost quite a bit of money.

At that time there was no mention of any indigenous policy, none, especially where I'm from in the southern area, in the south of Cauca. No one over there talked about an indigenous movement in those days, about finding ways to defend the people or to organize to demand any rights. No, there wasn't anything like that yet.

The fact is that in the south, the resguardos like Río Blanco, Guachicono, Pancitará, Caquiona, San Sebastián, these are very politicized. Some are Liberal and others are Conservative, committed to Liberal or Conservative party politics. So the indigenous people who joined the MRL were very brave because they knew they would be persecuted, but they still joined to defend what they thought at that time was the cause of the Liberal Party. They were very determined but there weren't very many of them, and from only about a fourth of the indigenous areas.

Working with the MRL and the Political Parties

When I was a member of the municipal council, the first thing I did was get the overdue bills paid. The municipios always operated that way, falling behind on paying people for their services, even though they have an obligation to pay the working people, the people who maybe work out of necessity. They owed a lot to the people who had been working for the municipio, and that was the first thing I did.

Another thing I did was not have municipal employees appointed just because they were from a particular party. They had to be people who would really work for the good of the municipio. I understood that municipal politics was manipulated by the local caciques, you know? The so-called Liberals and Conservatives. These caciques saw their opportunity to gain an advantage when it came to naming municipal workers. That's why they went for political power, to be able to name their brothers or sons, nephews and sometimes their political clients for municipal jobs, not to mention their party underlings.

We began to separate all these things from party politics and the council began to take the positions I was proposing. The other councilors, the members of the council, they gradually came to see that politics wasn't like everyone had always said. It wasn't just partisan, hateful, or vengeful people; it was to serve the needs of the population.

Another thing is about the improvements. In those four years, first the *Caja Agraria*, the Agricultural Bank, was set up, and producers who needed it got access to small amounts of credit. The caciques opposed the Caja Agraria because they were also the ones who were exploiting people. They lived off what the working class produced by farming. So they didn't like this idea, but nevertheless we succeeded and the Caja Agraria was set up. Not everyone was happy, and it was very hard, but we struggled until it was established.

Thanks to our strong criticisms of the municipal and national leaders of the National Front they released funds to fix the municipal building. We succeeded at that and we also got an appropriation to erect a building for the public market.

I was the council president when the contracts were drawn up to build the first floor of the market building. I worked very closely with the community, and I also proposed that a school be built. But the caciques were vocal and stubborn in opposing the school, and in the end it didn't get built. I thought it was very important for the people's education and it was a popular proposal, but we weren't successful. It was a first step, though, and after I left office the people got organized. It was a grassroots effort, not a case of organizing by political bosses but by the people themselves. They saw that there was a need for a school and they got it.

Why did the caciques oppose the school and the Caja Agraria? Well, they were against the bank because they had a little capital, a small amount of capital, and they bought agricultural products, like coffee for example—they bought products ahead of time. In effect, they lent money to producers until the harvest came in. Afterward the producers had to sell them the products directly, either in bulk weight or by the load. The cacique would then sell these products at the best prices and make a fat profit. Sometimes if a quantity of produce was worth say 20 pesos, the cacique could pay the producer as little as two to five pesos in advance. Over the course of a year and with the quantity of goods being resold they would make a bundle of money. So that's why they opposed the Caja Agraria, you see?

As for the school, they were against it because they were the ones in charge; they were unchallenged, and they didn't want anyone to oppose them. That's how things had worked for fifty years, ever since the founding of the municipio of La Sierra. Then they saw that fifty years after the founding of the municipio, here comes this Indian to cause them trouble. This drove them crazy because after all, the last thing most of them wanted was for people to get educated. It was better for them to stay ignorant so they could be taken advantage of economically, so the people who controlled the municipio could enforce local laws to manipulate them. That's why they didn't want the local Caja Agraria or the school.

I also found that the policy of the National Front as expressed in municipal legislation was to divide up among just a few people what was produced by everybody in the municipio, in the department, and in all of Colombia. But it was never to help the people. Very little funding ever went to improvements for the people. Everything that's been done to improve people's lives has been because of their own efforts, their own demands, and their own work. I mean like decent roads and schools, these are all the fruit of the people's efforts. That's why when I lent my support to starting a school in the area where I live now, in Timbío,[64] the caciques put up a lot of opposition.

I've never been a mouthpiece for any fat cat, landowner, or politiquero; I've never been a pawn of anyone like that. So my freedom of action helped me get the school started here where I live now. Despite all the opposition, we won and got the school. Now we've had high school graduates, we've educated teachers at the normal school, and some are even at the university.

To me the way the system works, the way the government works is that it keeps the people marginalized, and they don't get up the energy to do anything because they're kept ignorant. Then they're exploited because they don't have any way to defend themselves. Just think, if I hadn't gone up against them and made the effort to struggle for education in this area, we wouldn't have those high school graduates or university students.

To understand why this politiquería was so ingrained in people you have to realize what they've been conditioned to think. If you belong to the Liberal or Conservative party then that's the cause you have to defend. The people are indoctrinated to believe a lot of those kinds of things. I mean people think if you don't vote you'll die or you'll go to hell, like the priests used to say. Some of these people if they don't vote they get sick, so they vote because they're so easily manipulated, they're so submissive, and this despite the fact that they don't get anything. They vote obediently, afraid that if they don't vote, or if we don't vote, there won't be anything for them in the budget; they're not going to give them a school; they're not going to give them the health clinic they've been promised in every election.

These politiqueros would say, "Well, there are going to be bridges here," and the community would respond, "But there aren't any rivers"; so the politicians say, "We'll build the bridges and the rivers, too."[65] These politicians are demagogues, you know? Politiqueros always help themselves and find whatever way they can to fool people. You already know that.

There's a sickness. It's present in the whole ruling class in relation to the class they dominate—it's really because they establish these compadrazgo[66] relationships, you know? Another thing is they used the most visible campesinos as their mouthpieces in the debate. They would send them a letter saying "Well then, you're going to lead the debate." And they told them they were important people, capable people, and maybe, just maybe we can help you get a scholarship, a job, or help you in some other way. Ignorant people thought these promises would be kept; they'd be offered jobs or scholarships, all that kind of crap. It's almost like they want to believe them, you know, like they're happy to be fooled. That's how they keep them subservient. But then when they ask about getting that work, that job with the municipio, they say, "Well, there wasn't enough, it didn't come through, it's not gonna happen right now because you know you have to give it to the people who've worked the most, so you have to keep on working, but maybe in the future it'll come through." In any case if the school had actually been founded, that would be one thing, but there wasn't any school anyway, so what kind of scholarships? And at the departmental level it was impossible because there wasn't enough [to work with]. They got nothing.

Compadrazgo relationships with the town's caciques and manipulators were very effective, because they told their compadres it was a great honor and very advantageous to have that connection with a cacique. The Church also approved of these relationships. The priests told people that the compadre and the comadre[67] had to be treated very respectfully, the ahijado[68] also had to be treated very respectfully, and one compadre had to be at the service of the other. And the ahijado had to show great respect and be completely at the service of the padrino and the madrina. So people were taken in by all these relationships that were an obligation, but also an honor. They felt honored to be a compadre of one of the caciques, one of their exploiters. And I do mean exploiters, because they were people who took advantage of the people's ignorance.

The Management Class of the Catholic Religion

I can also say that I too was very submissive to the question of the Catholic religion. When I organized meetings at the school, I called upon the priest and the mayor, so the priest thought I was a little naïve, domesticated, at their service. When there were celebrations for Saint Isidro, the Blessed Virgin, or the Sacred Heart, the Father would send a note saying "You're put in charge of collecting funds for such and such a celebration."

But what happened was one day the priest slipped up. There was a meeting at the school we founded and he found a newspaper that talked about the opposition in other countries. It talked about communism, socialism, and democracies. It talked about dictatorships and all that kind of thing. So I asked the priest, "Well, but you're talking against communism, against dictatorships. Why don't you do me a favor and explain to me what that is?" Actually I knew something about socialism, and I thought that socialism had to do with getting united and working together, all for one and one for all. So we got a discussion going right there at a lunch, and suddenly the priest decided that he couldn't discuss that with me any more because I knew a few things about what they call socialism. So what he did was, he didn't even finish eating, because he was too agitated. He just got up and started doing something else.

Right then and there his image of me had changed; in his eyes, the mystique was gone, and he never sent me another letter telling me to collect funds for any saint he wanted to honor. He didn't want anything more to do with me after that. I saw that it was a phony thing they did, a scam they have to fool the campesinos.

I can't denounce all the priests in Colombia or say they're all bad, you know? It seems to have occurred to some of the clergy that ministering to the group of people who adhere to the Holy Catholic Apostolic Roman Church, as they call it—that it's deceitful if it doesn't truly match up with the mission they should be following. So there have been some different types, and I can't say at this time that all of them are exploiters.

Some of them have thought differently and have seen things more clearly, starting for example with Father Camilo Torres.[69] He proposed to defend the working class, to work with marginalized people, with people under the spell of politiqueros, and with people who had been deceived in all kinds of ways. He began to struggle and I don't know to what extent he had faults, but he struggled in the interests of a social class because he understood that the country was governed by another class of people who dominated society throughout their lives, you know. And the system and the state didn't provide any services to the proletariat, which was the class that produced all the wealth the state ever had. So I recognize that.

And there are others who've kept coming along, more than one, who worked with the people, with humanity, and maybe not to hoodwink anyone but who actually wanted to work with what's real, and with dedication. Maybe they don't work for their own personal interests or their regional interests, but to keep moving forward.

I say this because take for example the case of our compañeros, the proletarian class, like the people in El Salvador. There was a priest there and there are priests who support the [working] class. In El Salvador they killed the archbishop while he was giving mass, the one who was defending the working class, the laboring class, the dispossessed.[70] So this means they're thinking differently and seeking change, and they're keeping the pledge they made to the Church, to be the heirs or sons of Christ, right? We think they're doing what history says Christ did. In Nicaragua, too, some of the priests confronted the government in the overthrow of Anastasio Somoza. Some nuns who realize that innocent people, simple people, are being persecuted, sometimes they help. And because they help they're accused of being guerrillas.

So I think things are reaching this level, this group that manages the Catholic religion, they're getting to the place where they should be, you know? To serve the people.

We've gotten very few of them here in Cauca. It seems the archbishops who came before and even the current ones have kept their people very, very focused on a way of exploiting people, not on a way of helping them. Maybe now very recently there's people who are beginning to see if they can [change], but we still can't see who is who.

Another thing is that having had hope, as indigenous people with hope, as campesinos, as an exploited class, what we have are the so-called ministers of the Church such as Arce Vivas, who was the archbishop of Popayán. By necessity we were forced to take back a piece of land he had taken away from the communities of Coconuco.[71] And that was a pretty tough fight. Even though he asked various government agencies to defend that land, they couldn't defend it. What happened was the land passed into the hands of the community but with a lot of persecution, also very strong, because there was an alliance between the civilian government, the military government, and the Church hierarchy, the archbishop.

There was also the case of Tierradentro, where it was necessary to fight pretty hard and confront Monsignor Vallejo with a number of criticisms. His many misdeeds were so widely publicized that he had to go. So, this "pillar of the Church" was of no use to humanity, none at all. We can say, on the other hand, that the compañero who was in Corinto, we could truly call him compañero. Compañero Pedro León Rodríguez[72] was a man who unlike the others went out among the indigenous communities to teach, to say that the essential message of the Catholic religion was not being upheld, and to comply with this obligation one should state clearly who was in the right. One should defend that class, because the idea of the Catholic religion was to make sacrifices, to become not a landowner, a capitalist, or a cacique so you could lord it over people, but one who imparts Catholic social justice.

Looking for an Organization: The Campesino Association and the Indigenous Organization

As I observed how things worked, I found discrimination everywhere. I also found there was administrative discrimination when poor people made use of the justice system, whether to file a complaint or make any demand. Whoever had even slightly greater economic possibilities, that's who they paid attention to. And even if a poorer person, someone from the most disadvantaged class was legally in the right, they still didn't take him at all seriously and no justice was done, none at all. I thought this showed a lot of inequality in how things worked, but I didn't realize at all what was in fact behind this.

I kept looking at this and I came to understand what it really meant to acquire economic and administrative power. Economic power was money. Administrative power was that administrators only dispensed justice to people who could give them some chicken for example or buy them drinks if they went out to do an on-site inspection. And denigrate the people who worked the hardest or denigrate the poor, or slander them, and so on. So I found the situation extremely degrading, very much the fault of the administrators.

Politically I found that political power, whether you're talking about the cacique of a town, of a province—a department that is—or some powerful figure or big shot in the country, that person, that official, would use his power to serve the interests of that class. Anyone who got involved in politics, whether in the Liberal or Conservative party, even if he was the biggest fraud, a person whose only achievement was getting people to give him what he wanted on election day, even if he was totally ignorant, even if he didn't know how to sign his name, they put him in office. They named him to a government position; he became an inspector for the judicial police or he became mayor. All that mattered was that he was partisan for the right partisan group.

To me this was a warped way to govern. It was a deceitful government that deceived people just so they'd come out on election day, so they'd come out and give them their votes. And what did the people get in return for standing behind a party or a political leader? It was very dishonest because naming illiterates as administrators meant nothing got done clearly or correctly. They didn't have the ability to administer things as they should. And I don't mean that this happened just once or just in one place. Until recently, before mayors were elected, they put in mayors who when they got in office, at first they didn't even know where to sign a payroll. And they botched up the payrolls of teachers and other departmental and municipal employees because they didn't know what they were saying or what they were doing.

So I began to see that traditional party politics didn't have anything to offer the common people or the campesinos. There was a national party committee at the highest level where they looked for ways to deceive people and then blame someone's ignorance, saying something like "Well, the person who screwed up or who didn't act properly was so and so." But why do they put such ignorant people into office? If so and so screwed up why can't he go to jail? Why can't they punish him? Why can't the people take him down a peg? This is one example of the things I thought were all wrong in this kind of governing system.

Including, let me say, the shameful way they treated me when I was campaigning for the MRL, hounding me in every imaginable way for their own sectarian purposes. For one thing they laughed off whatever I said, because since I was a stupid Indian, a savage, what would I know anyway? An Indian without a peso to his name, what could he possibly know? So that demoralized me, but I didn't let it get to me too much because I knew, I understood that there was such a thing as human rights and a person had to struggle to defend the rights of man, for himself and for others.

I was demoralized by all this—I mean this kind of politics and the government of Lleras Restrepo. Then he organized the National Association of Campesinos. People started saying things about it and my friends said "Come on, Palechor, work with us organizing the association of campesinos. Now we're going to straighten out our situation; now we're going to have things." So I asked them, "So how do you obtain those things the government has offered you? They're not going to give away cattle or land to anyone and everyone with a card. They're not going to give everyone sheep or mules, burros, none of that kind of credit." Then, well, you had to join and you had to buy that membership card, which cost five pesos.

I was so disillusioned with being governed by the Camargo family, the Lleras family, and the López family, and lastly with Alfonso López Michelsen and the fraud he pulled, that I didn't want any part of this. In fact, I was thinking that it really was time to go back to private life. Whoever has to die, let them die, I thought, because in politics they're all frauds. No one's honest, everyone lies, and they all get ahead on someone else's back, on the backs of the ignorant.

But there was a peasant movement. Some people were very happy with Lleras Restrepo's policies toward campesinos. What they didn't like about Lleras Restrepo was the Agrarian Reform. They didn't like that part very much because it wasn't really clear how it worked. As I said, the campesinos thought about all the credits the government had offered them. Some of them believed what they heard and got involved with the program. There was an organization, but people asked for a lot of things, submitted a lot of petitions, but I think they got nothing out of it. Maybe it was like I thought; it was nothing but another trick. Get taken for another ride.

Why didn't they like the Agrarian Reform? People didn't like the Agrarian Reform because as I said, they didn't understand it. They thought it was the government negotiating with landowners over their lands, to distribute their lands to other people, but they didn't understand at all how that would be.

Plus they weren't that interested because there weren't large landowners in this area, just people who owned their own small properties. And as for the resguardos, the government knew the indigenous resguardos were never going to accept the government position; the resguardos were not going to let themselves be manipulated out of existence, because the cabildos in the south are very protective of resguardo land. No question, they defended the land like it was a part of themselves, and they didn't want any changes to take place under the name of the Agrarian Reform.

So I didn't get involved in the campesino organization at all, because again, as I say again, it was still part of the National Front program and still in the hands of Lleras Restrepo, and I no longer had any faith in the Liberals. That's why I refused to get involved.

But I was a very popular person, and one market day when they were having one of their meetings in town, in the cabecera, a friend took me by the hand to where they were meeting to see if I could help them, if there was any way I could help by speaking out in their favor. Once I was at the meeting, I could see that they were doing a lot of things poorly or at least poorly planned, so I made some short comments. The people at that meeting liked what I said, as they had before, and more than that they were glad to have me in the meeting, so they invited me to come to their regular biweekly meetings.

Two weeks later a man showed up, an Agrarian Reform coordinator for the southern region, including the departments of Valle del Cauca, Cauca, Nariño, Putumayo, and maybe Chocó. That was the region this coordinator was responsible for. He was one of the people I call the centralists, those full-time political opportunists. He was an educated man, though, a professional. As it turned out, he was there that day to get people to go to Popayán and take a six-day course being given to members of the campesino association. And they had called an election to choose who would be the local delegates to the course, who would then represent the political positions of the campesino association. Well, I came out on top. They elected me at the top of the list in the first vote, but I declined. Then they voted a second time and again I came out on the top of the list. I declined again. The third time they voted, they still put me at the top of the list. So that was three times. Well, the name of this gentleman was Álvarez, and Doctor Álvarez said, "If the people need you, if the campesinos need you, if they want to give you this job, then take the job. Go take the course and if you want to leave the organization after that, then leave. But go." So looking at it that way, I thought, well okay, I'll go.

And I did. I signed up and attended for the six days, and it turned out I pretty much understood it. The course was pretty clear; I mean I could understand it. Other people from the area including some of the campesinos didn't understand it so well and they asked me to explain things. So I told them a few things; they needed me to clarify some of the things that had been said in the course. Not that I agreed with it, I just happened to be there. But the other attendees wanted to elect me to the departmental campesino association. Somehow I got out of that one, but when I was called upon to speak at the closing ceremony I got a little carried away. Since it was July 20, the National Congress was holding its opening session, and at different points of my speech I said things like "Today is a patriotic holiday, or what they call the Twentieth of July, when Congress inaugurates a new session. Today as that den of scoundrels is divvying up the pork in Bogotá, let us raise high the red flag of the Colombian people's movement here in Popayán: To defend our own interests, the interests of the Colombian peasantry, of the indigenous people, but with no taint of any Liberal or Conservative party policies."

I did it like that, agitating, you know? So anyway the people saw I had convictions, you know? Convictions different from those of the Liberal or Conservative party. So it happened that the people at the course that day would remember my name, indigenous people from Tierradentro, from the north, east, and center of Cauca. My presence at that course made me very visible, and ever since that time people have listened when I speak. They're interested in my opinions.

I had already become well known in the MRL together with compañero Gustavo Mejía,[73] who like me was deceived into supporting that movement. But also like me he became frustrated and turned in another direction, doing union organizing in the north of Cauca, organizing farm workers. But this compañero saw that nothing was being changed by organizing campesinos, and he decided to organize among indigenous people. So he took up that work with a few friends from Silvia, Toribío, and Corinto. They talked to some indigenous people and decided to call an indigenous assembly for February 24, 1971. The assembly took place in Toribío, but what happened was that one of the speakers was a politiquero, not to be trusted. But he was an agitator, supposedly leftist and revolutionary and all that. Anyway, he stirred things up against the people who organized the Regional Indigenous Council. That was when the Regional Indigenous Council of Cauca (*Consejo Regional Indígena del Cauca*—CRIC) was established, on February 24, 1971.

My Work in CRIC

I didn't attend that assembly. I still wasn't known in the organization. And since there was a lot of persecution, the executive committee didn't get much done. The executive committee was made up of compañeros from the center and the north.

But they'd already seen me work effectively when I took the course, and another assembly was called to take place in La Susana, also in the north of Cauca. This time they invited me, because compañero Gustavo knew me very well, and supposedly they said they had to invite people from the south; to invite Palechor and some others. But the important thing was that Palechor should be there because they knew me as a decisive individual, a man who was ready for the struggle, and some of my experiences due to the problems I'd had—it seems they were good for something.

The compañeros came and invited me. I told them I couldn't go, not that I didn't like the organization, but I was completely disillusioned. I'd said previously that I wouldn't join any public organization because I was disillusioned with politics after my experiences in the Liberal Party and especially in the MRL, and I wanted no part of this kind of thing. I didn't want to hear anything about an organization, because I thought maybe its purpose was more backstabbing and I didn't want to be fooled again.

The assembly in La Susana was on September 6, 1971, that same year. I didn't attend that one either. But they named another executive committee made up of different people. And what they did was even though I wasn't there, because I didn't go to the assembly, nevertheless they elected me secretary of the Regional Indigenous Council of Cauca.

So they came to tell me I'd been elected—the assembly had elected me secretary of the council, or of the executive committee. I didn't want to, because I didn't want anything. I wanted nothing, not at all! But the compañeros persuaded me. "Go to a meeting once or twice," they said, "and if you don't like it just don't continue." So I had to say okay. And the fact that I said okay, I would go to one or two meetings, well since that meeting, I've been in this work for almost twenty years and those two meetings haven't ended yet.

I continue because the program of the Regional Indigenous Council of Cauca is completely different from working within the system, from working with politiqueros. And finding out about the seven points [of the CRIC program]; where we were going to struggle; what we were going to work on; it was all completely different. And what was most striking to me, what I demanded to know was, "What does this have to do with politicians or with the government?" "No," the compañeros told me, "This has nothing to do with the Liberal Party or the Conservative Party, nothing to do with Catholics or Evangelicals. This is an indigenous organization that we ourselves have proposed because as indigenous people we should start to work and struggle for all the rights they've taken away from us starting hundreds of years ago and right up to now. That's why we have to get it back." I looked very carefully into what they told me, and it was true that not a single politiquero was part of this, so I accepted and I thought if CRIC could do what was proposed then there would be a concrete reason for this struggle, and it would be something that should be done.

At that time it was thought that land should be reclaimed as part of the seven-point program, and the compañeros in the north began the work of reclaiming land. So the government detained compañero Gustavo Mejía and our members in the San Francisco, Toribío, and Tacueyó cabildos. They threw them in jail in Toribío. Since I was secretary of the executive committee, we started to struggle to get the compañeros out of jail, and in fact we succeeded in getting them out, because the case was heard in the Third Brigade.[74] From then on we were scared; it was frightening that an offense like that—over the reclaiming of land—would be taken to the Third Brigade, I mean threatened with a military trial.[75]

At first, not all the indigenous people were in CRIC, but at the end of 1972, or maybe it was in 1973, people in INCORA[76] began to see that there were a lot of problems in the indigenous areas, in the resguardos, because of the land question. They decided there had to be an indigenous census. At first we didn't want this because it would be part of the same system, the same government people. But together with all the indigenous compañeros we took a look at how this could help, and at the last minute we accepted the idea. So we came into contact with the rest of the indigenous people, the rest of the resguardos, and as a result CRIC was able to grow.

As CRIC grew, it quickly became popular with people because its reasons for being and its proposals came to seem ever more right. The organization began to develop a program including reclaiming land and not paying terrajes.[77] It was my responsibility to supervise the southern zone, made up of the resguardos of Río Blanco, Guachicono, Pancitará, Caquiona, and San Sebastián, in order to see what they thought about the organization. As we've discussed before, they were and continue to be dominated by politiquería. And since there aren't any landowners there, there was practically no one to contend with over the land.

So we said that in the north and in the center the priority would be on reclaiming land and not paying terraje, because there were beginning to be a lot of complaints and many cases of landlords confiscating land from their tenants. And we saw that the north, the center, and the west should be prioritized. At that point people in the south did not want to get organized in CRIC because they thought maybe our program was a trick or we were part of the Agrarian Reform policy. That's why they didn't believe in it. They're still Liberals and Conservatives. They're still, let's say, limited in their thinking, in thinking it has to be like that. Of course in the administration of the resguardos, yes. Their cabildos are very well organized and they demand respect for their communities.

It was the hardest work for me, so hard it prevented me from keeping other commitments to my own work. I suffered because of that. I went through a lot of crises in order to fulfill my work in the organization. But I kept my commitment. I'd made a commitment to my wife and children that I would make an effort, whether I had ten children or however many I had if it was less than that, a promise to pay for their schooling until every one of them finished high school.

Well at that time I didn't have many resources, and I didn't have enough time to work in artisanry, so I looked for some land to farm, even if it was just a few plants. And I made a great effort. My children worked hard. They didn't have very good clothes like other people who are, let's say, more comfortable economically. At times it was hard to scrape together enough for a pair of shoes and a shirt. But I have a very supportive brother, very honest and scrupulous, and also very dedicated to people being civilized and above all to the family. So he helped me send my children to the primary school where he worked, the El Crucero School in the corregimiento of Río Blanco, municipio of Sotará. In the meantime I was developing the small plot of land in the municipio of La Sierra.

Anyway, when they finished primary school, after fifth grade we had to think about their continuing education, years more of study for a diploma. But as I said, none of my goals in the council had been met, and that included founding the *colegio*, the middle and secondary school. Since there wasn't any option for their education in La Sierra, I decided to leave there and go to the municipio of Timbío. But I left La Sierra without a cent. I thought I'd be having to work to pay for my children's education, that my work would provide the money to support my children and pay for their education. That was my move to Timbío.

When my first son finished the fourth year of high school, he asked me to send him to a normal school. So I sent him to the normal school in the municipio of La Vega. Then my other son asked me to send him to the Normal for Men in Popayán, and that's why I moved to Popayán as well, to continue my children's education. The one who went into the Normal for Men also graduated, and I'm struggling for the other two that are left. But that's what kept me in Popayán. Apart from that I can't say I like it, being in cities and towns that is, because they may not like to hear it, but I think people in cities are lazy, you know? They're for lazy people. I really like farming; I really like working with my hands. So much so that I don't really feel like myself here[78] because I'm not doing farm work. I think after these kids finish, with luck I'll be going back to the country if I'm still alive. I did make a commitment to my wife and to my children when they were growing up, that I would pay for their education until they had a high school diploma. But if they have the intelligence to go to the university, it's on their own dime. It's up to them to see how they can take care of themselves, to get work and everything. My commitment was up to that point.

In any case they made that sacrifice, and I did too. Their mother was very dedicated. She took care of them to the best of her ability, but it was a very hard life, and it's hard still, because you know, because me being in the organization I don't have that option to make money in my private time. And that's caused me some really bad problems. My health has been affected. I'm not in good health. I've felt very sick and worn out. Physically, I don't have the energy I had ten years ago. But nevertheless I'm satisfied that through all my efforts and hard work I've supported my family, which was what they needed, which will make them their future. And I'm happy because I've contributed to their education.

The other thing is the effort I make for the organization, for my indigenous compañeros—it's like I'm slipping some money into a piggy bank, not to use for myself, but for the future needs of those indigenous compañeros, for them to use. That's why I'm so happy at this time with what I've done; I mean despite all the repercussions, the suffering I talked about. And I'll die happy if my indigenous compañeros throw off the yoke they've borne over the last five hundred years.

As I said, my wife has helped me because despite so many difficulties she never got discouraged. I was afraid to get married because you take on great responsibilities. There was a big difference in age; she was a little younger, but I was able to educate her. From the beginning I knew I should educate her because in the journey of life man should have short-term and long-term vision, and I was always searching. I absolutely wasn't one to rest on my laurels. On the contrary, I struggled, worked, spoke out, and didn't sleep. I got right up and thought about a lot of things—since I didn't have a formal education, that was my schooling. That was my education, what I was looking for. So I also succeeded in educating her, and now she knows there's a concrete reason why she suffers the economic repercussions, and what it means to work in indigenous organizing.

I think a woman's role after she's educated and becomes aware of what really needs to be done in public and private life—the woman's role is tremendously important. To me it's always been tremendously important. Since I got married thirty-six years ago, she hasn't caused a single problem; I haven't had a problem of any kind and I've been able to work for my family and for the organization.

The Struggles of CRIC and Indigenous Traditions

All in all I kept working in CRIC because I saw that things were completely different. It was a question of defending a race, defending a class—an organization that sought to reclaim what had been lost, such as by reclaiming land and not paying terraje. This clarified a lot of things for me.

You could say I'd struggled for change since long before, looked for another way forward. I'd been looking for the way to bring about social change, political change, administrative change, and for a government that would give indigenous people their rights along with those of the campesinos, workers, and students. So I decided to stay in the organization. And I did. I kept on working.

And even though it was hard, and even if it's still hard, I kept on working at it because now it wasn't something anyone was forcing me to do. It was something I chose to do as long as I was mentally and physically able, a process for indigenous people to get their rights. To me the defense of traditions and customs was a very important part of our struggle.

I considered us a bloodline that didn't come from anywhere else: a pure bloodline but the system made us ashamed of it. That's why I continued in the struggle, because by then I was liking it and liking a lot of other things, like reclaiming land. Seeing that my compañeros were completely enslaved to the landowners, and recognizing that it'd been five centuries since the Spanish arrived, and even though the land was theirs the Spanish made them slaves. Since that's the way things were, it seemed like a very good thing, and that's why I kept on working and that's why I'm here.

CRIC is made up of indigenous resguardos led by cabildos, but the resguardos that had that clarity. I mean the outstanding resguardos, the most visible ones, the ones that work the hardest and struggle the hardest, the ones in the north, in the center, and in Tierradentro, and the most steadfast and visible leaders have been the compañeros in Puracé, the compañeros in Coconuco, and in Paniquitá. Two executive presidents came from among the compañeros of Coconuco, the first of them compañero Marcos, elected to the position. After they sent compañero Marcos to jail he was replaced by compañero Jesús Avirama.[79] The compañeros from Paniquitá have also seen things clearly. Although most recently they haven't been very close to us, during a certain period of time they worked with us. The compañeros of the north were very motivated, they were part of what we were doing, also those of Tierradentro and of Chimborazo, Honduras, and Aguas Negras in the west. The compañeros from the east, Jambaló and Guambía, came in at first but maybe for some reasons they had to leave.

Some compañeros have stood out, compañero Manuel Trino Morales, for example, who is a very important person. He's a very capable person, very brave, who has learned a lot, and he's very honest, even though the enemy has tried to criticize him, and not with constructive criticism. In fact he's been a very honorable man, but some people have tried to criticize him, people on the inside and on the outside, I mean both indigenous people and mestizos, but he's always had a lot of prestige.

Compañeros from Jambaló, there are some compañeros that have understood things, and compañeros from Caldono. These were regions where people had been very deceived, very marginalized, really repressed by politiquería, but they've been very hard working, particularly in reclaiming land. They've gotten organized and they're working hard.

I wonder why some of the resguardos haven't joined CRIC. I think it's been some of the resguardos from here in the center and in Tierradentro that've been very taken in by politiquería. They still dream of having what these politiqueros dangle in front of them, an insignificant job like inspector de policía, or they may dream of being a mayor, or they think being a government official will be a great honor for them or very advantageous. And another thing is in those places where people still don't see things clearly, influenced by religion maybe or politics, they say CRIC is a bad influence; they say it's communist and communism is against the clergy, against religion, and communists organize to form things against the government. So we understand that they still lack an understanding of politics as it relates to identity.

As for some other places like the resguardo of Poblazón here in the center, some people own small pieces of land, but not enough. Meanwhile, they think the organization would come and take it away from them because that's what it does: it reclaims land. They think if an indigenous person owns 100 hectares, it would be taken over. So they don't understand, you know? I mean nobody can occupy a 100 hectare property because it's not enough to do anything with.

People who've been in the organization and who've left, well, some of them maybe were dishonest in a way, you know? Some of them were already accustomed to lying, too, just like those politiqueros or landowners; or like people who prefer to live off others, deceiving them in different ways. I say dishonest because after belonging to an organization as important as I think ours is, they've left to support the system, to get an inspección de policía[80] or some other little job, and I mean a really small one like personero.[81] Anyway that's the kind of thing, and they've left. And others because they thought the organization was going to accomplish everything overnight and they'd get rich along the way. So these things have hindered us.

Another reason why some compañeros have left has also been that they've been tricked by political groups that are mostly interested in ripping off the organization's values and work ethic. And because the organization wasn't meeting their political needs they seduced people away. They told these people that by going with them they'd get everything they wanted, and that people staying with CRIC weren't really demanding their rights anymore anyway, because we're just bureaucrats now and working within the system. That's how they convince some people to pull out of the organization.

What's been the women's role in the organization, in the struggle? Well up to now it's been very hard to make this happen in concrete terms because people still go by what's been instilled in them. They say things like women are inferior to men, and because they're inferior to men, they have to be under their control, be dominated by men and what men say.

And this is a result of everything I was saying before, that there was an earthly paradise and God put Adam there and then to form woman he took one of Adam's ribs and made the first woman from that rib. And then since Eve was the one who sinned, she would have to suffer all those punishments and it would be forever. And that was an original sin that stayed with people, especially women, but also men. So all these things implant that kind of idea, and then this thing called religion adds in that only women are sinners, without recognizing that by saying that women, or only women are sinners, they haven't shown human beings how things really are. They've blocked off the education that people should really have, both men and women, because both are human beings, and both sexes have a right to life.

Then there's this inferiority complex and that's why women still haven't been very visible in the work of the organization.[82] But as far as

Juan Gregorio Palechor: The Story of My Life 151

we're concerned, indigenous women have played a very important role. This despite suffering the effects of all the things I mentioned, because they've galvanized the men, they've made great contributions. When we were reclaiming land, they confronted the police, and they've been beaten and thrown in jail many times. Much younger women have also contributed, despite being clubbed and kicked, Rosalía Jesús, for example.

So I think if women don't play a more advanced role it's because we men have allowed ourselves to imply this message of inferiority, because we aren't educating them. I think we should educate the women. Women definitely need that. But educating them doesn't mean they should be educated into the system that's been imposed on us. I mean educating them to read and write. They should know how to do that. But what we want most is change. We want to recover our lost rights and women should contribute to that. And we haven't educated them in this sense. Sometimes we think if they aren't directly participating then they're not making any contribution. But conscious women, women who've been educating themselves to some degree, well, they're aware of what's being done.

Take my case, for example. My wife doesn't go out and club the enemy. She doesn't throw stones at them when we're reclaiming land. And she doesn't go to meetings, either. But she's committed in the educational sense. She's committed to me and she helps me. When it's my responsibility to be out in the struggle, she takes charge of everything in the house because that's part of what I've taught her.

I think we've been improving all along and after educating the women they should participate little by little in the organization's activities, even in the leadership. But again, the weakness is their education. What it comes down to is women have to become educated, very well educated. They have to know where they come from, where they are, and where they're going, right? I'd say this is a long-term process.

People have to learn all about the process of struggle, above all women. Every aspect of the struggle, I mean right on the ground where it takes place. As I was saying, we can see that they still need more education, more training. With the inferiority complex hammered into them and all the techniques that exploiters like priests and landlords use to frighten them with so many fears—like the devil is going to make off with you, that whole thing. So we're not there yet, but we think that before long women will be advantageous at the executive level.

As far as I know, in the old days there weren't any women in the cabildos. But to be clear, some individual women could be good at acquiring knowledge, because I remember that women played an important role in the ten-year-long struggle on the resguardo of Guachicono.[83] And there are some outstanding women who are physically and mentally very capable, and they're more adept, they understand things better. I see that women are very important, and they would play a major role if we brought them into the cabildos as well.

This wouldn't conflict with indigenous traditions as long as the person is educated. It would conflict if she isn't educated. If she thinks she's going to be in charge, that she's going to be giving orders, well that would be a problem, because I also understand and I've been in a position to see women's attitudes where sometimes they lose their temper for very minor reasons. Over a little thing they get exasperated, lose their temper or do violent things. In that kind of situation you need to respond calmly.

With respect to our traditions, I and others have proposed to fully research and compare the effectiveness of medicines. Looking at how the body works and comparing how traditional indigenous medicine works and how modern medicine works.

I think the most important medicine and the one that man, or human beings should be using and should never forget is plant or herbal medicine. Because in my experience I've seen when you take medicine for a sickness, if you take plant medicine and it doesn't have any effect, if it doesn't help with your sickness, at least it doesn't do you any harm. But in most cases, and this is for sure, plant medicine is safer.

When you use modern medicine on the other hand, or what they call chemical medicine because it's processed—even if it's extracted from some plants, it's processed, and I think it's not very effective. I think it congests your body because it might help you, the sickness might improve or at least you might get a little relief from it, because the medicine fights against it. But even if it's done right and it helps you and relieves that sickness, it does you harm with other sicknesses because it congests the organism. So I think the most important thing is to keep defending the custom of using traditional medicine; because another thing I've noticed is even if you get used to using a chemical medicine, it will still be obstructing certain things in the way the body works and bring on other sicknesses that haven't ever been seen before in living beings, in human beings. I think these are the consequences of taking or using chemical medicine.

That's the way it is with family planning. In my opinion there are certain other interests involved. It's almost like you wonder where all this comes from, this invention called family planning. I think this invention called family planning comes from outside, because the United States is a country that's been very interested in taking control of the South American countries, to have them under its control and now they've plowed in a lot of capital, so I think maybe it's to control even the territory. I think this family planning is so there aren't a lot of people, so the governments of these countries don't ask for so much credit, so many loans, or so there won't be so many problems. I hear people say you shouldn't have children, or only like one or two, so you can pay for their schooling. But I think it's not because you won't be able to pay for their schooling, but because the exploiters would lose what you produce for them. A father that's responsible and wants to see his children in school isn't going anywhere. He'll stay put, in a difficult situation but investing in his own land, in his own country, and not be going to the United States, which is where they horde most of the money, right?

There's another thing, and it's that family planning has to be by means of some pills or some other medical solution, so what is it really that they're putting in the women? A device they put in, another device supposedly so they won't have children. I think the purpose of those pills is to sterilize people, and if they do have children they come out useful idiots, I mean idiots, good for nothing.

Because that's what the enemy of the working class and what some people in other countries want to see come out of this invention: it should sterilize people and make them so they're no good for anything useful or only to serve the needs of capitalism. So in that sense, no.

But there are other immediate problems. For example, we've always seen that women are happy now not to have that problem; they don't have the pain of having kids. They use those pills, but what happens is when they stop using them or if they're careless and then remember and take two or three of them, then that's the situation where the organism gets congested, and I think that's a very bad thing.

I also understand that it sterilizes the blood; it sterilizes the person's body. And I'm not in favor of using chemicals for family planning because it sterilizes the blood or the woman's organism. Because it's the same as agricultural fertilizers. What I mean is if you buy processed chemical fertilizer for growing food crops what happens is you get a good harvest with the first crop. Then you apply the same amount of fertilizer for the second crop but the harvest is smaller. So you use more fertilizer for the third crop but it yields less. You harvest less food. Then you get nothing. The chemical fertilizer has completely sterilized the earth. Since the plant cover is gone there's no more organic matter. Your field is sterile and won't produce a thing: only indignation, if that. You have to wait some ten or twenty years till the new plant cover tells you it's productive again. I think it's the same way with chemical fertilizer in the human body, it obstructs it, it cuts it off, it wears it down, and you end up with a deteriorated race, a deteriorated family.

I believe that the state, the government, or a household take a different approach to family planning. There should be education about it because we shouldn't talk about anything without knowledge. We can't talk about what we don't know, rather about what we know. I know there's a lot of ignorance talking about the direct contact between men and women. People aren't educated. We aren't educated, and that's why there's a lot of family, because we're not educated in any sense and because there's this lack of education among lovers.

Politiqueros and Their Empty Words

I wouldn't say that I'm an enemy of any people, but an enemy of the system, of the way politics is practiced, you know? Because no way have I seen the so-called help of these politiqueros lead to any improvement for marginalized people, for underprivileged people.

I'm very dissatisfied with the way they talk, the speeches they give to the least educated groups, the way they make a lot of promises. They promise change for the better, improvements, all that kind of thing, and people believe them because they're kept in such a state of ignorance. They get people thinking that if they don't vote for the Liberal Party or the Conservative Party then somehow they're going to be left without a government and without any help, so people hear these speeches and they say, "Oh, this guy speaks very well, let's vote for him just because. It's not that we're Liberals or Conservatives; it's just that we're going to vote," even if they know that the Liberal bosses in the department get into the House of Representatives or the Senate and they pass any kind of law they want, whatever's good for themselves. Then after these laws are passed they say this was a legal reform or a constitutional amendment and so now it's a constitution for the people. I think a constitution should be made up of laws for the kind of government that looks at the problems in a country and how to solve these problems. But that's not what they do. Instead there's a way of talking that deceives people.

Now you don't see any help for the people. Work is done by the people themselves, for example the work organized by the Community Action Committee, the mingas, all that kind of thing. I don't know why some individuals trick people or why other people submit to them. I ask myself why they let themselves be manipulated by caciques with all those kinds of lies. How humiliating for Cauca!

Yes, it's a disgrace. That someone who's done absolutely nothing for the people, nothing for the region, who sets himself up like a king, just like a king sitting there, and people come up to him hat in hand begging for his good will. They're the ones who've elevated this guy up to where he is.

But it's a race of people, a family tradition. Because that old guy, what's his name? Tomás Cipriano de Mosquera; he was president for several terms and so people had to believe in his descendant, Víctor Mosquera Chaux. But what comes of trusting Mosquera Chaux, trusting in the politics of Mosquera Chaux? Nothing at all. And especially in indigenous areas, as for defending his people, the ones that vote for him, no. He does them just the same as the guy we talked about before: kicks their butts, knocks them around, and clubs them on the head. It's a sham and a fraud the game he plays. And it's something that'll never change as long as he lives. Like a cat toying with a mouse.

So that's the way here in Cauca. A gentleman by the name of Víctor Mosquera Chaux has been able to trick people and dominate them. And the people are so naïve, including some intellectuals in Popayán, or from regions like the municipio of Santander, or the municipio of Bolívar, or from other towns, you see, where they flock to him because he offers them some petty jobs, but in fact he gives jobs to some of them and doesn't give jobs to others: some people he just gives a kick in the ass.

But they don't learn, you see? I remember one guy for instance who was active in the MRL, working very hard against Víctor Mosquera Chaux. Well one morning he woke up and decided to go with Mosquera Chaux; he begged Mosquera Chaux to accept him. So what happened was all the people who were with this guy were duped and went right along with him into the ranks of Mosquera Chaux. But even after this man sold out, Mosquera Chaux kept him marginalized anyway. He didn't help him at all, in fact he still keeps him at arm's length.

And these intellectuals are the same, I mean some intellectuals have no political sense because even if you're ignorant, how can you put yourself in the hands of that kind of politician, knowing the way they take people in and use them? That's what they're famous for; it's how Víctor Mosquera Chaux made himself famous, without working, without helping anybody.

It's the politiqueros who completely oppose CRIC. They identify with their politiquería; never defend indigenous people. They deceive them, first saying that they're going to get them roads, then they're going to get them health clinics, they're going to get them land to work. But I understand that they're hypocrites, trying to build themselves up, maneuvering deceitfully—as always—to get power over others, occupy positions of administrative control, and then persecute us worse than before.

That's why politiqueros are less than zero as far as I'm concerned. They've never done anything to help campesinos, indigenous people, students, or anyone else. They want you to think they're talking about something but they just make a lot of empty sounds that don't even mean anything. And if you think you can depend on them you'll just be disappointed. They try to manipulate every part of indigenous and campesino society. They want us to forget that we're indigenous and do away with our organization. So whatever it is that comes out of their mouths, to us they're just full of it.

Why an Organization of Indigenous People?

Indigenous people have acted as individuals, struggled for their interests, but an organization is needed to learn to be leaders. If you depend on one leading figure, a caudillo, he dies and that's it. I don't approve of one person ordering everyone else around. The ethnic group needs to be educated to carry on a struggle for their rights. If it's just one person he can be undermined individually, or if they kill him or jail him; then it's over. That was the case with Manuel Quintín Lame[84] (see figure 3.3). If everyone gets educated though, and if you're organized, and there's not just one person giving orders, then when they kill or jail a leader everyone still knows what to do and the struggle goes on.

We've lost traditional customs including the use of the indigenous language in Guachicono and other resguardos. But we struggle to maintain our traditions and customs because the state and the mestizos want them to die out. The Paeces have always considered themselves indigenous, but these others don't take any of it into account: they're taking away their legal status, their rights, and their lands.

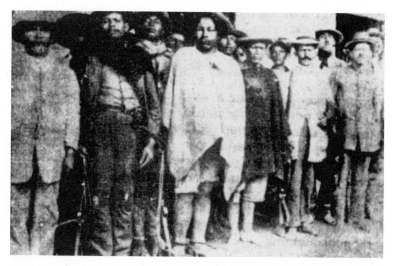

Figure 3.3. Photo of Quintín Lame under arrest in El Cofre, Popayán, 1915.

We Yanaconas insist on our indigenous identity because even though we've lost our language we're still protected by our indigenous structures. We're governed by a cabildo and we live on resguardos under Law 89 of 1890.[85] Despite having lost some customs, we believe that if we don't get organized, they'll wipe us out. But we want to survive. We're proud to still feel indigenous. We have our race, and as far as we're concerned, we're full-blooded indigenous.

Several assemblies were held in 1989 and 1990 on the Macizo Colombiano to make demands in the name of Río Blanco, Guachicono, Pancitará, Caquiona, and San Sebastián: the five resguardos of the south of Cauca. All of them are in the area of the Macizo Colombiano. We're asking for better education. How so? Provide complete primary school education and establish secondary schools specializing in agriculture and industrial arts oriented to the improvement of the region and also the culture in the sense of recovering lost customs and traditions.

We're also asking the government to give us enough land to enlarge the resguardos or establish resguardos in the Bota Caucana. The government is committed to providing economic and social assistance to the resguardos until they produce enough to sustain themselves. Going forward, these settlements will be the state's responsibility since there are no large landowners on the Macizo Colombiano.

Resguardos can be established in the Bota Caucana, and the one in Río Blanco can be expanded because it has land adjacent to it. The movement there hasn't asked for advice from CRIC, but it has its own organization, which is new.

About the origins of the five resguardos, nobody can say for sure. They have a name that they call us, which is Yanaconas, but that's all we know—it's thanks to historian Juan Friede.

When I was a boy no one ever said we were anything but indigenous. This was so because we were under Law 89 of 1890, but no one ever said we had a name as an ethnic group. We didn't know about the survival of other ethnic groups. We didn't know anything about Putumayo, about the Paeces, or the Guambianos. At the beginning of the century people focused on their work and didn't know anything else. Those of us on the resguardos of the Macizo did know about each other, but we held separate meetings on each resguardo.

A cabildo was elected every year at the end of December by a popular vote of males over the age of fifteen. The governor [of the cabildo] summoned the entire community to elect the new cabildo on a given day, usually Christmas, December 25. Voters came out with their wives and children and cast their votes according to rules set by the existing cabildo. That meant signing their names or making a mark to indicate who they wanted to vote for. Women didn't take part in that.

The new cabildo took office on January 1 after being sworn in by the inspector de policía. The outgoing cabildo delivered an official report that day, but there was no special ceremony or celebration. We didn't have ceremonial staffs[86] like others did. Mestizos were excluded; people didn't let them come near. The cabildo always defended the land. Their mission was to defend the land and enforce the law.

The cabildo heard the petitions of landless members of the resguardo, and it had to look for an indigenous person who had a lot of uncultivated land that could be divided in order to grant some land to the petitioner. Of course there were boundary disputes, and there still are. One person wants to move the line over toward someone else and take some land away from him. But nobody has monopolized a lot of land there. Of course there are those who have more, but it's not like on other resguardos where some people have unscrupulously accumulated land at the expense of the weakest. Another responsibility of the cabildo was to inspect land boundaries and adjudicate when there were disputes. Their decisions were always respected and they still are.

Ever since I can remember there was migration. Young people didn't have work and went to Valle, Antioquia, or Caldas departments as day laborers. Some returned and others stayed there. More than anything it was the women who went. They wanted to get ahead and be able to dress well, to look modern.

Another important thing for the cabildo was to build animal trails. This work was sometimes done by mingas or some people were required to do it.

A minga is an event in which a group of indigenous people get together to work on a project, a section of road for example. People would bring their tools and women would cook a corn or potato soup. Everyone chewed coca but drank only chicha, no other alcoholic beverage. Some played music on flutes and drums to accompany the work. They brought children along so they would get used to working. After work everyone went home.

I consider myself a person who thinks first. First I look at where the problem is and where the deception is. Then I speak and I provide leadership by my teaching. When my time comes I will pass, but the world keeps on going. But you have to point things in the right direction so they don't go backward. If they'd taught me something I would've been able to do more. That's my grievance with the government; that's the anger of Palechor.

What am I afraid of? Of betraying what I stand for. But I haven't worried about that because I've felt good about my work. I've thought about every step.

APPENDIX

CRIC Documents

Document 1. Front cover of 1979 CRIC pamphlet *CRIC Denounces*.

INDIGENAS DEL CRIC ASESINADOS EN LOS ULTIMOS
5 AÑOS EN EL CAUCA

		RESGUARDO	FECHA
1.	GUSTAVO MEJIA	Corinto	Marzo 1/74
2.	LUIS E. TAQUINAZ	Corinto	Octubre 2/74
3.	ALFONSO DAGUA	Corinto	Diciembre 6/74
4.	MAURICIO DAGUA	Corinto	Diciembre 6/74
5.	LISANDRO CRUZ TALAGA	Caloto	Agosto /74
6.	MARCO TULIO TALAGA	Caloto	Agosto /74
7.	JOSE LONDOÑO	Caloto	Agosto /74
8.	JOAQUIN MARINO YONDA	Santander	Octubre 18/74
9.	LUIS F. RAMOS	Santander	Octubre 18/74
10.	EMILIO ULCUE	Caldono	Octubre 8/74
11.	LUIS E. PRADO	Purace	Diciembre 8/74
12.	EMILIANO MESA	Huila	Diciembre /75
13.	MARCO MELENGE	Coconuco	Abril 19/75
14.	PABLO QUINTO	Inza	Enero /76
15.	ISIDRO PILCUE	Tacueyo	Abril /76
16.	BENJAMIN CUETIO	Caldono	Octubre /76
17.	ANTONIO YULE	Jambalo	Noviembre /76
18.	ANGEL MESTIZO	Jambalo	Julio /76
19.	BERNARDO IPIA	Jambalo	Noviembre /76
20.	LUCIANO RAMOS	Jambalo	Noviembre /76
21.	JUSTINIANO LAME	Popayan	Febrero /77
22.	FRANCISCO FERNANDEZ	Santander	Marzo /77
23.	ERNESTO GUEJIA	Toribio	Julio /77
24.	BALBINO QUIHUAPUNGO	Corinto	Diciembre /77
25.	DIONICIO IPIA	Santarrosa	Diciembre /77
26.	LISANDRO CASO	Jambalo	Octubre /78
27.	JUAN CASO	Jambalo	Octubre /78
28.	N. CASO	Jambalo	Octubre /78
29.	AVELINO UL	Toribio	Diciembre /78
30.	BENJAMIN DINDICUE	Huila	Febrero /79

Document 2. Back cover of 1979 CRIC pamphlet CRIC *Denounces*. "Indigenous members of CRIC murdered in the last five years in Cauca," listed by their respective resguardo and month or date of death.

Dr. VANIN TELLO
GERENTE GENERAI INCORA
C.A.N BOGOTA

† ¹¹⁰ Junio 21 /-75
& Sandoz:

1° _____ por medio de este memorial
Y a gradeciendo el interes Que el instituto
mostró en su visita a nuestra región, —
Queremos plantear. Lo siguiente: _____
1 _____ Según reuniones Que Hemos tenido
Los representantes de la Comunidad de los nosotro
Piapoco, Hemos Decidido seguir Haciendo un —
esfuerso para que el Gobierno Nal. reconosca
La propiedad de nuestras tierras, y nos Conceda
los titulos Correspondientes. &o _____

2° Nuestra Historia Ha sido Una de persecuciones y
Carreras A Huyentados por el avance del Colono
Que Desde Hace Años nos acosa Con sus Ganado
Sus armas y sus " leñas. Nuestros abuelos Comensaro
sus Contenuos trasteos en las sabanas del meta y
Casanare y Hoy, Despues de muchos trabajos Hemos
llegado Ya al final de las sabanas del Vichada.
Muchos de nuestras gente Han muerto; otros se
han Visto Obligados A Cambiar sus Vidas en la
sabana por las de las selvas del Guaviare, Orinol.
y Guainia. Nosotros, los Que hemos Decidido
Quedarnos en la sabana, nos Vemos obligados A
detener ese avance en nuestros linderos, y A —
defeander nuestros derechos Sobre nuestras tierras.
~~3° ~~~~~~~~~~~~~~~~~~~~~~~~~~~~

(Above and overleaf) **Document 3.** Letter from Piapoco Indians to the director of INCORA demanding their territorial rights, 1975, pages 1 and 2.

3: Por esto, hace ya varios años venimos apelando al Gobierno, atraves del Incora, y otros institutos.

Hasta ahora el instituto ha practicado 3 visitas a nuestras tierras y hoy, Despues de largo tiempo, ya parece verse una solución cercana.

Con la ayuda del instituto hemos desarrollado un mapa delineando la región habitada por nosotros. Donde trabajamos y vivimos mas de Dos mil personas.

A continuación incluimos este mapa:

MONTE INARIABO

CAFETERA
CERCA ORIGINAL RAFAEL PEREZ
CERCA RAFAEL PEREZ
PEÑARON
CASA RAFAEL
CASA TEOFILO
CAITASIQUE
SUR
CHIMIELI
ATASUATO
CERCA QUE TUMBARON
ALIPICHI
CAÑO AMUQUANA
EN AZUL, LAS CERCAS Y CASAS ORIGINALES DE LOS INDÍGENAS.
LAS CERCAS Y CASAS EN ROJO SON LAS QUE HAN HECHADO LOS COLONOS.
ORIENTE

Dr. VANIN TELLO   F110 June 21, 1_75
INCORA GENERAL MANAGER   Dr Sanchez
C.A.N. BOGOTA

1st. by means of this brief and thankful for the interest That the institute showed on its visit to our region, We wish to state. The following:

1. Based on meetings that we have held The representatives of our community of Piapoco, We have Decided to continue making an effort to convince the Nat. Government to recognize the property of our lands, and Grant us the corresponding titles.

2nd. Our History Has been one of persecutions and Hurried Flight from advancing settlers Who for Many Years have harassed us with their Cattle, Their weapons, and their "laws." Our grandparents began their continuous movements around the savannas of [the departments of] meta and Casanare, and Today, After much work, we Have come to the end of the savannas of Vichada. Many of our people Have died; others have had to give up their Lives on the savanna for new lives in the tropical forests of Guaviare, Orinoco, and Guainía. We, those Who have Decided to Stay on the savanna, we have no choice but to put an end to this advance on our borders, and to defend our right to our lands.

3rd. For this reason, we appealed to the Government Through INCORA and other institutes several years ago now.

Up to the present time, the Institute has visited our lands three times, and today After a long time, a Solution now appears to be Near.

With the Help of the Institute we have made a map delineating the region inhabited by us. Where more Than Two thousand of us work and live.

We include this map below:

[map labels]

INARIABO MOUNTAIN
SOUTH
ORIGINAL INDIAN HOUSES AND FENCES IN BLUE.
HOUSES AND FENCES BUILT BY SETTLERS IN RED.
EAST

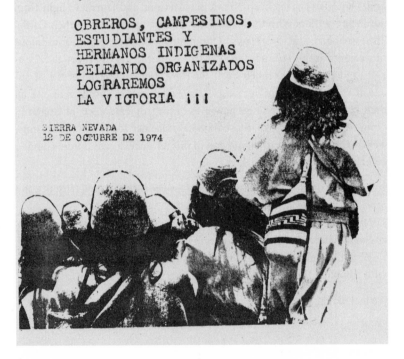

NOSOTROS HACEMOS UN LLAMADO
A NUESTROS HERMANOS INDIGENAS,
A LOS OBREROS, CAMPESINOS,
ESTUDIANTES Y TODAS LAS GENTES
DEL PUEBLO OPRIMIDO PARA
QUE SE SOLIDARICEN CON
NUESTRA JUSTA LUCHA.

POR LA RECUPERACION DE
NUESTRAS TIERRAS Y DEFENSA
DE NUESTRA CULTURA.
¡¡¡ ADELANTE ¡¡¡

OBREROS, CAMPESINOS,
ESTUDIANTES Y
HERMANOS INDIGENAS
PELEANDO ORGANIZADOS
LOGRAREMOS
LA VICTORIA ¡¡¡

SIERRA NEVADA
12 DE OCTUBRE DE 1974

Document 4. Mimeographed pamphlet distributed by a solidarity group in Bogotá denouncing persecution in the Sierra Nevada de Santa Marta, a mountainous area near the Caribbean coast that is home to several ethnicities, October 1974.

WE CALL ON OUR INDIGENOUS BROTHERS AND SISTERS
ON THE WORKERS, CAMPESINOS, STUDENTS,
AND ALL OPPRESSED PEOPLE
TO JOIN IN SOLIDARITY WITH OUR JUST STRUGGLE.

FOR THE RECOVERY OF OUR LANDS
AND THE DEFENSE OF OUR CULTURE
FORWARD TOGETHER!!!

WORKERS, CAMPESINOS, STUDENTS,
INDIGENOUS BROTHERS AND SISTERS,
ORGANIZED TOGETHER IN THE STRUGGLE,
WE WILL ACHIEVE VICTORY!!!

SIERRA NEVADA
OCTOBER 12, 1974

Third Indigenous Encounter of Cauca, July 15–17, 1973.
First public act of CRIC. *Photo:* CRIC Archives.

El programa del CRIC presenta nuestras luchas de hoy en siete puntos :

1. Recuperar las tierras de los resguardos.
2. Ampliar los resguardos.
3. Fortalecer los cabildos indígenas.
4. No pagar terrajes.
5. Hacer conocer las leyes sobre indígenas. y exigir su justa aplicación.
6. Defender la historia, la lengua y las costumbres indígenas.
7. Formar profesores indigenas para educar de acuerdo con la situación de los indígenas y en su respectiva lengua.

Document 5. CRIC program distributed to participants at the Third Indigenous Encounter of Cauca, 1973.

....

The CRIC program summarizes our struggles today in seven points:

1. Recover *resguardo* lands.
2. Enlarge the *resguardos*.
3. Strengthen the indigenous *cabildos*.
4. Do not pay *terrajes*.
5. Make the laws dealing with indigenous people known and demand their just application.
6. Defend indigenous history, language, and customs.
7. Train indigenous educators to teach in a way that is appropriate to the situation of indigenous people, and [to do so] in their respective languages.

COMO NACIO EL CRIC

1. **EL CRIC NACIO DE LA LUCHA
    DE LOS TERRAJEROS**

Antes de constituírse el CRIC, habían comenzado las
luchas de los terrajeros de **Chimán y del Credo**, en tierras de
los resguardos de Guambía y Tacueyó, arrebatadas por
terratenientes.
Mientras que los compañeros del Credo contaban con el
apoyo decidido del Cabildo de Tacueyó, los de Chimán
estaban respaldados por los Guambianos que habían
constituído la cooperativa de Las Delicias. Pero se hacía
sentir la necesidad de una unión para reforzar estas luchas.
Este fué uno de los principales objetivos de la Asamblea de
Toribío en que se creó el CRIC y su bandera fué el "no pago
de terrajes".

2. **EL CRIC NACIO PARA UNIR**

El 24 de febrero de 1971, se reunieron delegaciones
indígenas del Norte y del Oriente del Cauca en Toribío en lo

1

Document 6. First page of the booklet "How We Got Organized,"
CRIC, no. 2, 1974.

THE BIRTH OF CRIC

1. CRIC EMERGED FROM THE STRUGGLE OF THE TERRAJEROS

Before CRIC was established the struggles of *terrajeros* had begun in **Chimán** and **Credo** on lands that landlords had usurped from the *resguardos* of Guambía and Tacueyó.

While the *compañeros* in Credo had the steadfast support of the *cabildo* of Tacueyó, those in Chimán were supported by the Guambianos who had established the Las Delicias cooperative. But a union was needed to strengthen these struggles. This was one of the principal goals of the Assembly of Toribío where CRIC was established under the banner "no *terraje* payments."

2. CRIC WAS ESTABLISHED TO UNITE

On February 24, 1971, indigenous delegations from northern and eastern Cauca met in Toribío.

Memorial elevado por los mandones de los pueblos de indígenas de San Sebastián, Caquiona, Pancitará y Guachicono al Gobernador de la Provincia, pidiendo su intervención para lograr la suspensión de las leyes de reparto. (Año de 1833. — Archivo del Cabildo de San Sebastián).

"Señor Gobernador de la Provincia del Cauca.

Los mandones de los pueblos de indígenas de Caquiona, San Sebastián, Pancitará y Guachicono, comprendidos en el Cantón de la ciudad de Almaguer ante VS con debido respeto y conforme a derecho decimos, que en cumplimiento de la ley sobre repartimiento de tierras de indios, se nos ha intimado por el Alcalde Municipal Segundo de esta ciudad, que debía pasar a practicar el de las tierras de nuestro pueblo y en ésto emprender esta diligencia en los de San Sebas-

tián y Guachicono la que no pudo verificar por las dificultades... (ilegible);

"Pero hoy se siguen los derechos que ya hemos reclamado y lo mandan devolver, para evitar el perjuicio que se nos causa, pero como... (roto) se ha de... (roto) el que se cumpla la disposición de la ley, ocurrimos a la piedad de VS, suplicándolo que, en vista de las razones que vamos a proponer y de los conocimientos que le asisten de nuestra deplorable situación y demás circunstancias, que imposibilitan el expresado repartimiento, se digne él usar nuestra representación al próximo Congreso por el conducto... (roto) apoyándola con el informe que estima de justicia.

"Es bien notorio, que nuestros pueblos y los demás de este Cantón están situados en montañas y riscos, cuya mayor parte es sumamente estéril, no solamente por ser terrenos de páramo muy rígido, sino por lo escarpado de éllos y por las muchas peñas áridas e inaccesibles que contienen. También lo es, que los terrenos correspondientes a cada pueblo no tienen mucha extensión, que los indios que los habitan son bastantes en número y que tánto por ésto, como por lo que queda expuesto, nos vemos sumamente estrechos y reducidos a cultivar sólamente aquellas partes de los referidos terrenos, que producen algunos frutos, sin poder adelantar nuestras sementeras, sino a lo que permite la tierra fértil, las que por consiguiente son pequeñas y apenas producen lo más necesario, para nuestro escaso y ordinario alimento y el de nuestras familias; y... (ilegible) que nuestra pobreza y miseria es general, porque ni hay proporción de dar ensanche a nuestros trabajos de campo, ni de aumentar nuestras facultades con crías de animales, por no permitir la estrechez y situación de los terrenos, y si se ve alguna u ótra cabeza de ganano vacuno o lanar, o alguna otra bestia, son en muy poco número, porque no tenemos tierras abundan de crías.

"Esta su... (roto) discreción, tan cierta como notoria, es demasiado suficiente, para que se conozca, que si se llevará a efeto el repartimiento quedamos reducidos a un estado el más deplorable, que multiplicando nuestra pobreza, nos reduciría a la última y acaso nos obligaría, para no morir de necesidad, a abandonar nuestros pueblos, para buscar en otras partes nuestra subsistencia, para no ver perecer nuestra familia; porque ceñidos a los límites del corto (pedazo de tierra)

Petition submitted by the authorities of the San Sebastián, Caquiona, Pancitará, and Guachicono indigenous communities to the Governor of the Province, requesting his intervention to suspend the laws on the distribution of lands (Archive of the *cabildo* of San Sebastián, Year of 1833)

"Your Honor the Governor of the Province of Cauca.

The authorities of the Caquiona, San Sebastián, Pancitará, and Guachicono indigenous communities in the Canton of the city of Almaguer before Your Honor with all due respect and in conformity with the law we say that in keeping with the law on the division of Indian lands, it has been made known to us by the Second Municipal Mayor of this city that this law should have been applied to the lands of our community and at the same time undertaken on the lands of San Sebastián and Guachicono indigenous communities, which due to the difficulties could not be verified. . .[illegible];

"But today we retain the rights that we have requested to be respected and that they be ordered to be returned to us in order to avoid the damages that are caused us, but since [torn] it must be [torn] that the provisions of the law must be respected, we appeal to the mercy of Your Honor, begging you that in light of the arguments that we will elaborate upon and of the knowledge of our deplorable situation and other circumstances that make the referenced land distribution impossible, that you communicate our representations to the next Congress through the offices of [torn] supported by a report on the matter that you consider to be just.

"It is well known that our communities and the others in this canton are located on mountains and cliffs, areas which for the most part are exceedingly unfertile, due not only to the severe *páramo* climate but because they are so rugged and craggy and due to their dry, inaccessible, and rocky landscape. In addition, the lands corresponding to each community are not very extensive and the Indians that inhabit them are many in number, so for this reason and others described above we are exceedingly constrained and

....

(*Opposite and overleaf*) **Document 7.** Petition submitted by the authorities of the indigenous communities of San Sebastián, Caquiona, Pancitará, and Guachicono to the provincial governor requesting his intervention to suspend the laws on the distribution of lands (Archive of the cabildo of San Sebastián, 1833). Cited in Friede, 1944, pages vi and 2.

que se señale a cada úno, cuya mayor parte debe ser inútil, ni podre-
los animales precisos para nuestro alivio. Nuestros hijos, que si se ca-
san y forman nuevas familias, no tendrán ya en donde establecerse.
porque enajenados los terrenos no le quedará la libertad que ahora
tenemos de terminar sus casas y posesiones en aquellas partes más
útiles. que no están ocupadas por otros y se verán obligados a expa-
triarse para buscar subsistencia. A más de ésto nos veremos obligados
a experimentar la introducción de otras gentes en nuestros pueblos y
los perjuicios que a ósta son contingentes; para que destinándose una
parte de los terrenos para las comunidades en su división, es natural
que éstos elijan para sí lo mejor, que pongan en éllos su posesión, a
que las vendan a otros extraños, porque nosotros carecemos de facultades para comprarles el terreno que les toque; a más de vernos privados con dolor de esta parte útil en que les toque y a más de vernos
privados con dolor de esta parte en que podríamos trabajar, experi-
mentaríamos muchas inquietudes y perjuicios.

"Podríamos... (roto) aquí otras razones que se presentan a la vista. que favorecen nuestro reclamo, pero las omitimos porque éllas no
escápanse de la penetración de VS ni de nuestros representantes en
el Congreso, de cuya benignidad esperamos que así contuvieren... el
procurar una felicidad para establecer la expresada ley, así también
procurarán el remedio de nuestros males en vista de las razones que
proponemos a manifestar, que es inaceptable en estos pueblos, cuyas
circunstancias quizá no... (ilegible) prever. Por tanto humildemen-
te suplicamos, que se digne a ceder a nuestra solicitud por un efecto
de la notoria bondad con que se interesa para la felicidad de esta raza
de los miserables indios que, destituídos de amparo y recurso, nos aco-
gemos a la protección de VS para que se compadezca de nuestra amar-
ga situación. — Almaguer, 26 de agosto de 1833.

"A ruego del Gobernador de Caquiona, Florencio Quinayás, Pedro
Nieto. A ruego de regidor de Caquiona, Julián Córdoba. El Gobernador de San Sebastián. Custodio Anacona. El Gobernador de Pancitará. Marcelino Jiménez. El Alcalde de Pancitará, Javier Palechor. Joseph María Lupo, el regidor mayor de San Sebastián, Silvestre Anacona. El regidor mayor de Pancitará, Pablo Jiménez. El Gobernador
de Guachicono. Joseph Paniquitá. Alcalde, Valerio Palechor a nombre
de regidor mayor, Efraim Jiménez.

Fermín Cuspián. — Derechos ocho reales"

reduced to cultivating only those parts of the referred lands that produce a few fruits, unable to plant our crops other than to the extent possible on the fertile land which for the above reasons is limited in area and barely produces what is absolutely necessary to provide for our scant and coarse food needs and those of our families; and [illegible] that our poverty and misery is prevalent because the proportions don't exist to expand our agricultural endeavors, nor to increase our possibilities through animal husbandry because the limited quantity and quality of the lands would not permit us to do so. and if one or more head of bovine or ovine livestock or some other creature is seen, they are very few in number because we don't have land [that can] support very many.

"It is your [torn] discretion, as certain as it is well known, it is more than sufficient so that you know that if the division of lands is carried out, we will be reduced to the most deplorable condition, our poverty will be multiplied and we will be reduced to the worst consequences imaginable and in order not to die due to unmet needs we may be obliged to abandon our communities in order to seek our subsistence in other parts, in order to work sufficiently to achieve our subsistence, and to not see our family perish, because limited to work within the boundaries of the small (piece of land) that is assigned to each one, the greatest part of each will necessarily be useless even to support the animals necessary to relieve our distress. Our sons, if they marry and form new families, will have nowhere to establish themselves because once the lands are taken from us there will not be the freedom that we have today to establish their houses and possessions in the most propitious areas that are not occupied by others, and they will be obliged to leave our communities in order to find a way to subsist. In addition to this, it will be incumbent upon us to experience the introduction of new persons in our communities and the negative consequences that this entails, because directing a part of the lands to the communities when they are divided, it is natural that they will choose the best for themselves, that they would put them in their own possession and would sell them to other outsiders, because we do not have the capacity to buy the land from those to whom it has been distributed; in addition to finding ourselves painfully deprived of those productive lands that go to the others and in addition to finding ourselves painfully deprived of this part that we could work, we would experience many damages and perturbations.

"We could [torn] here other pertinent arguments to favor our appeal to you, but we will not do so because they will not be overlooked in Your

Honor's penetrating analysis of the situation nor that of our representatives in Congress, who we hope will act with kindness in order to procure a happy outcome to establish the referenced law, and also that they procure the solution to our problems in light of the arguments that we propose to manifest, that it is unacceptable in these settlements, whose circumstances perhaps are not [torn] to predict. For these reasons we humbly beg that you deign to yield to our petition as an example of the kindness that you are known to hold for the happiness of this race of miserable Indians who deprived of protection and with nowhere else to turn we appeal for the protection of Your Honor and that you take pity on us in our painful situation. — Almaguer, August 26, 1833.

"At the petition of the Governor of Caquiona, Florencio Quinayás, Pedro Nieto. At the petition of Julián Córdoba, Councilor of Caquiona. The Governor of San Sebastián, Custodio Anacona. The Governor of Panicitará, Marcelino Jiménez. The Mayor of Panicitará, Javier Palechor. Joseph Maria Lupo, Senior Councilor of San Sebastián, Sylvestre Anacona. Pablo Jiménez, Senior Councilor of Panicitará. The Governor of Guachicono, Joseph Paniquitá, Mayor, <u>Valerio Palechor</u> in representation of the Senior Councilor, Efraím Jiménez.

Fermín Cuspián. — Fee eight reales.

Document 8. Mimeograph announcing the establishment of a solidarity group at the Department of Anthropology of the National University in Bogotá. Probable date is 1974.

The Committee in Solidarity with Indigenous Struggles at the Department of Anthropology, National University of Colombia, has organized this politico-cultural event including ethno-cultural presentations by indigenous groups and black communities.

The committee was established to act in solidarity with resistance struggles and the organization of indigenous groups against exploitation and domination by imperialism and by the land owning bourgeoisie that does its bidding.

Because the struggle of indigenous groups is part of the revolutionary struggle of the Colombian people it demands the revolutionary solidarity of the Colombian people for its development and consolidation under the proletarian ideology of the fundamental forces of the Colombian revolution (workers and campesinos).

From colonial times to our days and throughout their long struggle of resistance against the abuses of the dominant ideology, indigenous groups have produced culturally rich manifestations such as the one being presented here today, testimony to their will to organize and fight.

Committee in Solidarity with Indigenous Struggles

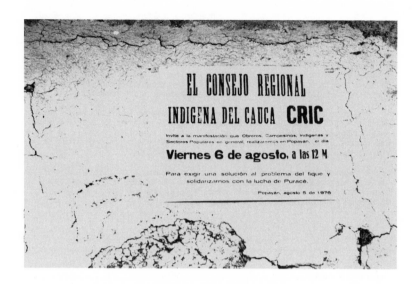

Document 9. Poster announcing an indigenous mobilization to support sisal growers, 1976. Photo by author.

The Regional Indigenous Council of Cauca CRIC

Invites you to the demonstration being held in Popayán by Workers, Campesinos, Indigenous People, and Popular Sectors in general on

Friday, August 6 at 12 noon

To demand a solution to the sisal problem and express our solidarity with the struggle in Puracé.

Popayán, August 5, 1976

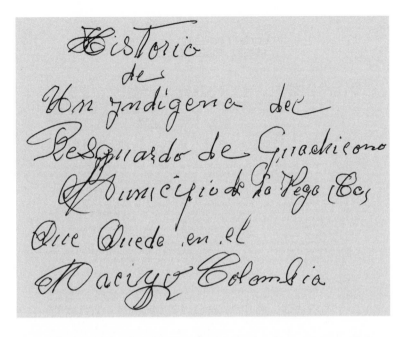

Document 10. Handwritten note by Palechor in which he suggested a title for his autobiography: *History of an Indigenous Man from the Resguardo of Guachicono, Municipio of La Vega, located on the Macizo Colombia* [sic].

Silvia, julio 15 de 1.973

CUANDO NACE EL CONSEJO REGIONAL INDIGENA DEL CAUCA. El 24 de febrero de 1.971 nos reunimos en Toribío en una gran asamblea de Indígenas del Cauca, para protestar y reunir nuestras luchas de indígenas campesinos, sobre todo las de recuperar las tie rras y terminar con el pago de terrajes. Después, el 6 de septiembre de 1.971 reu- nimos la Segunda Asamblea, en la Susana, resguardo de Tacueyó (Cauca). El 15 de ju- lio de 1.973 realizamos en Silvia (Cauca), el III Encuentro Indígena del Cauca y - Primer Encuentro Indígena Nacional.

El Consejo Regional Indígena del Cauca (CRIC) es una organización manejada por los Campesinos Indígenas. Por eso es una organización independiente de los partidos y del gobierno.

Haciendo crecer el CRIC mostramos el interés que tenemos los Indígenas en organizar- nos nosotros mismos. Estas luchas de hoy, como las de ayer, nos han costado muchos sufrimientos, cárceles y persecusiones, y nos costarán más antes del triunfo, pero nos vamos fortaleciendo y seguimos la lucha sin miedo. "Ahora la juventud indígena debe despertar y buscar su camino. Seguir la lucha y no caer en la oscuridad" (1). De la raza secularmente aplastada surgen día tras día nuevos dirigentes de primera línea, a los que nuestra organización debe tareas abnegadas y una enorme base de a- poyo en nuestra lucha anti-imperialista y antifeudal.

"De los vientres del sexo femenino indígena nacerán nuevas flores de inteligencia que llamarán la atención a toda la civilización de explotadores, calumniadores, usu reros y ladrones, quienes han desterrado de los bosques, de las llanuras y de las selvas a nuestros padres, hijos y esposos; engañándolos con licores alcohólicos para poderlos despojar de sus hogares, de sus cultivos y de sus tierras" (2).

CONCLUSIONES

INTRODUCCION

El Consejo Regional Indígena del Cauca (CRIC) está actualmente elaborando unos docu mentos de análisis de la situación de las comunidades indígenas, para discutirlos - en su próximo Congreso. Las presentes conclusiones comprende los problemas más ur- gentes denunciados por los distintos delegados y algunas recomendaciones dirigidas sobre todo a los organismos gubernamentales.

Se ha tratado aparte la región de Tierradentro, pues tiene características en algu- nos aspectos muy diferentes al resto del departamento del Cauca y porque precisamen- te en Tierradentro programó el CRIC este Encuentro, pero ante la oposición tan intran sigente como infundada del gobierno departamental, tuvo que aceptar el cambio de sede En lo que respecta al problema indígena a nivel nacional, no hay elementos de juicio suficientes para dar una visión de conjunto. Aquí se recogen simplemente algunas de- nuncias presentadas por los voceros de las comunidades asistentes y se dan una reco- mendaciones de carácter muy general.

T I E R R A D E N T R O

ANALISIS DE LA SITUACION

1.- Tierradentro es una región subdesarrollada cuya población vive en la miseria y donde el atraso es evidente en lo económico, social, cultural y demás órdenes. La primera causa de esta situación está, en el régimen de opresión de tipo feu- dal que ejerce allí una pequeña élite, encabezada por Monseñor Enrique Vallejo, Prefecto Apostólico de Tierradentro, y de la cual hacen parte también el doctor Lordy Noriega de la División de Asuntos Indígenas y los Alcaldes de Belalcázar e Inzá.

2.- Este grupo dominante se opone ferozmente a cualquier intento de organización del sector indígena que no esté manipulado por los amos anteriores y denuncia como subversivos y comunistas a los dirigentes auténticos de las comunidades. Los indígenas no tienen ni voz ni voto en los asuntos de Tierradentro a pesar de constituir la mayoría de la población.

3.- No existe realmente libertad de movilización para los indígenas de Tierradentro. Es muy difícil que un indígena logre entrar o salir de la zona sin ser interro- gado y remprendido por el respectivo Alcalde, Inspector de Policía o Cura Párro- co.

(1) Manuel Quintín Lame
(2) Manuel Quintín Lame

Document 11. First page of the document produced for the 1973 Week in Solidarity with the Struggle of the Indigenous Campesino, distributed at the Third Indigenous Encounter of Cauca in Silvia the same year.

THIRD INDIGENOUS ENCOUNTER OF CAUCA

FIRST NATIONAL INDIGENOUS ENCOUNTER

Silvia, July 15, 1973

WHEN WAS THE REGIONAL INDIGENOUS COUNCIL OF CAUCA ESTAB-
LISHED. We came together in a great assembly of Indigenous People of
Cauca in Toribío on February 24, 1971 to protest and unite in our struggles
as indigenous campesinos, and above all to reclaim the land and end the
payment of *terraje*. We met again in a Second Assembly on September 6, 1971
in La Susana, on the *resguardo* of Tacueyó in Cauca. We met in the Third Indigenous Encounter of Cauca–First National Indigenous Encounter on July
15, 1973, in Silvia, Cauca.

The Regional Indigenous Council of Cauca (CRIC) is an organization
run by Indigenous Campesinos. Thus it is independent of the parties and
the government.

By working to enlarge CRIC we Indigenous People demonstrate our
interest in self-organization. The struggles of today, like those of yester-
year, have cost us a lot of suffering, jailings, and persecution, and they will
cost us even more before our victory, but we continue to get stronger and we
will continue in the struggle without fear. "It is time for indigenous youth
to awaken and find their path. To continue in the struggle and not succumb
to the darkness." (1) Day after day outstanding leaders also arise from out of
our perpetually humiliated race. Our organization owes them an enormous
base of support and owes it to them to selflessly undertake its tasks in its
anti-imperialist and anti-feudal struggle.

"From the wombs of indigenous womanhood new blossoms of intelligence will spring forth and rebuke the entire civilization of exploiters, de-
famers, usurers, and thieves who have uprooted our parents, children, and
spouses from the forests, plains, and jungles; deceiving them with drink to
dispossess them of their homes, their crops, and their lands." (2)

CONCLUSIONS

INTRODUCTION

The Regional Indigenous Council of Cauca (CRIC) is currently working to
produce several documents analyzing the situation of the indigenous communities for discussion at its next Congress. The conclusions presented

here represent the most urgent problems reported by the different delegates and some recommendations intended above all for government agencies.

The Tierradentro region has been dealt with separately since in a number of respects it has characteristics that are very different from the rest of the Department of Cauca and because in fact CRIC intended for this Encounter to take place in Tierradentro but was forced to move it to another location due to the completely baseless and intransigent opposition of the departmental government. With respect to the indigenous problem at the national level, we lack sufficient evaluative elements with which to provide an overall perspective. Instead we simply present several grievances expressed by representatives of the communities attending and provide some very general recommendations.

TIERRADENTRO

ANALYSIS OF THE SITUATION

1.—Tierradentro is an underdeveloped region whose residents live in dire poverty. Its backwardness is indisputable with respect to social, cultural, economic, and other conditions. The most significant reason for this is the feudal-like control, oppressive in every respect, exercised by a small elite headed up by Monsignor Enrique Vallejo, the Apostolic Prefect of Tierradentro, with the additional participation of Dr. Lordy Noriega of the Division of Indigenous Affairs and the mayors of Belalcázar and Inzá.

2.—This dominant group ferociously opposes any attempt to organize indigenous sectors not manipulated by those who were once its unquestionable masters, and denounces the authentic leaders of the communities as communists and insurgents. Despite making up the majority of the population in Tierradentro, indigenous people have no voice and play no role in regional decision making.

3.—There is no real freedom of movement for the indigenous people of Tierradentro. It would be unusual for an indigenous person to be able to enter or leave the zone without being questioned and rebuked by a local mayor, *inspector de policía*, or parish priest.

---

(1) Manuel Quintín Lame
(2) Manuel Quintín Lame

Document 12. First page of a mimeographed pamphlet in support of the Third Indigenous Encounter of Cauca produced in 1973 by a solidarity group in Bogotá. It is signed by CRIC President Julio Tunubalá, Vice President Manuel Trino Morales, and Secretary Juan Gregorio Palechor.

WEEK OF SOLIDARITY
WITH THE STRUGGLE
OF THE INDIGENOUS CAMPESINO
COMMITTEE OF SOLIDARITY WITH ANUC

Document 13. Poster by the solidarity group Yaví of Bogotá calling for solidarity with CRIC prisoners, 1980.

....

IN THE INTERNATIONAL YEAR OF THE CHILD . . .
My dad is in → jail
FREE INDIGENOUS PRISONERS
CRIC

CRIC

MENSAJE PRESENTADO POR LOS PRESOS DEL CONSEJO REGIONAL INDÍGENA DEL CAUCA -CRIC- ANTE EL CONSEJO DE GUERRA QUE JUZGA A LOS SINDICADOS DE PERTENECER AL M-19

Document 14. First page of message mimeographed by CRIC prisoners, 1981.

CRIC

Message presented by the prisoners of the Regional Indigenous Council of Cauca–CRIC–to the Military Court judging those accused of belonging to M-19.

"YO NO SOY PROFETA, PERO SI HE SIDO Y SOY EL APOSTOL DE MI RAZA"

MANUEL QUINTIN LAME

El indio busca el mejor sitio para construir su casa, consulta al médico
tradicional y de acuerdo al consejo que le dé, la hace y arma el fogón
que sirve para dar calor y alimento. Levantar una casa se puede llevar
toda la vida, eso depende de la forma como se construya, la cantidad de
manos que trabajen y el tamaño de la casa.
La casa de un indio es humilde pero grande.

Y hoy estamos despidiendo a "PALECHOR", el indio que construyó una casa
grande para todos los indios, una casa abierta y con muchos habitantes...
estamos los indios y los amigos de los indios para acompañarlo en su -
partida de este mundo, pero no del corazón y la mente de quienes fuimos
sus aprendices, compañeros y hermanos de raza.

Es difícil hacer un discurso para hablar del viejo "PALECHOR", más -
bien queremos decirle algunas cosas al viejo: Lo más valioso que usted
nos ha dejado JUAN GREGORIO, son las ideas y el amor a la lucha indígena,
las ideas están escritas y grabadas en la memoria de muchos, pero el amor
y la entrega a la lucha de los indios es un ejemplo de vida que no se -
graba facilmente, pues debe pasar primero por el corazón.......

Vinimos sus amigos para decirle gracias por su vida, por esa vida que
compartió y puso al servicio de los indios, usted Palechor con su paso
por este mundo dejó huellas de libertad y lucha.

Murió el 12 de Febrebrero /92
Elizabeth Castillo
Avelina pancho

Document 15. The words of Avelina Pancho, Paez of Tierradentro, at the funeral
of Juan Gregorio Palechor on February 13, 1992, in Popayán.

"I AM NOT A PROPHET, BUT I HAVE BEEN AND I AM
AN APOSTLE FOR THE CAUSE OF MY RACE"
MANUEL QUINTÍN LAME

The Indian looks for the best site to build his house, he consults a traditional healer and in keeping with the advice that he is given he builds the
hearth that will provide warmth and sustenance. Building a house may take
a lifetime; this depends on the way it is built, the number of hands at work,
and the size of the house.
The Indian's house is humble but it is a great thing.

And today we bid farewell to "PALECHOR," the Indian who built a great
house for all Indians, a house that is open and has many inhabitants . . . we
Indians and friends of Indians are here today to accompany him as he de-
parts from this world, but not from the hearts and minds of we who have
learned from him, of we who have been his compañeros, or of we his brothers
and sisters of the race.

It's difficult to give a speech to talk about "PALECHOR." It's more that we
want to tell the old man a few things: the most valuable things that you've
left us JUAN GREGORIO are your ideas and your love for the indigenous
struggle. Your ideas are engraved in the memory of many people, but your
love for the Indian struggle and your dedication to that struggle are an example, a way of life not so easy to instill. It's something that comes from
the heart.

We your friends have come to thank you for your life, the life you shared and
put at the service of the Indian. In your passage through this world, Palechor, you've marked out a trail of struggle and freedom.

Died on February 12, '92

Elizabeth Castillo
Avelina Pancho

GLOSSARY

Ahijado (masculine) or ahijada (feminine); a godson or goddaughter.

Cabañuelas A weather forecasting system originating in Spain and adopted in its colonies in which the weather on specific days of January is believed to be reproduced in corresponding months of the year.

Cabecera The town that serves as an administrative center where the governing bodies of a municipio are located and meet.

Cabildo An elected council, the governing body in a resguardo that exercises leadership, resolves conflicts, and administers territory.

Cacique Originally a word in the Taíno language for the leader of an indigenous community, it is now widely used to refer to a political boss with broad local power and authority.

Comadre A ceremonial comother in the compadrazgo relationship.

Compadrazgo The coparent relationship. This lifelong relationship between the parents and godparents of an individual may entail significant responsibilities. In some cases, the relationship may be established as a means to impose obligations and loyalty between people with differing interests.

Compadre A ceremonial cofather in the compadrazgo relationship.

Compañero A comrade or colleague, fellow participant in any activity; a word often used by political and social activists to refer to fellow participants and members of their communities of interest.

Corregimiento A subdivision of a municipio that may include several veredas and one or more small villages or settlements, one of which serves as its administrative center.

Inspección de policía An administrative subdivision of a municipio smaller than a corregimiento. Despite the name, inspecciones bear no relation to the National Police.

Macizo Colombiano The Colombian Massif or Nudo de Almaguer is a cluster of mountains in southwestern Colombia where the central and eastern subranges of the Colombian Andes converge. It is mainly located in the departments (provinces) of Cauca, Huila, and Nariño and is home to numerous páramos and mountain lakes that provide the headwaters of major rivers draining west into the Pacific Ocean, southeast into the Amazon River, and north into the Caribbean Sea.

Madrina Godmother.

Mestizo In English and Spanish, mestizo usually refers to a person of mixed Iberian and Amerindian ancestry. In Colombia, however, the word is used to refer to people not identified as indigenous or as Afro-descended.

Minga The long-standing indigenous Andean tradition of coming together for communal labor. The work itself may be on community projects or may focus on individual needs.

Municipio An administrative subdivision of a Colombian department similar to the county as an administrative subdivision of a U.S. state.

Padrino Godfather.

Páramo A high-elevation ecological community in the northern Andes located above the continuous tree line and below the permanent snow line and characterized by glacially formed valleys and plains with numerous lakes, bogs, and grasslands intermingled with shrub and forest patches.

Politiquería Opportunistic, hypocritical, and manipulative political practices.

Politiquero An opportunistic, hypocritical, and manipulative politician or political activist.

Resguardo An indigenous territorial unit comprising communally held lands and administered by an elected council called a cabildo.

Terraje The fulfillment of labor and crop-sharing obligations under the terrajería system.

Terrajería A system of tenancy under which indigenous tenants provided labor and a percentage of their harvest to nonindigenous landowners in return for the right to live on their property and farm it to meet their own needs.

Terrajero A tenant under the system of terrajería.

Tinterillo A person without a formal legal education who drafted petitions and provided other paralegal services for largely illiterate clients in a rural community.

Vereda Literally a rustic road or trail, now used to mean a rural area within a municipio or corregimiento that includes agricultural land and scattered dwellings.

NOTES

Foreword

....

1. Myriam Jimeno, "Colombia: Citizens and Anthropologists," in *Companion to Latin American Anthropology*, ed. D. Poole (Oxford: Blackwell, 2008), 72–89.

2. Lorenzo Muelas Hurtado, Lorenzo Urdaneta Franco, and Martha Urdaneta Franco, *La fuerza de la gente: Juntando recuerdos sobre la terrajería en Guambía, Colombia* (Bogotá: Instituto Colombiano de Antropología e Historia, 2005).

3. Christian Gros and Trino Morales, *¡A mí no me manda nadie! Historia de vida de Trino Morales* (Bogotá: Instituto Colombiano de Antropología e Historia, 2009).

Introduction

....

1. The Foundation for Colombian Communities (Fundación para las Comunidades Colombianas) devoted much of its energy in those times to legal advocacy in defense of the country's indigenous population.

2. For a history of CRIC see Consejo Regional Indígena del Cauca, *Caminando la palabra de los Congresos del Consejo Regional Indígena del Cauca CRIC, de febrero de 1971 a marzo de 2009* (Popayán: PEBI-CRIC, 2009); and Catherine González and Mauricio Archila, *Movimiento indígena caucano: historia y política* (Bogotá: Universidad Santo Tomás, 2010).

3. Myriam Jimeno and Adolfo Triana, *Estado y minorías étnicas en Colombia* (Bogotá: Cuadernos del Jaguar, 1985).

4. Paul Radin, *Crashing Thunder: The Autobiography of a Winnebago Indian* (New York: D. Appleton and Co., [1920] 1963).

5. John G. Neihardt, *Black Elk Speaks: Being the Life Story of a Holy Man of the Oglala Sioux* (Lincoln: University of Nebraska Press, [1932] 1988).

6. Ricardo Pozas, *Juan Pérez Jolote* (Mexico City: Fondo de Cultura Económica, [1952] 1975).

7. See León Zamosc, "La cuestión agraria y el movimiento campesino en Colombia: Luchas de la Asociación Nacional de Usuarios Campesinos (ANUC), 1967–1981" (Geneva and Bogotá: United Nations Research Institute for Social Development and Centro de Investigación y Educación Popular, 1987). See also *Estructuras agrarias y movimientos campesinos en América Latina (1950–1990)* coordinated by Manuel Chiriboga V., León Zamosc, and Estela Martínez Borrego (Madrid: Ministerio de Agricultura, Alimentación y Medio Ambiente, 1976), 75–132.

8. Víctor Daniel Bonilla, *Historia política de los Paeces* (Bogotá: Nuestras Ediciones, 1982).

9. Monica Espinosa, "Of Visions and Sorrows: Manuel Quintín Lame's Indian Thought and the Violences of Colombia" (January 1, 2004), Electronic Doctoral Dissertations, University of Massachusetts, Amherst, Paper AAI3152691, and *La civilización montés: La visión india y el trasegar de Manuel Quintín Lame en Colombia* (Bogotá: Universidad de los Andes, 2009); see also Diego Castrillón Arboleda, *El indio Quintín Lame* (Bogotá: Tercer Mundo, 1983); Piedad Tello, *Vida y lucha de Manuel Quintín Lame*, thesis, Universidad de los Andes, 1983; and Fernando Romero Loaiza, *Manuel Quintín Lame Chantre: el indígena ilustrado, el pensador indigenista* (Pereira: Consejo Regional Indígena del Cauca, CRIC, 2006).

10. Judith Okely, "Anthropology and Autobiography: Participatory Experience and Embodied Knowledge," in *Anthropology and Autobiography*, eds. Judith Okely and Helen Callaway (London: Routledge, 1992).

11. See Françoise Morin, "Praxis antropológica e historia de vida," in *Historia Oral*, ed. Jorge Aceves (Mexico City: Instituto Mora, Universidad Autónoma Metropolitana, 1993).

12. Edward Bruner, "Ethnography as Narrative," in *The Anthropology of Experience*, eds. Victor Turner and Edward Bruner (Chicago: University of Illinois Press, 1986).

13. Carlos Zambrano, ed., *Hombres de páramo y montaña, los Yanaconas del Macizo Colombiano* (Bogotá: ICAN, Colcultura, PNR, 1993).

14. Arnold Krupat, *For Those Who Come After: A Study of Native American Autobiography* (Berkeley: University of California Press, 1985), 30.

15. Krupat, *For Those Who Come After*, 30.

16. Brian Swann and Arnold Krupat, eds., *I Tell You Now: Autobiographical Essays by Native American Writers* (Lincoln: University of Nebraska Press, 1987).

....

1. David Bynum, "Oral Evidence and the Historian: Problems and Methods," in Folklore and Traditional History, ed. Richard Donson (The Hague: Mouton, 1973).

2. The name of Arnold Krupat's 1985 book For Those Who Come After is a quote from Paul Radin's Crashing Thunder: The Autobiography of an American Indian.

3. Arnold Krupat, For Those Who Come After: A Study of Native American Autobiography (Berkeley: University of California Press, 1985), 64–65.

4. Roger Sanjek, "The Secret Life of Fieldnotes," in Fieldnotes: The Makings of Anthropology, ed. Roger Sanjek (Ithaca, NY: Cornell University Press, 1990).

5. See Krupat, For Those Who Come After; and L. L. Langness, The Life History in Anthropological Science (New York: Holt, Rinehart and Winston, 1965).

6. Paul Radin, Crashing Thunder: The Autobiography of an American Indian (New York: D. Appleton and Co., 1926. For discussions and analyses of this book and its influence see Krupat, For Those Who Come After, and David Brumble, American Indian Autobiography (Berkeley: University of California Press, 1988).

7. Radin, quoted in Lawrence C. Watson and Maria Barbara Watson-Franke, Interpreting Life Histories: An Anthropological Inquiry (New Brunswick, NJ: Rutgers University Press, 1920), 383.

8. Krupat, For Those Who Come After, 75–106.

9. Clifford Geertz, Local Knowledge (New York: Basic Books, 1983); Geertz in Eickelman 1985; Carlos Reynoso, comp., El surgimiento de la antropología posmoderna (Barcelona: Gedisa, 1992); and Paul Rabinow, Reflexiones sobre un trabajo de campo en Marruecos (Madrid: Jucar Universidad, 1992).

10. See for example Vincent Crapanzano, Tuhami: Portrait of a Moroccan (Chicago: University of Chicago Press, 1980); and Renato Rosaldo, "Ilongot Hunting as Story and Experience," in The Anthropology of Experience, eds. Victor Turner and Edward Bruner (Champaign: University of Illinois Press, 1986).

11. Judith Okely, "Anthropology and Autobiography: Participatory Experience and Embodied Knowledge," in Anthropology and Autobiography, eds. Judith Okely and Helen Callaway (London: Routledge, 1992), 8–24.

12. Crapanzano, Tuhami: Portrait of a Moroccan.

13. Françoise Morin, "Praxis antropológica e historia de vida," in Historia Oral, ed. Jorge Aceves (Mexico City: Instituto Mora, Universidad Autónoma Metropolitana, 1993), 101.

14. Rabinow in Caplan 1992, 80.

15. Pat Caplan, "Spirits and Sex: A Swahili Informant and His Diary," in Judith Okely and Helen Callaway, Anthropology and Autobiography (London: Routledge, 1992), 80.

16. Edward Bruner, "Ethnography as Narrative," in *The Anthropology of Experience*, eds. Victor Turner and Edward Bruner (Champaign: University of Illinois Press, 1986).

17. Bruner, "Ethnography as Narrative."

18. Watson and Watson-Frank, *Interpreting Life Histories*, 12.

19. Ángel Loureiro, "Introducción: Problemas teóricos de la autobiografía," in *La autobiografía y sus problemas teóricos*, Suplementos Anthropos 29, December 1991, 7.

20. Watson and Watson-Franke, *Interpreting Life Histories*.

21. Rosaldo, "Ilongot Hunting as Story and Experience."

22. Watson and Watson-Frank, *Interpreting Life Histories*.

23. Langness, *The Life History in Anthropological Science*.

24. Paul Bellaby, "Histories of Sickliness: Making Use of Multiple Accounts of the Same Process," in *Life and Work History Analyses: Qualitative and Quantitative Developments*, ed. Shirley Dex (London: Routledge, 1991), 22.

25. Ronald Frankenberg quoted in Bellaby 1991, 22.

26. Mitterand, "Todos los días los compañeros caminan a un café," 1987, 304; see also Rousseau 1983, Rousseau 1783.

27. Mitterand 1987. See also Rousseau 2009.

28. Bellaby 1991, 23.

29. Adam Kuper and Jessica Kuper, eds., *The Social Science Encyclopedia* (London: Routledge and Kegan Paul, 1985).

30. L. L. Langness, *The Life History in Anthropological Science*.

31. For more on North American Indian biographies and autobiographies see Krupat, *For Those Who Come After*; and Brumble, *American Indian Autobiography*. For the role of these works in anthropology see Langness, *The Life History in Anthropological Science*; and Okely, "Anthropology and Autobiography."

32. Langness, *The Life History in Anthropological Science*.

33. See, for example, Shirley Dex, ed., *Life and Work History Analyses: Qualitative and Quantitative Developments* (London: Routledge, 1991); and Raphel Samuel and Paul Thompson, eds., *The Myths We Live By* (London: Routledge, 1990).

34. On the family, see for example Echeverry de Ferrufino 1988.

35. See Alfredo Molano and Fernando Rozo, "Observaciones sobre el Proyecto de Sustitución de Cultivos de Coca en el Sur del Departamento del Cauca," in Work Report for the United Nations, Bogotá, 1990; and Alfredo Molano, "Mi historia de vida con las historias de vida," in Thierry Lülle, Pilar Vargas, and Lucero Zamudio, *Los usos de la historia de vida en las ciencias sociales*, vols. 1–2 (Barcelona: Anthropos Molano, 1998), among other works.

36. Molano, "Mi historia de vida con las historias de vida," 104.

37. Myriam Jimeno, "Colombia: Citizens and Anthropologists," in *A Companion to Latin American Anthropology*, ed. Deborah Poole (Malden, MA: Blackwell Publishing, 2008), 72–89.

38. Davi Kopenawa and Bruce Albert, *La chute du ciel: Paroles d'un chaman Yanomami* (Paris: Plon, Collection Terre Humaine, 2010).

39. Samuel and Thompson, *The Myths We Live By*.

40. Samuel and Thompson, *The Myths We Live By*.

41. Samuel and Thompson, *The Myths We Live By*.

42. Bill Nasson, "Abraham Esau's War, 1899–1901," in *The Myths We Live By*, eds. Samuel R. and P. Thompson (London: Routledge, 1990).

43. See Okely, "Anthropology and Autobiography"; Jorge Aceves, *Historia oral e historias de vida: Teoría, métodos y técnicas: Una bibliografía comentada* (México City: Centro de Investigaciones y Estudios Superiores en Antropología Social, 1991); and Mauricio Archila, "Fuentes orales e historia obrera," in *Los usos de la historia de vida en las ciencias sociales*, vol. I–II, comps. Thierry Lülle, Pilar Vargas, and Lucero Zamudio (Barcelona: Anthropos Editorial Archila, 1998).

44. Aceves, *Historia oral e historias de vida*, 7.

45. Aceves, *Historia oral e historias de vida*, 7.

46. Archila, "Fuentes orales e historia obrera," 291.

47. Nasson, "Abraham Esau's War, 1899–1901."

48. Bruner, "Ethnography as Narrative."

49. Bruner, "Ethnography as Narrative."

50. Edward Bruner, "Introduction," in *The Anthropology of Experience*, eds. Victor Turner and Edward Bruner (Champaign: University of Illinois Press).

51. Sarah Lamb, "Being a Widow and Other Life Stories: The Interplay between Lives and Words," *Anthropology and Humanism* 26, no. 1 (2001): 16–34.

52. Lamb, "Being a Widow and Other Life Stories," 16.

53. Lamb, "Being a Widow and Other Life Stories," 16.

54. Samuel and Thompson, *The Myths We Live By*.

55. Samuel and Thompson, *The Myths We Live By*.

56. James Olney, "Algunas versiones de la memoria / Algunas versiones del bios: la ontología de la autobiografía," *Suplementos Anthropos 29, La autobiografía y sus problemas teóricos*, December 1991.

57. In Loureiro 1991.

58. In Loureiro 1991, 5.

59. Mikhail Bakhtin, *The Dialogic Imagination: Four Essays*, ed. Michael Holquist (Austin: University of Texas Press, 1981).

60. Bakhtin, *The Dialogic Imagination*.

61. Bakhtin, *The Dialogic Imagination*.

62. Georges Gusdorf, "Condiciones y límites de la autobiografía," in *La autobiografía y sus problemas teóricos, Suplementos Anthropos* 29, December, 1991.

63. Richard Werbner, "Contending Narrators: Personal Discourse and the Social Biography of a Family in Western Zimbabwe," University of Illinois Center for African Studies Spring Symposium, April 11–13, 1991.

64. Bakhtin, *The Dialogic Imagination.*

65. Kuper and Kuper, *The Social Science Encyclopedia,* 94–95.

66. Morin, "Praxis antropológica e historia de vida," 90.

67. Okely, "Anthropology and Autobiography," 24.

68. Molano, "Mi historia de vida con las historias de vida," 103.

69. Molano, "Mi historia de vida con las historias de vida," 15.

70. Joanne Rappaport, *The Politics of Memory* (New York: Cambridge University Press, 1990).

71. Bruner, "Introduction," in *The Anthropology of Experience.*

72. Lamb, "Being a Widow and Other Life Stories," 22.

73. Crapanzano, *Tuhami.*

74. Watson and Watson-Franke, *Interpreting Life Histories,* 46.

75. Watson and Watson-Franke, *Interpreting Life Histories,* 46.

76. Lamb, "Being a Widow and Other Life Stories," 20.

77. Lamb, "Being a Widow and Other Life Stories," 23.

Part 2: Juan Gregorio Palechor: Between the Community and the Nation

··

1. Joanne Rappaport, *The Politics of Memory* (Cambridge: Cambridge University Press, 1990; see also Rappaport, "Hacia la decolonización de la producción intelectual indígena en Colombia," in *Modernidad, identidad y desarrollo,* ed. María Lucía Sotomayor (Bogotá: Instituto Colombiano de Antropología and Colciencias, 1998).

2. Kay Warren, "Mayan Multiculturalism and the Violence of Memories," in *Violence and Subjectivity,* ed. Veena Das, Arthur Kleinman et al. (Berkeley: University of California Press, 2000), 309; see also Warren, *The Symbolism of Subordination: Indian Identity in Guatemala* (Austin: University of Texas Press, 1989).

3. Warren, "Mayan Multiculturalism and the Violence of Memories."

4. In both English and Spanish, *mestizo* usually refers to a person of mixed Iberian and Amerindian ancestry. In Colombia, however, the Spanish word is used to refer to any people not identified as indigenous or of African descent.

5. Myriam Jimeno and Adolfo Triana, *Estado y minorías étnicas en Colombia* (Bogotá: Cuadernos del Jaguar, 1985); Raúl Arango and Enrique Sánchez, *Los pueblos*

indígenas de Colombia (Bogotá: Tercer Mundo Editores, DNP, 1998); and Virginia Laurent, *Comunidades indígenas, espacios políticos y movilización electoral en Colombia, 1990–1998* (Bogotá: Instituto Colombiano de Antropología e Historia [ICANH] and French Institute for Andean Studies [IFEA], 2005).

6. DANE, 2008; *Censo General 2005: nivel nacional* (Bogotá: DANE, 2005).

7. The *resguardo* is an indigenous territorial unit comprising communally held lands and administered by an elected council called a *cabildo*.

8. Raúl Arango and Enrique Sánchez, *Los pueblos indígenas de Colombia* (Bogotá: Tercer Mundo Editores DNP, 1998).

9. Arango and Sánchez, *Los pueblos indígenas de Colombia*.

10. DANE, *Censo General 2005*.

11. Alcida Ramos, *Indigenism: Ethnic Politics in Brazil* (Madison: Wisconsin University Press, 1998); and Ramos, "Los dilemas del pluralismo en Brasil," Presentation to the Masters in Anthropology Program, Universidad Nacional de Colombia, Bogotá, October 11, 2002.

12. This is not to minimize the intense activity of other indigenous people, for example, in the Sierra Nevada de Santa Marta or on the Guajira Peninsula in northern Colombia, or those in the Amazon region. Nonetheless, the role of indigenous organizations in the southwest stands out.

13. Myriam Jimeno, "Reforma constitucional na Colômbia e povos indígenas: Os limites da lei," in *Constituições Nacionais e Povos Indígenas: Os limites da lei,* coord. Alcida R. Ramos (Belo Horizonte: Editora UFMG, 2012).

14. Joanne Rappaport, *Intercultural Utopias: Public Intellectuals, Cultural Experimentation, and Ethnic Pluralism in Colombia* (Durham, NC: Duke University Press, 2005).

15. Pierre Bourdieu, *Ce que parler veut dire: L'économie des échanges linguistiques* (Paris: Fayard, 1982).

16. Virginie Laurent, *Comunidades indígenas, espacios políticos y movilización electoral en Colombia, 1990–1998* (Bogotá: Instituto Colombiano de Antropología e Historia [ICANH] and French Institute for Andean Studies [IFEA]), 2005.

17. Esther Sánchez, *Derechos propios: Ejercicio legal de la jurisdicción especial indígena en Colombia* (Bogotá: Procuraduría General de la Nación, 2004); and Sánchez, *Entre el juez Salomón y el dios Sira: Decisiones interculturales e interés superior del niño* (Bogotá: UNICEF, Universiteit van Amsterdam, 2006).

18. Jimeno, "Reforma constitucional na Colômbia e povos indígenas."

19. Rappaport, *Intercultural Utopias*.

20. Jean Jackson, "Rights to Indigenous Culture in Colombia," in *The Practice of Human Rigths: Tracking between the Local and the Global*, comps. Mark Goodale and Sally Merry (Cambridge: Cambridge University Press, 2007), 204, 212–14.

21. Jimeno, "Reforma constitucional na Colômbia e povos indígenas."

22. Elizabeth Tonkin, Maryon McDonald, and Malcom Chapman, eds., "Introduction: History and Social Anthropology," in *History and Ethnicity* (London: Routledge, 1989), 1–22; Myriam Jimeno, "Juan Gregorio Palechor: tierra, identidad y recreación étnica," in *Journal of Latin American Anthropology* 1, no. 2 (spring 1996): 46–77; for contextual identity see the classic work of Fredrick Barth, "Introducción," in *Los grupos étnicos y sus fronteras* (México: Fondo de Cultura Económica, 1976); and Greg Urban and Joel Sherzer, eds., *Nation-States and Indians in Latin America* (Austin: University of Texas Press, 1991).

23. Peter Burke, *Formas de hacer historia* (Madrid: Alianza Editorial, 1993), 297.

24. Warren, *The Symbolism of Subordination.*

25. Warren, "Mayan Multiculturalism and the Violence of Memories."

26. This section is adapted from my comments in response to the lecture "*Los dilemas del pluralismo en Brasil*" (The Dilemmas of Pluralism in Brazil), given to master's degree students in anthropology at the National University of Colombia by Alcida Ramos in October 2002.

27. See also Ramos, *Indigenism.*

28. Jimeno, "Juan Gregorio Palechor."

29. Zygmund Bauman, *Culture as Praxis* (London: Routledge and Kegan Paul, 1973), 1.

30. Bauman, *Culture as Praxis*, 23.

31. H. G. Wells, *Anticipations of the Reactions of Mechanical and Scientific Progress upon Human Life and Thought* (London: Chapman and Hall, 1901), 317.

32. Friedrich Nietzsche, *The Will to Power* (London: Weidenfield and Nicholson, 1968), 476.

33. Norbert Elias, *The Germans: Power Struggles and the Development of Habitus in the Nineteenth and Twentieth Centuries* (New York: Colombia University Press, 1996).

34. Elias's footnote refers to Friedrich Schiller, "Was heißt und zu welchem Ende studiert man Universalgeschichte?" in *Schillers Werke: Nationalausgabe* (Weimar: Hermann Bölhaus Nachfolger, 1970), vol. 17, part 1: 365, 367 ff.

35. Elias's footnote refers to Dietrich Schäfer, *Deutsches Nationalbewusstsein im Licht der Geschichte* (Jena: G. Fischer, 1884), 1 ff.

36. Schäfer 1884: 1 ff., quoted in Elias, 132.

37. Elias, 136.

38. Francisco Colom, "La política del multiculturalismo," unpublished presentation, Bogotá, 2002.

39. Part of this text was published in the *Journal of Latin American Anthropology* 1, no. 2 (spring 1996): 46–77, under the title "Juan Gregorio Palechor: Tierra, identidad y recreación étnica."

40. A *cabildo* is an elected council, the governing body in a *resguardo* and exercises leadership, resolves conflicts, and administers territory.

41. Jimeno, "Juan Gregorio Palechor."

42. Jimeno and Triana, *Estado y minorías étnicas en Colombia*; Germán Colmenares, *Terratenientes, mineros y comerciantes* (Cali: Universidad del Valle, 1975); and Juan Friede, *El indio en lucha por la tierra: Historia de los resguardos del macizo central colombiano* (Bogotá: Espiral, 1944).

43. An administrative subdivision of a Colombian department similar to the county as an administrative subdivision of a U.S. state.

44. The Colombian Massif or Nudo de Almaguer is a cluster of mountains in southwestern Colombia where the central and eastern subranges of the Colombian Andes converge. It is mainly located in the departments (provinces) of Cauca, Huila, and Nariño and is home to numerous *páramos* and mountain lakes that provide the headwaters of major rivers draining west into the Pacific Ocean, southeast into the Amazon River, and north into the Caribbean Sea.

45. A bloody civil war fought from 1899–1902 between the Conservative Party government and Liberal Party rebels who rejected Conservative Party policies and their own exclusion from power.

46. Valerio Palechor's signature appears as the governor of the indigenous cabildo on the resguardo of Guachicono.

47. Herbert Braun, *Mataron a Gaitán: Vida pública y violencia urbana en Colombia* (Bogotá: Universidad Nacional de Colombia, 1987), 25.

48. Braun, *Mataron a Gaitán*.

49. The violent explosion of popular anger in the capital on April 9, 1948, is known as the *Bogotazo*.

50. A person without a formal legal education who drafted petitions and provided other paralegal services for largely illiterate clients in a rural community.

51. Font Castro, José, "Qué fue, qué hizo y qué dejó el MRL," *El Tiempo*, November 23, 1997. http://www.eltiempo.com/archivo/documento/MAM-692737.

52. A lot has been written about this period. See, among other sources, Daniel Pécaut, *Orden y violencia: Colombia 1930–1953*, 2 vols. (Bogotá: Siglo XXI Editores, 1987); James Henderson, *Modernization in Colombia: The Laureano Gómez Years 1889–1965* (Gainesville: University Press of Florida, 2001); and Gonzalo Sánchez, *Ensayos de historia social y política del siglo XX* (Bogotá: Áncora Editores, 1985). For an economic analysis of the events see Eduardo Sáenz Rovner, *La ofensiva empresarial: Industriales, políticos y violencia in los años 40 in Colombia* (Bogotá: Tercer Mundo, 1992).

53. León Zamosc, "La cuestión agraria y el movimiento campesino en Colombia: Luchas de la Asociación Nacional de Usuarios Campesinos (ANUC), 1967–

1981" (Geneva: United Nations Research Institute for Social Development and Centro de Investigación y Educación Popular, 1987); and Zamosc, *Estructuras agrarias y movimientos campesinos en América Latina (1950–1990)*, coordinated by Manuel Chiriboga V., León Zamosc, and Estela Martínez Borrego, 1996), 75–132.

54. As stated above, the cabildo is an institution that was imposed by the Spanish for the governance of the indigenous population. It functions as a local authority and represents indigenous communities to the outside world.

55. A tenant under the system of *terrajería* where indigenous campesinos provided labor and a percentage of the harvest to nonindigenous landowners in return for the right to live on their property and farm it to meet their own needs. Italics addded.

56. The fulfillment of the labor and crop-sharing obligations under the terrajería system.

57. Lorenzo Muelas Hurtado (2005).

58. Lorenzo Muelas Hurtado (2005), 45.

59. CRIC, *Caminando la palabra de los Congresos del Consejo Regional Indígena del Cauca CRIC, febrero de 1971 a marzo de 2009*, Graciela Bolaños, coord. (Popayán: Consejo Regional Indígena del Cauca—CRIC, Universidad Autónoma Indígena Intercultural, Programa de Educación Bilingüe e Intercultural, 2009); Catherine González and Mauricio Archila, *Movimiento indígena Caucano: Historia y política* (Bogotá: Universidad Santo Tomás, 2010); and Daniel Ricardo Peñaranda, *Organizaciones indígenas y participación política en Colombia* (Bogotá: La Carreta Editores, 2009).

60. CRIC, *Caminando la palabra de los Congresos*.

61. The Emberá-Eperara people on the Pacific Coast subsequently joined.

62. Guillermo Bonfil Batalla, *México profundo: Una civilización negada* (Mexico City: SEP-CIESAS, 1987).

63. Kay Warren and Jean Jackson, eds., "Introduction: Studying Indigenous Activism in Latin America," in *Indigenous Movements, Self-representation, and the State in Latin America* (Austin: University of Texas Press, 2002), 1–46.

64. Rappaport, *Intercultural Utopias*.

65. Victor Turner, *The Ritual Process* (Ithaca, NY: Cornell University Press, 1969).

66. For the ethnohistory of the region see Friede, *El indio en lucha por la tierra*; Duque Gómez 1955; Kathleen Romoli, "El suroeste del Cauca y sus indios al tiempo de la conquista española," in *Revista Colombiana de Antropología* (Bogotá: Instituto Colombiano de Antropología, 1962), 9, 239–301; Colmenares, *Terratenientes, mineros y comerciantes*; Franz Faust, "Etnografía y etnoecología de Coconuco y Sotará," in *Revista Colombiana de Antropología* (Bogotá: Instituto Colombiano de Antropología, 1989–1990), 27, 53–90; and María Clemencia Ramírez, *Frontera fluida entre Andes, Piedemonte y selva* (Bogotá: Instituto de Cultura Hispánica, 1996).

67. Duque Gómez 1955.

68. Duque Gómez 1955.

69. Escobar [1582] 1983, 291.

70. Friede, El indio en lucha por la tierra; and Colmenares, Terratenientes, mineros y comerciantes, 1979.

71. Friede, El indio en lucha por la tierra.

72. Romoli, "El suroeste del Cauca. . . ."

73. The encomienda was a grant by the Spanish crown to a resident of its American colonies of power over indigenous people living in a particular area. The recipient was authorized to exact tribute from the natives in gold, in kind, or in labor, and was required to protect them and instruct them in the Christian faith.

74. Romoli, "El suroeste del Cauca. . . ."

75. Romoli, "El suroeste del Cauca. . . ."

76. Friede, El indio en lucha por la tierra.

77. Romoli, "El suroeste del Cauca. . . ."

78. Franz Faust, "Etnografía y etnoecología de Coconuco y Sotará." In Revista Colombiana de Antropología 27 (1989–1990): 53–90.

79. Faust, "Etnografía y etnoecología de Coconuco y Sotará."

80. Friede, El indio en lucha por la tierra.

81. In a 1931 affidavit the Almaguer Circuit Notary presented the text of a March 1833 document produced by appraiser-surveyors Lorenzo Muñoz and Toribio de Abella, for the "act of dividing the resguardo and setting boundaries." This document stated that boundaries were set "solely at the request of the authorities and elders of this settlement with the previous presence of the entire body of indigenes in common without having produced any document to support [their claim]." In the course of subsequent legal arguments it is also mentioned that the original title or founding document of the resguardo had not been found, and indeed it has not been found to this day. In some legal documents its loss has been attributed to events related to the many Colombian civil wars ("Report on the Boundaries of the Indigenous Resguardo of Guachicono" [Bogotá: Agustín Codazzi Geographical Institute, 1983]).

82. Agustín Codazzi, Jeografía física i política de las provincias de la Nueva Granada (Bogotá: Banco de la República, 1959).

83. Dominguez and Gomez, 1990.

84. The relevant judicial rulings appear in a 1983 compilation by the Instituto Agustín Codazzi (document 4); and in Friede, El indio en lucha por la tierra.

85. Friede, El indio en lucha por la tierra, 16.

86. Romoli, "El suroeste del Cauca . . . ," 245.

87. Alfredo Molano and Fernando Rozo, Molano, "Observaciones sobre

el Proyecto de Sustitución de Cultivos de Coca en el Sur del Departamento del Cauca," in *Work Report for the United Nations*, Bogotá, 1990.

88. Christian Gros, "Los campesinos de las cordilleras frente a los movimientos guerrilleros y a la droga. ¿Actores o víctimas?" *Revista Análisis Político* 16 (May–August, 1992): 34–54.

89. Benedict Anderson, *Imagined Communities: Reflections on the Origin and Spread of Nationalism* (London: Verso, 1983); and Ramos, *Nações dentro da Nação: Um desencontro de ideologias*, Anthropological Series (Brasilia: Universidad de Brasilia, 1993).

90. David Gow and Joanne Rappaport, "The Indigenous Public Voice: The Multiple Idioms of Modernity in Native Cauca," in *Indigenous Movements, Self-Representation, and the State in Latin America*, ed. Kay Warren and Jean Jackson (Austin: University of Texas Press, 2002), 47–80.

91. Joanne Rappaport, *The Politics of Memory* (Cambridge: Cambridge University Press, 1990).

92. Degregori, 1990.

93. Joanne Rappaport, "Mythic Images, Historical Thought, and Printed Texts: The Paez and the Written Word," *Journal of Anthropological Research* 43, no. 1: 43–61; and Rappaport, *The Politics of Memory*.

94. Rappaport, "Mythic Images. . . ."

95. Ramos, *Nações dentro da Nação*, 11.

96. See Gow and Rappaport, "The Indigenous Public Voice"; Jean Jackson, "Contested Discourses of Authority in Colombian National Indigenous Politics: The 1996 Summer Takeovers," in *Indigenous Movements, Self-Representation, and the State in Latin America* (Austin: University of Texas Press, 2002); and María Lucía Sotomayor, ed., *Modernidad, identidad y desarrollo* (Bogotá: Instituto Colombiano de Antropología, Colciencias, 1998).

97. For information on indigenous organizations in the more recent past see Gow and Rappaport, "The Indigenous Public Voice"; Warren and Jackson, "Introduction: Studying Indigenous Activism in Latin America"; and Sotomayor, *Modernidad, identidad y desarrollo*.

98. Warren, *The Symbolism of Subordination*.

99. Spoken at Palechor's funeral, on February 13, 1992.

Part 3: Juan Gregorio Palechor: The Story of My Life

1. The *resguardo* is an indigenous territorial unit comprising communally held lands and administered by a *cabildo*.

2. The *municipio* is an administrative subdivision of a Colombian department similar to the county as the administrative subdivision of a U.S. state.

3. The Macizo Colombiano or Colombian Massif is also known as the Nudo de Almaguer. It is a cluster of mountains in southwestern Colombia where the central and eastern ranges of the Colombian Andes converge. It is mainly located in the departments (provinces) of Cauca, Huila, and Nariño and is home to numerous *páramos*. The páramo is a high-elevation ecological community located above the continuous tree line and below the permanent snow line. It is characterized by glacially formed valleys and plains with numerous lakes, bogs, and grasslands intermingled with shrub and forest patches. Mountain lakes on the Macizo Colombiano provide the headwaters of major rivers draining west into the Pacific, southeast into the Amazon, and north into the Caribbean.

4. An indigenous council, the governing body in a resguardo that exercises leadership, resolves conflicts, and administers territory.

5. In English and Spanish, *mestizo* usually refers to a person of mixed Iberian and Amerindian ancestry. In Colombia, however, the word is often used to refer to any people not identified as black or indigenous.

6. An *inspector de policía* is the administrator of an *inspección de policía*, a sub-municipal administrative division smaller than a *corregimiento*. Despite their names, *inspectores* and *inspecciones* bear no relation to the National Police.

7. *Politiqueros* are opportunistic, hypocritical, and manipulative politicians or political activists.

8. The common name for a large number of plant species belonging to the genus Espeletia and endemic to the Andes of Venezuela, Colombia, and northern Ecuador at altitudes more than ten thousand feet above sea level.

9. A *páramo* is a high-elevation ecological community in the northern Andes located above the continuous tree line and below the permanent snow line. *Páramos* are characterized by glacially formed valleys and plains with numerous lakes, bogs, and grasslands intermingled with shrub and forest patches.

10. The Bota Caucana is the southern panhandle of Cauca department, named for its shape resembling a boot.

11. A *compañero* is a comrade or colleague, a fellow participant in any activity. It is a word often used by social movement activists to refer to fellow participants and members of their communities of interest.

12. *Mingas* are work days in the long-standing indigenous tradition of coming together for communal labor in the rural Andes. The work may be on collective projects such as maintaining roads or may focus on individual needs.

13. A bloody civil war fought from 1899 to 1902 between the Conservative Party

government and Liberal Party rebels who rejected Conservative policies and their own exclusion from power.

14. Any town that serves as an administrative center where the governing bodies of a municipio are located and meet.

15. A subdivision of a municipio that may include several *veredas* and one or more small villages or settlements, one of which serves as its administrative center.

16. A *compadre* is a ceremonial cofather. See *compadrazgo* for further description of the relationship.

17. Literally a rustic road or trail, a *vereda* is a rural section within a municipio or corregimiento that includes agricultural land and scattered dwellings.

18. A fermented beverage made from corn.

19. Examining the urine was a traditional diagnostic technique.

20. Opportunistic, hypocritical, or manipulative political discourse and practices.

21. A person without a formal legal education who drafted petitions and provided other paralegal services for largely illiterate clients in a rural community.

22. In the documentary appendix to his book El indio en lucha por la tierra: Historia de los resguardos del macizo central colombiano (Bogotá: Espiral, 1944), Juan Friede cites an 1883 petition from the leading citizens, or comuneros, of the resguardo of Guachicono to the mayor of the municipio signed by several people including Valerio Palechor, the leading official of the indigenous cabildo, who held a position called *gobernador* (governor) today, and *alcalde* (mayor) at that time.

23. In the Central Archives of Cauca there is an 1888 Last Will and Testament from a certain Gregorio Palechor (No. 572, vol. 1, page 23, 1892), but this does not appear to be the same person. There is also a 1919 deed belonging to a Salvador Palechor, who appears to have been the brother of this other Gregorio Palechor.

24. Colombia and Peru fought a border war over Amazonian territory in 1932–33.

25. In El indio en lucha por la tierra, Juan Friede notes that in 1942 the Catholic Church owned two grain mills and several pieces of land on the resguardo.

26. The tiple is a guitarlike musical instrument, the Colombian variety of which has twelve strings.

27. The bandolín is a musical instrument primarily found in the Andean region of Ecuador. It is shaped like a mandolin and has fifteen strings.

28. Literally "inhabitants of a warm region," that is, "lowlanders," in opposition to the indigenous *fríanos* who live at higher altitudes and a cooler climate. The connotations of *calentano* include the cultivation of plantain and yuca (cassava)

as opposed to corn and participation in the capitalist wage-based economy as opposed to mutual aid and the communal economy of the minga.

29. Palechor laughs as he says this.

30. *Panela* is a hard cake of raw brown sugar, pieces of which are dissolved to make a sweet hot drink that is often consumed daily.

31. The *Caja Agraria* was the state-owned bank that granted credit for agricultural production between the 1940s and the 1990s, when it was replaced by the *Banco Agrario de Colombia*.

32. The Colombian Institute for Agrarian Reform (*Instituto Colombiano de Reforma Agraria*—INCORA) was established in the 1960s and was later restructured as the Colombian Institute for Rural Development (*Instituto Colombiano para el Desarrollo Rural*—INCODER).

33. A weather forecasting system originating in Spain and adopted in its colonies in which the weather on specific days of January is believed to be reproduced in corresponding months of the year.

34. Alfonso López Pumarejo (1886–1959) was a businessman and politician who served twice as Colombian president, in 1934–38 and 1942–45. In his first presidency he sponsored social reforms under what he called the Revolution on the March (*Revolución en Marcha*). In his second presidency he was beset by strong political opposition and popular discontent in the context of economic difficulties related to the Second World War. On July 10–11, 1944, López Pumarejo was held prisoner in the southern city of Pasto by a dissident colonel demanding his resignation. López Pumarejo refused and the uprising was resolved within forty-eight hours. Nevertheless, López resigned the following year before completing his term in office. López Pumarejo was the father of Alfonso López Michelsen, who is mentioned by Palechor in connection with the Liberal Revolutionary Movement (*Movimiento Revolucionario Liberal*—MRL).

35. Gabriel Turbay (1901–46) was a medical doctor, politician, and Liberal leader in the Senate who aspired to his party's nomination for the presidency in competition with Jorge Eliécer Gaitán (1903–48). This division among the Liberals led to the election of a Conservative, Mariano Ospina (1891–1976) as president from 1946–50, a time of intense inter-party violence throughout much of the country.

36. A popular radio station in Popayán.

37. Antonio is a successful radio journalist, and Libio works on educational programs for CRIC.

38. Colombians often insert an honorific *doctor* or *doctora* preceding the name of individuals perceived as being highly educated, whether or not they have acquired a doctoral degree.

39. As presidential designate (similar to vice president), Liberal leader Darío Echandía (1897–1989) had served as acting president of Colombia between October 1943 and May 1944, during the absence of President Alfonso López Pumarejo. He also served as acting president on three subsequent occasions.

40. Laureano Gómez (1889–1965) was a Conservative legislator, the principal Conservative leader of his time, and a frequent cabinet minister known for his eloquent and heated oratory. Gómez was the sole candidate for president in the election of December 1949 because Liberal candidate Darío Echandía withdrew after an assassination attempt against him resulted in the death of his brother. The Liberal Party decided that conditions did not exist for their participation due to the assassination attempt and the wave of violence being perpetrated against them. Gómez served as president from 1950–51, at which time poor health prevented him from continuing to perform his duties. Roberto Urdaneta took over as acting president. In subsequent years the wave of interparty violence reached unprecedented proportions, especially in the countryside. Gómez resumed his presidency in June 1953 but was deposed in a military coup led by General Gustavo Rojas Pinilla, who governed until 1957 (see James D. Henderson, *La modernización de Colombia: Los años de Laureano Gómez, 1889–1965* (Medellín: Editorial Universidad de Antioquia, 2006).

41. Mosquera Chaux was a leading Liberal Party politician in Cauca department. He was a member of the Liberal Party National Directorate and served in both chambers of Congress, as minister of justice, and as a diplomat. He was the presidential designate in 1980–82 and 1986–90. The indigenous movement considered him one of its major opponents.

42. Paez Indian Benjamín Dindicué was from the resguardo of Huila in Tierradentro and was a member of the CRIC Executive Committee. He was assassinated at his home on February 4, 1979. Dindicué related this story in 1978.

43. The terms *chulavitas* and *policía chulavita* both refer to a politicized police unit associated with the Conservative Party during the first several years of violence following the 1948 assassination of Liberal leader Jorge Eliécer Gaitán.

44. The Moras vereda is in a high-altitude section of the resguardo of Mosoco in Tierradentro.

45. A euphemism used to refer to the guerrillas.

46. *Mambe* is an alkali that is mixed with coca leaf to moderate its flavor and activate the alkaloids that are its active ingredients.

47. *Alpargatas* are the locally made espadrilles used by campesinos in various parts of rural South America.

48. The National Front was the name given to a political agreement signed in 1957 between the leaders of the two traditional parties, the Liberal Party and the

Conservative Party. The goal of this political pact was to end the bloodletting of the interparty confrontation that had led to thousands of deaths between 1946 and 1957, and that had devastating consequences for the country, particularly in rural areas east and west of Bogotá.

49. Originally a word in the Taíno language for the leader of an indigenous community, *cacique* is now widely used to refer to a political boss with broad local power and authority.

50. The Liberal Revolutionary Movement (*Movimiento Revolucionario Liberal*— MRL) was a dissident movement within the Liberal Party that was formed in 1957. The MRL survived until 1967, when it dissolved into the Liberal Party during the government of President Carlos Lleras Restrepo.

51. *Indio* may simply mean "Indian"; but sometimes, such as in this context, it is used as a pejorative.

52. The reference is to the resguardo of Guachicono since Palechor was still living in La Sierra.

53. Gustavo Rojas Pinilla was the commander of the Colombian army who led a 1953 military coup against President Laureano Gómez. Rojas Pinilla was himself deposed in 1957 by five officers representing the different branches of the armed forces, who organized legislative and presidential elections several months later. Alberto Lleras Camargo was elected president and the Liberal and Conservative parties reached the agreement known as the National Front, under the terms of which they agreed to alternate in the presidency between 1958 and 1974.

54. The Community Action Committees (*Juntas de Acción Comunal*) are composed of local community representatives. According to a 1979 law, they are intended to promote citizen participation in community management and to seek solutions to local needs in dialogue with the municipal, departmental, and national governments. Their origin dates to 1958 when they were proposed as a mechanism to promote peaceful governance in the wake of the violent confrontation between the two traditional parties. They continue to be active, particularly in poor and working-class areas, both rural and urban. Critics have accused them of being susceptible to manipulation by local politicians and interest groups.

55. *La Violencia* (the Violence) was a period of widespread and brutal conflict between the Liberals and Conservatives that lasted from 1946 to 1956. It was especially intense between 1950 and 1953.

56. It is common to use this number with reference to the number of dead in the confrontation between Liberals and Conservatives from 1946 to 1956. Empirical evidence for the number has been hotly debated but some researchers estimate that the dead numbered between 150,000 and 200,000 (see Henderson, *La modernización de Colombia*; Daniel Pécaut, *Orden y violencia: Colombia 1930–1943*, 2 vols.

(Bogotá: Siglo XXI, 1987); and Gonzalo Sánchez, *Ensayos de historia social y política del siglo XX* (Bogotá: El Áncora, 1985).

57. The Campesino Congresses were organized by the National Association of Campesinos (*Asociación Nacional de Usuarios Campesinos*—ANUC), an organization that was growing in size and importance at that time. The members of ANUC were campesinos who were organizing to reclaim land.

58. July 20 is a national holiday celebrating Colombian independence from Spain.

59. The Sincelejo group constituted the radical wing of ANUC. Sincelejo is a city near the Caribbean coast, which at the time being discussed here was the center of a movement to take back land through militant action rather than negotiating with the government for its return.

60. A plebiscite was held in December 1957 in accordance with the terms of the June 1956 Benidorm Agreement signed in Spain by Laureano Gómez for the Conservatives and Alberto Lleras Camargo for the Liberals. It was the first time that the franchise was extended to Colombian women. The plebiscite asked voters to ratify the preliminary agreement establishing the National Front, the first paragraph of which included the following: "We can declare with great mutual satisfaction that we have reached full agreement on the immediate need to recommend to the historical parties a joint action destined to achieve a rapid return to the institutional forms of political life and the recovery of the freedom and the legal protections that for generations and up to the present time have been the proudest accomplishment of the Colombian people" (Translation by Andy Klatt).

61. A *godo* is a member of the Conservative Party, especially an extreme social and political conservative with an authoritarian worldview.

62. Palechor blames the Conservatives for not having defended Colombian territorial control of its southern border with Peru, leading to the Colombia–Peru War of 1932–33.

63. Palechor laughs when he says this.

64. Palechor had a house for many years in Timbío, which is near Popayán, the capital of Cauca. His wife still lives there.

65. Palechor laughs as he says this.

66. *Compadrazgo* is the coparent relationship. This lifelong relationship between the parents and godparents of a baby, child, or adolescent may entail significant responsibilities, and the relationship may be established as a means to impose obligations and loyalty between people with differing interests.

67. Comadre is a ceremonial comother (see compadrazgo for further description of the relationship).

68. *Ahijado* is a godson or a goddaughter.

69. Camilo Torres (1929–66) was a Colombian Catholic priest who espoused the tenets of liberation theology, a movement that attempted to reconcile Marxism and Christianity and to prioritize social problems. Torres briefly led a movement against the National Front called the *Frente Unido*, or United Front, but decided to join the guerrillas of the National Liberation Army (*Ejército de Liberación Nacional—*ELN) and died in a February 1966 confrontation with the Colombian Army.

70. Archbishop Oscar Romero of El Salvador was assassinated while offering mass in 1980 during the 1980–92 civil war. Romero advocated "the preferential option for the poor," a key tenet of liberation theology. Then-retired Army Major Roberto D'Abuisson, now deceased, has been attributed with planning the archbishop's murder, which was carried out by a right-wing death squad with links to the army.

71. The local Catholic hierarchy expropriated community lands in Coconuco in 1973.

72. Pedro León Rodríguez was a parish priest in the town of Corinto in the north of Cauca who died in 1975.

73. Gustavo Mejía was a leader of the campesino organization in the north of Cauca and subsequently of the indigenous movement. He was assassinated in Corinto, in the north of Cauca, in 1979.

74. The Third Brigade of the Colombian army.

75. A state of siege was in effect at this time. Individual rights had been suspended and mechanisms were in place for expedited trials of individuals considered a threat to public order.

76. The Colombian Institute for Agrarian Reform (*Instituto Colombiano de Reforma Agraria—*INCORA) was established in 1961 in order to address the question of land ownership. From the beginning it was met with strong political opposition that significantly limited its ability to act. A 1974 law seriously limited its powers and successive laws hobbled it even further until it was replaced by the Colombian Institute for Rural Development (*Instituto Colombiano de Desarrollo Rural—*INCODER).

77. The fulfillment of the labor and crop-sharing obligations under the terrajería system of tenancy under which indigenous campesinos, known as terrajeros, provided labor and a percentage of their harvest to nonindigenous landowners in return for the right to live on their property and farm it to meet their own needs.

78. This part of the testimony was recorded in 1980 when Palechor was living in Popayán and working full time for CRIC. He lived in a modest house that he later lost when it was taken over by squatters after a 1983 earthquake.

79. This part of the conversation was recorded in 1980 when several CRIC leaders were in prison.

80. The name of a subdivision of a municipio smaller than a corregimiento. The job Palechor refers to would be inspector de policía, the administrator of an inspección de policía.

81. A *personero* is a municipal human-rights ombudsman.

82. The participation of women in the organization and its leadership has increased significantly in recent years.

83. The reference is to a struggle in the 1930s to defend a piece of land on the resguardo.

84. Manuel Quintín Lame (1880–1967) spearheaded an indigenous rebellion in Cauca in 1910–1915 and led a long-standing movement for territorial rights in the western department of Tolima in 1930–1950 (see Manuel Quintín Lame, *Las luchas del indio que bajó de la montaña al valle de la civilización. Selección, arreglo y notas de Gonzalo Castillo Cárdenas* (Bogotá: Comité de defensa del indio, 1973); Fernando Loaiza Romero, *Manuel Quintín Lame Chantre: el indígena ilustrado, el pensador indigenista* (Pereira: CRIC, 2006); Mónica Arango Espinosa, "Of Visions and Sorrows: Manuel Quintín Lame's Indian Thought and the Violences of Colombia," *Electronic Doctoral Dissertations for the University of Massachusetts, Amherst*, Paper AAI3152691, January 1, 2004; Piedad Tello, *Vida y lucha de Manuel Quintín Lame* (Bogotá: Universidad de los Andes, 1983), Department of Anthropology thesis; and Diego Castrillón Arboleda, *El indio Quintín Lame* (Bogotá: Tercer Mundo, 1973).

85. This law classified indigenous peoples as "savages" and those being transitioned to "civilized life." The two groups were granted different rights and different government policies were authorized with respect to each of them.

86. In some indigenous groups, members of the cabildo use ceremonial staffs that symbolize their leadership and their communication with the spiritual forces of nature. These staffs have deep symbolic meaning for the groups who use them.

REFERENCES

Archival Documents Consulted

....

1. Memoria testamentaria de Gregorio Palechor, vecino del Distrito de Ríoblanco, no. 572, 1892, vol. 1, Folio 23. Archivo Central del Cauca.

2. Escritura no. 420, Salvador Palechor, 1919, vol. 1, Folio 2215. Archivo Central del Cauca.

3. Memorial elevado por los mandones de los pueblos indígenas de San Sebastián, Caquiona, Pancitará y Guachicono al gobernador de la Provincia, pidiendo su intervención para lograr la suspensión de las leyes de reparto. In Juan Friede, *El indio en lucha por la tierra: Historia de los resguardos del macizo central colombiano.* Bogotá: Espiral, 1944.

4. Informe de límites del resguardo indígena de Guachicono, municipio de La Vega, departamento del Cauca. Instituto Geográfico Agustín Codazzi, Subdirección de Catastro Nacional, Bogotá, 1983 (108 pp., maps and aerial photography).

5. Diligencia del 3 de marzo de 1833 practicada por los agrimensores del resguardo de Guachicono, inscrita in 1924, in el libro duplicado no. 2, 1934—Notaría Pública del Circuito no. 2, Almaguer. In IGAC, Informe de límites, documento no. 4.

6. Escritura de junio 5 de 1924, Notaría del Circuito de La Vega. In IGAC, Informe de límites, documento no. 4.

7. Escritura no. 31 de junio de 1924 de la Notaría del Circuito de La Vega. In IGAC, Informe de límites, documento no. 4.

8. Sentencia del Juzgado 1ro. del Circuito de Bolívar, octubre de 1934 en proceso de deslinde propuesto por el cabildo indígena de Guachicono, contra el cabildo indígena de Pancitará. In IGAC, Informe de límites, documento no. 4.

9. Sentencia del Tribunal del Distrito Judicial de Popayán de diciembre de 1935, del proceso anterior. In IGAC, Informe de límites, documento no. 4.

10. Escrituras de 1939, 1941, and 1966, sobre terrenos cedidos al resguardo de Guachicono. In IGAC, Informe de límites, documento no. 4.

11. Actas de deslinde del resguardo, de 1978. In IGAC, Informe de límites, documento no. 4.

General Works
....

Aceves, Jorge. 1991. *Historia oral e historias de vida: Teoría, métodos y técnicas: Una bibliografía comentada*. México City: Centro de Investigaciones y Estudios Superiores en Antropología Social.

Aceves, Jorge. 1993. *Historia oral*. México: Instituto Mora, Universidad Autónoma Metropolitana.

Anderson, Benedict. 1983. *Imagined Communities: Reflections on the Origin and Spread of Nationalism*. London: Verso.

Arango, Raúl and Enrique Sánchez. 1998. *Los pueblos indígenas de Colombia*. Bogotá: Tercer Mundo Editores, DNP.

Archila, Mauricio. 1998. "Fuentes orales e historia obrera." In *Los usos de la historia de vida en las ciencias sociales*, vols. 1–2. Compiled by Thierry Lulle, Pilar Vargas, and Lucero Zamudio. Barcelona: Anthropos Editorial.

Archila, Mauricio, and Nidia Catherine González Piñeros. 2010. *Movimiento Indígena Caucano: Historia y Política*. Tunja: Sello Editorial Santo Tomás.

Bakhtin, Mikhail. 1981. *The Dialogic Imagination: Four Essays*. Ed. Michael Holquist. Austin: University of Texas Press.

Barnet, Miguel. 1968. *Biografía de un cimarrón*. México: Siglo XXI Editores.

Barth, Fredrick. 1976. "Introducción." In *Los grupos étnicos y sus fronteras*. México: Fondo de Cultura Económica.

Bauman, Zygmund. 1973. *Culture as Praxis*. London: Routledge and Kegan Paul.

Bellaby, Paul. 1991. "Histories of Sickliness: Making Use of Multiple Accounts of the Same Process." In *Life and Work History Analyses: Qualitative and Quantitative Developments*. Ed. Shirley Dex. London: Routledge.

Bertaux, Daniel. 1991. "Social Genealogies, Commented and Compared: An Instrument for Observing Social Mobility Processes in the 'longue durée,' conference on 'Social Inequality in Historical and Comparative Perspective,'" Prague, June 18–21.

Bertaux, Daniel. 1992. "Les transmissions familiales intergenerationnelles:

esquisse d'une approche comparative." French-Soviet Conference "Psycho-analyse et sciences sociales," Moscow, March 30–April 5.

Bonfil Batalla, Guillermo. 1987. *México profundo: Una civilización negada*. Mexico City: SEP-CIESAS.

Bonilla, Víctor Daniel. 1982. *Historia política de los paeces*. Bogotá: Nuestras Ediciones.

Bourdieu, Pierre. 1982. *Ce que parler veut dire: L'économie des échanges linguistiques*. Paris: Fayard.

Braun, Herbert. 1987. *Mataron a Gaitán: Vida pública y violencia urbana en Colombia*. Bogotá: Universidad Nacional de Colombia.

Brumble, David. 1988. *American Indian Autobiography*. Berkeley: University of California Press.

Bruner, Edward. 1986 (a). "Ethnography as Narrative." In *The Anthropology of Experience*. Eds. Victor Turner and Edward Bruner. Champaign: University of Illinois Press.

Bruner, Edward. 1986 (b). "Introduction." In *The Anthropology of Experience*. Ed. Victor Turner and Edward Bruner. Champaign: University of Illinois Press.

Burke, Peter. 1993. *Formas de hacer historia*. Madrid: Alianza Editorial.

Bynum, David. 1973. "Oral Evidence and the Historian: Problems and Methods." In *Folklore and Traditional History*. Ed. Richard Donson. The Hague: Mouton.

Caja Agraria, INCORA et al. 1990. *Políticas del Gobierno Nacional para la Defensa de los Derechos Indígenas y la Conservación de la Cuenca Amazónica*. Bogotá: Caja Agraria.

Caplan, Pat. 1992. "Spirits and Sex: A Swahili Informant and His Diary." In Judith Okely and Helen Callaway, *Anthropology and Autobiography*. London: Routledge.

Castrillón Arboleda, Diego. 1973. *El indio Quintín Lame*. Bogotá: Tercer Mundo.

Clark, Katherine and Michael Holquist. 1984. *Mikhail Bakhtin*. Cambridge, MA: Harvard University Press.

Codazzi, Agustín. 1959. *Jeografía física i política de las provincias de la Nueva Granada*. Bogotá: Banco de la República.

Colmenares, Germán. 1975. *Terratenientes, mineros y comerciantes*. Cali: Universidad del Valle.

Colmenares, Germán. 1979. *Historia económica y social de Colombia*. Bogotá: La Carreta Editores.

Colom, Francisco. 2002. *La política del multiculturalismo*. Unpublished Presentation. Bogotá.

Consejo Regional Indígena del Cauca (CRIC). 2009. *Caminando la palabra de los Congresos del Consejo Regional Indígena del Cauca–CRIC, febrero de 1971 a marzo de 2009*. Coor. Graciela Bolaños. Popayán: PEBI-CRIC, Universidad Autónoma Indígena Intercultural, Programa de Educación Bilingüe e Intercultural.

Crapanzano, Vincent. 1980. *Tuhami: Portrait of a Moroccan.* Chicago: University of Chicago Press.

Crapanzano, Vincent. 1992. "Les transmissions familiales intergenerationnelles: esquisse d´une approche comparative." French-Soviet Conference "Psycho-analyse et sciences sociales." Moscow, March 30–April 5.

Degregori, Carlos Ivan. 1990. *Qué difícil es ser Dios: Ideología y violencia Política en Sendero Luminoso.* Peru: Ed. Zorro de Abajo.

Departamento Administrativo Nacional de Estadística—DANE. 2008. *Censo General 2005: nivel nacional.* Bogotá: DANE.

Dex, Shirley, ed. 1991. *Life and Work History Analyses: Qualitative and Quantitative Developments.* London: Routledge.

Duque Gómez, Luis. 1955. *Colombia. Monumentos históricos y arqueológicos.* Mexico City: Instituto Panamericano de Geografía e Historia.

Echeverry de Ferrufino, Ligia. 1988–1991. "Socialización y vejez: una explicación teórica para el caso empírico colombiano." In *Maguaré* 6, Departamento de Antrolopogía, Universidad Nacional de Colombia, no. 6–7: 33–47.

Elias, Norbert. 1996. *The Germans: Power Struggles and the Development of Habitus in the Nineteenth and Twentieth Centuries.* New York: Colombia University Press.

Escobar, Fray Gerónimo. [1582] 1983. "Relación para los muy poderosos señores del Real Consejo de Indias, ansi de la descripción de la tierra que llaman Gobernación o Provincia de Popayán, como de los individuos que hay en ella, como de algunas cosas que convino hacerse para su buen gobierno, ansi en lo temporal como en lo espiritual," in *Cespedesia* no. 45–46, suplemento no. 4, January–June 1983. Espinosa Arango, Mónica. 2004. "Of Visions and Sorrows: Manuel Quintín Lame's Indian Thought and the Violences of Colombia." Electronic Doctoral Dissertations for the University of Massachusetts, Amherst. Paper AAI3152691, January 1.

Escobar, Fray Gerónimo. 2009. *La civilización montés: La visión india y el trasegar de Manuel Quintín Lame en Colombia.* Bogotá: Universidad de los Andes.

Faust, Franz. 1989–1990. "Etnografía y etnoecología de Coconuco y Sotará." In *Revista Colombiana de Antropología*, vol. 27: 53–90. Bogotá: Instituto Colombiano de Antropología.

Ferguson, Brian R. and Neil Whitehead. 1992. "The Violent Edge of Empire." In *War in the Tribal Zone: Expanding States and Indigenous Warfare.* Santa Fe, NM: School of American Research Press, Advanced Seminar Series.

Font Castro, José. "Qué fue, qué hizo y qué dejó el MRL?" *El Tiempo*, November 27, 1997. http://www.eltiempo.com/archivo/documento/MAM-692737.

Friede, Juan. 1944. *El indio en lucha por la tierra: Historia de los resguardos del macizo central colombiano.* Bogotá: Espiral.

Geertz, Clifford. 1983. *Local Knowledge*. New York: Basic Books.

Godard, Francis. 1996. "El debate y la práctica sobre el uso de las historias de vida en las ciencias sociales." In *Uso de las historias de vida en las ciencias sociales*. Godard, Francis, and Robert Cabanés. Cuadernos del CIDS, no. 1 series 2. Bogotá: Universidad Externado de Colombia.

González, Catherine and Mauricio Archila. 2010. *Movimiento indígena caucano: historia y política*. Bogotá: Universidad Santo Tomás.

Gow, David and Joanne Rappaport. 2002. "The Indigenous Public Voice: The Multiple Idioms of Modernity in Native Cauca." In *Indigenous Movements, Self-Representation, and the State in Latin America*. Ed. Kay Warren and Jean Jackson, Austin: University of Texas Press.

Griaule, Marcel. 1965. *Conversation with Ogotemmeli: An Introduction to Dogon Religious Ideas*. Oxford: Oxford University Press.

Gros, Christian. 1991. *Colombia indígena: Identidad cultural y cambio social*. Bogotá: Cerec.

Gros, Christian. 1992. "Los campesinos de las cordilleras frente a los movimientos guerrilleros y a la droga. ¿Actores o víctimas?" In *Revista Análisis Político* 16 (May–August): 34–54.

Gros, Christian and Trino Morales. 2009. *¡A mí no me manda nadie! Historia de vida de Trino Morales*. Bogotá: Instituto Colombiano de Antropología e Historia, 2009.

Gusdorf, Georges. 1991. "Condiciones y límites de la autobiografía." In *La autobiografía y sus problemas teóricos*. Suplementos Anthropos 29, December.

Gutiérrez, Francisco. 1998. "Historias de vida: notas acerca de la tradición polaca." In *Los usos de la historia de vida en las ciencias sociales*. Eds. Thierry Lülle, Pilar Vargas, and Lucero Zamudio. Barcelona: Anthropos Editorial.

Henderson, James D. 2006. *La modernización de Colombia: Los años de Laureano Gómez, 1889–1965*. Medellín: Editorial Universidad de Antioquia.

Jackson, Jean. 2002. "Contested Discourses of Authority in Colombian National Indigenous Politics: The 1996 Summer Takeovers." In *Indigenous Movements, Self-Representation, and the State in Latin America*. Ed. Kay Warren and Jean Jackson. Austin: University of Texas Press.

Jackson, Jean. 2007. "Rights to Indigenous Culture in Colombia." In *The Practice of Human Rigths: Tracking between the Local and the Global*. Comps. Mark Goodale and Sally Merry. Cambridge: Cambridge University Press.

Jimeno, Myriam and Adolfo Triana. 1985. *Estado y minorías étnicas en Colombia*. Bogotá: Cuadernos del Jaguar.

Jimeno, Myriam and Adolfo Triana. 1996. "Juan Gregorio Palechor: tierra, identidad y recreación étnica." *Journal of Latin American Anthropology* 1, no. 2 (spring): 46–77.

Jimeno, Myriam and Adolfo Triana. 2004. "El indigenismo como espejo de la nación: Comentario al texto "Los dilemas del pluralismo brasileño, de Alcida Ramos." *Revista Maguaré* 18: 26–32. Bogotá: Universidad Nacional de Colombia, Departamento de Antropología.

Jimeno, Myriam and Adolfo Triana. 2008. "Colombia: Citizens and Anthropologists." In *A Companion to Latin American Anthropology*. Ed. Deborah Poole. Malden, MA: Blackwell.

Jimeno, Myriam and Adolfo Triana. 2012. "Reforma constitucional na Colômbia e povos indígenas: Os limites da lei." In *Constituições Nacionais e Povos Indígenas: Os limites da lei*. Coor. Alcida R. Ramos. Belo Horizonte: Editora UFMG.

Kofes, Suely. 1998. "Experiencias sociales, interpretaciones individuales: posibilidades y límites de las historias de vida en las ciencias socials." In *Los usos de la historia de vida en las ciencias sociales*, vol. 1. Eds. Thierry Lülle, Pilar Vargas, and Lucero Zamudio. Bogotá: Anthropos, IFEA, CIDS.

Kopenawa, Davi and Bruce Albert. 2010. *La chute du ciel: Paroles d'un chaman Yanomami*. Paris: Plon (Collection Terre Humaine).

Krupat, Arnold. 1985. *For Those Who Come After: A Study of Native American Autobiography*. Berkeley: University of California Press.

Kuper, Adam and Jessica Kuper, eds. 1985. *The Social Science Encyclopedia*. London: Routledge and Kegan Paul.

Kuper, Hilda. 1978. *Shobuza II: Ngwenyama and King of Swaziland: The Story of an Hereditary Ruler and His Country*. London: Duckworth.

Labov, William. 1972. "The Transformation of Experience in Narrative Syntax." In *Language in the Inner City: Studies in the Black English Vernacular*. Philadelphia: University of Pennsylvania Press.

Lamb, Sarah. 2001. "Being a Widow and Other Life Stories: The Interplay between Lives and Words." In *Anthropology and Humanism* 26, no. 1: 16–34.

Lame, Manuel Quintín. 1973. *Las luchas del indio que bajó de la montaña al valle de la civilización. Selección, arreglo y notas de Gonzalo Castillo Cárdenas*. Bogotá: Comité de defensa del indio.

Langness, L. L. 1965. *The Life History in Anthropological Science*. New York: Holt, Rinehart and Winston.

Laurent, Virginia. 2005. *Comunidades indígenas, espacios políticos y movilización electoral en Colombia, 1990–1998*. Bogotá: Instituto Colombiano de Antropología e Historia (ICANH) and French Institute for Andean Studies (IFEA).

Loureiro, Ángel. 1991. "Introducción: Problemas teóricos de la autobiografía." In *La autobiografía y sus problemas teóricos*. Suplementos Anthropos no. 29, December.

Mitterand, Henri, ed. 1987. *Littérature. Textes et documents S. XVIII*. Paris: Éditions Nathan Littérature.

Molano, Alfredo and Fernando Rozo. 1990. "Observaciones sobre el Proyecto de Sustitución de Cultivos de Coca en el Sur del Departamento del Cauca." *Work Report for the United Nations*. Bogotá.

Molano, Alfredo. 1998. "Mi historia de vida con las historias de vida." In *Los usos de la historia de vida en las ciencias sociales*, vols. 1–2. Ed. Thierry Lülle, Pilar Vargas, and Lucero Zamudio. Barcelona: Anthropos.

Morin, Françoise. 1993. "Praxis antropológica e historia de vida." In *Historia Oral*. Ed. Jorge Aceves. Mexico City: Instituto Mora, Universidad Autónoma Metropolitana.

Muelas Hurtado, Lorenzo, Lorenzo Urdaneta Franco, and Martha Urdaneta Franco. 2005. *La fuerza de la gente: Juntando recuerdos sobre la terrajería en Guambía, Colombia*. Bogotá: Instituto Colombiano de Antropología e Historia.

Nasson, Bill. 1990. "Abraham Esau's War, 1899–1901." In *The Myths We Live By*. Ed. Samuel Raphael and Paul Thompson. London: Routledge.

Neihardt, John G. [1932] 1988. *Black Elk Speaks: Being the Life Story of a Holy Man of the Oglala Sioux*, Lincoln: University of Nebraska Press.

Nietzsche, Friedrich. 1968. *The Will to Power*. London: Weidenfield and Nicholson.

Okely, Judith. 1992. "Anthropology and Autobiography: Participatory Experience and Embodied Knowledge." In *Anthropology and Autobiography*. Ed. Judith Okely and Helen Callaway. London: Routledge.

Olney, James. 1991. "Algunas versiones de la memoria / Algunas versiones del bios: la ontología de la autobiografía." *Suplementos Anthropos 29, La autobiografía y sus problemas teóricos*. December 1991.

Pécaut, Daniel. 1987. *Orden y violencia: Colombia 1930–1943*, 2 vols. Bogotá: Siglo XXI.

Peñaranda, Daniel Ricardo. 2009. *Organizaciones indígenas y participación política en Colombia*. Bogotá: La Carreta Editores.

Pereira de Queiroz, Maria Isaura. 1983. *Variações sobre a técnica de gravador no registro da informação viva*. São Paulo: CERU and FF LCH/USP.

Pineda Camacho, Roberto, L. Cardona, M. Chávez, et al. 1990. "Evaluación Cualitativa del Plan Nacional de Rehabilitación (PNR)." In *Comunidades Indígenas*. Working Document. Bogotá: Universidad de los Andes, Departamento de Antropología, PNR.

Pozas, Ricardo. [1952] 1975. *Juan Pérez Jolote*. Mexico City: Fondo de Cultura Económica.

Rabinow, Paul. 1992. *Reflexiones sobre un trabajo de campo en Marruecos*, Madrid: Jucar.

Radin, Paul. 1926. *Crashing Thunder: The Autobiography of an American Indian*. New York: D. Appleton and Co.

Ramírez, María Clemencia. 1996. *Frontera fluida entre Andes, piedemonte y selva*, Bogotá: Instituto de Cultura Hispánica.

Ramos, Alcida. 1993. *Nações dentro da Nação: Um desencontro de ideologias*. Anthropological Series. Brasilia: Universidad de Brasilia.

Ramos, Alcida. 1998. *Indigenism. Ethnic Politics in Brazil*. Madison: University of Wisconsin.

Ramos, Alcida. 2002. "Los dilemas del pluralismo en Brasil." Bogotá: Universidad Nacional de Colombia. Presentation to the Masters in Anthropology Program, October 11.

Rappaport, Joanne. 1987. "Mythic Images, Historical Thought, and Printed Texts: The Paez and the Written Word." *Journal of Anthropological Research* 43 no. 1: 43–61.

Rappaport, Joanne. 1990. *The Politics of Memory*. Cambridge: Cambridge University Press.

Rappaport, Joanne. 1998. "Hacia la decolonización de la producción intelectual indígena en Colombia." In *Modernidad, identidad y desarrollo*. Ed. María Lucía Sotomayor. Bogotá: Instituto Colombiano de Antropología and Colciencias.

Rappaport, Joanne. 2005. *Intercultural Utopias: Public Intellectuals, Cultural Experimentation, and Ethnic Pluralism in Colombia*. Durham, NC: Duke University Press.

Reynoso, Carlos, comp. 1992. *El surgimiento de la antropología posmoderna*. Barcelona: Gedisa.

Romero Loaiza, Fernando. 2006. *Manuel Quintín Lame Chantre: el indígena ilustrado, el pensador indigenista*. Pereira: CRIC.

Romoli, Kathleen. 1962. "El suroeste del Cauca y sus indios al tiempo de la conquista española." In *Revista Colombiana de Antropología*, no. 9: 239–301. Bogotá: Instituto Colombiano de Antropología.

Rosaldo, Renato. 1986. "Ilongot Hunting as Story and Experience." In *The Anthropology of Experience*. Eds. Victor Turner and Edward Bruner. Champaign: University of Illinois Press.

Rousseau, Jean Jacques. 1783. *The Confessions of Jean Jacques Rousseau: With the Reveries of the Solitary Walker*. London: Printed for J. Bew.

Rousseau, Jean Jacques. 1983. *Las confesiones*. Madrid: Espasa-Calpe.

Rousseau, Jean Jacques. [1762] 2009. "As Quatro Cartas A Malesherbes." In *Textos Autobiográficos e Outros Escritos*. São Paulo: Editora UNESP.

Samuel, Raphael and Paul Thompson, eds. 1990. *The Myths We Live By*. London: Routledge.

Sánchez, Esther. 2004. *Derechos propios: Ejercicio legal de la jurisdicción especial indígena en Colombia*. Bogotá: Procuraduría General de la Nación.

Sánchez, Esther. 2005. *Los pueblos indígenas en Colombia: Derechos, políticas y desafíos.* Bogotá: UNICEF/ Editorial Gente Nueva.

Sánchez, Esther. 2006. *Entre el juez Salomón y el dios Sira: Decisiones interculturales e interés superior del niño.* Bogotá: UNICEF, Universiteit van Amsterdam.

Sánchez, Gonzalo. 1985. *Ensayos de historia social y política del siglo XX.* Bogotá: El Áncora.

Sanjek, Roger. 1990. "The Secret Life of Fieldnotes." In *Fieldnotes: The Makings of Anthropology.* Ed. Roger Sanjek. Ithaca, NY: Cornell University Press, 1990.

Shostak, Marjorie. 1983. *Nisa: The Life and Words of a !Kung Woman.* New York: Random House.

Smith, Sidonie. 1991. "Hacia una poética de la autobiografía de mujeres." In *La autobiografía y sus problemas teóricos.* Barcelona: Suplementos Anthropos, no. 29, December.

Sotomayor, María Lucía, ed. 1998. *Modernidad, identidad y desarrollo.* Bogotá: Instituto Colombiano de Antropología, Colciencias.

Swann, Brian and Arnold Krupat, eds. 1987. *I Tell You Now: Autobiobiographical Essays by Native American Writers.* Lincoln: University of Nebraska Press.

Tello, Piedad. 1983. *Vida y lucha de Manuel Quintín Lame.* Bogotá: Universidad de los Andes, Department of Anthropology, master's thesis.

Tonkin, Elizabeth, Maryon McDonald, and Malcom Chapman, eds. 1989. "Introduction: History and Social Anthropology." In *History and Ethnicity.* London: Routledge.

Triana, Adolfo. 1989. "El Estado y el Derecho Frente a los Indígenas." In *Etnia y Derecho.* Mexico City: Instituto Indigenista Interamericano.

Turner, Terence. 2002. "Representation, Poliphony, and the Construction of Power in a Kayapó Video." In *Indigenous Movements, Self-Representation, and the State in Latin America.* Eds. Kay Warren and Jean Jackson. Austin: University of Texas Press.

Turner, Victor. 1967. *The Forest of Symbols: Aspects of Ndembu Ritual.* Ithaca, NY: Cornell University Press.

Turner, Victor. 1969. *The Ritual Process.* Ithaca, NY: Cornell University Press.

Urban, Greg and Joel Sherzer (Eds.). 1991. *Nation-States and Indians in Latin America.* Austin: University of Texas Press.

Uribe, María Tila. 1994. *Los años perdidos.* Bogotá: CESTRA, CEREC.

Wachtel, Nathan. 1992. "Note sur le probleme des identités collectives dans les Andes méridonales" in *L'Homme*, no. 122–124, Year 31, April–December.

Warren, Kay. 1989. *The Symbolism of Subordination: Indian Identity in Guatemala.* Austin: University of Texas Press.

Warren, Kay. 2000. "Mayan Multiculturalism and the Violence of Memories." In *Violence and Subjectivity*. Ed. Veena Das, Arthur Kleinman, et al. Berkeley: University of California Press.

Warren, Kay and Jean Jackson. 2002. "Introduction: Studying Indigenous Activism in Latin America." In *Indigenous Movements, Self-Representation, and the State in Latin America*. Eds. Kay Warren and Jean Jackson. Austin: University of Texas Press.

Watson, C. W. 1992. "Autobiography, Anthropology and the Experience of Indonesia." In *Anthropology and Autobiography*. Eds. Judith Okely and Helen Callaway. London: Routledge.

Watson, Lawrence C. and Maria Barbara Watson-Franke. 1985. *Interpreting Life Histories: An Anthropological Inquiry*. New Brunswick, NJ: Rutgers University Press.

Wells, H. G. 1901. *Anticipations of the Reactions of Mechanical and Scientific Progress upon Human Life and Thought*. London: Chapman and Hall.

Werbner, Richard. 1991. "Contending Narrators: Personal Discourse and the Social Biography of a Family in Western Zimbabwe." In University of Illinois Center for African Studies Spring Symposium, April 11–13.

Whitten, Norman. 1975. *Jungle Quechua Ethnicity: An Ecuadorian Case*. The Hague: Mouton.

Zambrano, Carlos, ed. 1993. *Hombres de páramo y montaña, los Yanaconas del Macizo Colombiano*. Bogotá: ICAN, Colcultura, PNR.

Zamosc, León. 1987. La cuestión agraria y el movimiento campesino en Colombia: Luchas de la Asociación Nacional de Usuarios Campesinos (ANUC), 1967–1981. Geneva and Bogotá: United Nations Research Institute for Social Development and Centro de Investigación y Educación Popular.

Zamosc, León. 1996. *Estructuras agrarias y movimientos campesinos en América Latina (1950–1990)*. Coor. Manuel Chiriboga V., León Zamosc, and Estela Martínez Borrego. Madrid: Ministerio de Agricultura, Pesca y Alimentación.

INDEX

Agricultural Bank. See *Caja Agraria*
AICO. *See* Movement of Indigenous Authorities of Colombia
Albert, Bruce, 17
Amórtegui, Guillermo, 1
Anaconas. *See* Yanacona people
ANUC. *See* National Association of Campesinos
Apache culture, 10
Arhuaco people, 30
Asociación National de Usuarios Campesinos. *See* National Association of Campesinos
autobiographies: authorship, 21–22; as dialogue, 12–14; ethnographic canon and, 23–24; identity in, 21; as research material, 14–17; tradition in, 18. *See also* life stories
Avirama, Edgard, 1
Avirama, Jesús, 2, 149
Avirama, Marcos, 1

Bakhtin, Mikhail, 21, 22–23
Barí people, 30
Barrett, S. M., 10
Bauman, Zygmund, 39, 42
Bellaby, Paul, 14

Beltrán. *See* Papamija (Beltrán)
biographies, 14–17. *See also* autobiographies; life stories
Black Elk Speaks (Niehardt), 3
Blowsnake, Sam, 11
Boas, Franz, 11
Bolaños, Graciela, 1
Bonfil Batalla, Guillermo, 52
Bourdieu, Pierre, 33
Bruner, Edward, 13, 20, 24
Bruss, Elizabeth, 21
Burke, Peter, 36
Bynum, David, 10

cabildos, 44–45, 76, 86–87, 204n54
caciques, power of, 56, 127–29, 132–33, 135
Caja Agraria, 132–33
campesinos, 29, 50, 117
Castillo, Elizabeth, 73, 188–89
Catholic Church, 31, 51–52, 64, 69, 85, 89–90, 107–8, 125, 135–38
Cauca region, 54–60, 55
Chicangana, Moisés, 76–77
Children of Sánchez, The (Lewis), 16
coca, use of, 65, 86, 93–94, 161
Codazzi, Agustín, 62
Colom, Francisco, 42

Colombian Institute for Agrarian Reform (INCORA), 52, 95, 140–41, 213n76

Colombian Institute for Rural Development (INCODER), 72

Committee in Solidarity with Indigenous Struggles, 179

Community Action Committees, 120

compadrazgo relationships, 134–35

Confessions of St. Augustine, 14

Consejo Regional Indígena del Cauca. See Regional Indigenous Council of Cauca

Conservative Party, 49

Constitution (Colombia, 1991), 32–34, 67

Cortés, Pedro, 71

Crashing Thunder (Radin), 3, 11, 16. See also Blowsnake, Sam

CRIC. See Regional Indigenous Council of Cauca

CRIC Denounces, 163–64

CRIC Handbook, 51

Cuene, Maximina, 109–10

culture: concept of, 39–42; right to difference, 34–35, 67

Culture as Praxis (Bauman), 39

Davis, Natalie, 19

Degregori, Carlos Ivan, 69

de Mosquera, Tomás Cipriano, 157

Derrida, Jacques, 13

Dewey, John, 19–20

difference, right to, 34–35, 67

"Digression on Nationalism, A" (Elias), 40

Dilthey, Wilhelm, 19–20

Dindicué, Benjamín, 1, 108, 210n42

discrimination, 101, 102, 119, 138

Du Bois, Cora, 16

Eakin, Paul John, 21

Echandía, Darío, 106, 210n39

education, indigenous, 52, 69, 113–14, 159–60

Elias, Norbert, 40–42

el indio. See Gaitán, Jorge Eliécer

Emberá people, 30

Esau, Abraham, 18–19

Escobar, Jerónimo de, 56

Escué, Julio, 1

Escué, Mario, 1

ethnicity: cultural plurality and, 42; identity, reinvention of, 65–73; as organizing principle, 50; use of term, 35–36

family planning, 154–55

Faust, Franz, 59–60, 61

forgetting, 17

For Those Who Come After (Krupat), 10

Foundation for Colombian Communities, 195n1

Friede, Juan, 56, 61, 63–64, 160

FUNCOL, 1–2

Fundación para las Comunidades Colombianas. See Foundation for Colombian Communities

Gaitán, Jorge Eliécer, 47–48, 65–66, 100, 100, 105–6, 121, 209n35, 210n43

García Márquez, Gabriel, 8, 17

Geronimo's Story of His Life (Barrett), 10

Ginzburg, Carlo, 19

gold mining, 56, 62

Gómez, Laureano, 106, 121, 122, 210n40
Guachicono *resguardo*, 56–57
Guajiro people, 30
Guambiano people, 33, 50, 52
Guaviare, indigenous people of, 30
Guerre, Martin, 19
Gusdorf, Georges, 22

Hipia, Dionisio, 1
Hugh-Jones, Stephen, 3–4

Ijkas. *See* Arhuaco people
INCODER. *See* Colombian Institute for Rural Development
INCORA. *See* Colombian Institute for Agrarian Reform
indigenism, use of term, 37–38, 42
indigenous movements: ethnic identity and, 38–39; growth of, 3, 33, 72–73; as imagined community, 66; land occupations by, 71; leaders' memoirs, 17; legal changes enacted, 33; memoirs of founders, 17; nature of, 52–53; organizations, need for, 158–61; on pluriethnicity, 38; on repression, 1–2; sisal grower support, 180. *See also* specific organizations
indigenous peoples: census of, 52; diversity of, 29–30; identity of, 28–29, 33, 59–60, 65–73; land rights, 31, 32, 67, 87, 107, 161; smallpox epidemics and, 58; women, role of, 148, 150–53, 160
indio, el. See Gaitán, Jorge Eliécer
Instituto Colombiano de la Reforma

Agraria. *See* Colombian Institute for Agrarian Reform
Instituto Colombiano para el Desarrollo Rural. *See* Colombian Institute for Rural Development

Jackson, Jean, 34–35
Jesús, Rosalía, 152
Juan Pérez Jolote (Burns), 3

Kankuamo people, 30
Kardiner, Abraham, 16
Kogui people, 30
Kopenawa, Davi, 17
Krupat, Arnold, 7, 10–11
Kuna people, 30
Kuper, Adam, 15
Kuper, Jessica, 15

Lamb, Sarah, 20, 25, 26
land rights: distribution laws, 61–65, 174–78; of indigenous peoples, 31, 32, 67, 87, 107, 160–61; struggle for, 61; *terraje* and, 50–51, 56
Langness, L. L., 15–16
language and expression, 16–17
Laurent, Virginie, 33
Law 89 (1890), 61, 87, 159, 160
La Violencia. *See* Violencia, La
Lejeune, Philippe, 21
Le Roy Ladurie, Emmannuel, 19
Lewis, Oscar, 16
Liberal Party, 47, 49–50, 84, 104–5, 106, 130
Liberal Revolutionary Movement (MRL), 49, 66, 116–17, 121–22, 126–35, 211n50

life stories: by indigenous leaders, 17; by Palechor, 76–161; as research material, 14–17; statistical inferences from, 23; technique in, 22–26. *See also* autobiographies; oral history

Lleras Camargo, Alberto, 121, 122, 124

Lleras Restrepo, Carlos, 49, 122, 130, 140–41

López Michelsen, Alfonso, 49–50, 70, 121–22, 126–31, 140, 209n34

López Pumarejo, Alfonso, 98–99, 121, 124

M-19 guerrilla movement, 1, 3, 72, 187

Maya people, 28–29, 36

Mejía, Gustavo, 50, 143, 145, 213n73

memory, 20–21. *See also* forgetting

Menoccio, 19

mestizaje, ideology of, 31–32, 207n5

migrations, 161

Ministry of Government, 52

missionaries, 31, 38, 69

Molano, Alfredo, 16, 23–24

Monroy, Luis Ángel, 1

Montaillou region, 19

Morin, Françoise, 12

Mosquera Chaux, Víctor, 106, 157, 210n41

Movement of Indigenous Authorities of Colombia (AICO), 32

Movimiento de Autoridades Indígenas de Colombia. *See* Movement of Indigenous Authorities of Colombia

Movimiento Revolucionario Liberal. *See* Liberal Revolutionary Movement

MRL. *See* Liberal Revolutionary Movement

Muelas, Lorenzo, 17, 51, 71–72

multiculturalism, 42

Muñoz, Manuel, 62

Nasson, Bill, 18

National Association of Campesinos (ANUC), 50, 70

National Constituent Assembly, 32

National Front, 49, 114–15, 123–24, 129, 130, 133, 210–11n48

National Indigenous Organization of Colombia (ONIC), 52

Neruda, Pablo, 9

News of a Kidnapping (García Márquez), 16

Nietzsche, Friedrich, 40

nongovernmental organizations (NGOs), 39, 53

Ñuscué, Mario, 1

Ñuscué, Miguel, 1

Ñuscué, Taurino, 1

Occidental Petroleum Company (OXY), 31

oil industry, 31

Okely, Judith, 5, 23

Olaya Herrera, Enrique, 124

ONIC. *See* National Indigenous Organization of Colombia

oral history: authorship, 19–22; reality and fantasy in, 17–18

Organization Nacional Indígena de Colombia. *See* National Indigenous Organization of Colombia

Ospina Pérez, Mariano, 100, 105, 121

OXY. *See* Occidental Petroleum
Company

Paez people, 1, 30, 33, 50, 52, 107, 158
Palechor, Juan Gregorio, 41, 43, 60,
63, 64; as activist, 48–49, 66, 119–
24, 138–43; agricultural work, 81,
93–96; architectural and carpentry
work, 102–3; background, 76–78;
birth and family, 41, 45, 54, 64,
81–85, 92–93, 103–4; in CRIC, 143–
50; on education, 113–14, 159–60;
on family planning, 154–55; identity and ethnicity, 28–35, 117–18;
on indigenous organization,
158–61; on indigenous women,
148, 150–53; as leader, 46, 68–69;
life history, relating, 2–3, 24–25,
76–161, 181; on medicine, 153–54;
military service, 46–47, 96–102;
in MRL, 131–35; multicultural approach of, 39; on politics, 125–31,
156–58; public life, 104–10; on religion, 124–25, 135–38; on *resguardo*,
80–88; schooling, 88–92; as *tinterillo*, 48, 69–70, 84, 107, 110–19.
See also specific topics
Palechor, Juan Gregorio (forebear),
85
Palechor, Matías, 85
Palechor, Miguel, 85
Palechor, Silvestre, 85
Palechor, Valerio, 45–46, 61, 76, 85
Pancho, Avelina, 73, 188–89
Papamija (Beltrán), 84
Parra, José María, 62–63
Parra, Pedro, 62–63
Pedro Martínez (Lewis), 16

People of Alor, The (du Bois), 16
Piapoco people, letter, 165–67
Piñacué, Jesús, 71–72
pluralism, 39, 42
politiqueros, 76, 114–15, 120, 125–26,
134, 156–58
Poloche, Adolfo, 2
Prado, Aníbal, 121, 127–28
Psychological Frontiers of Society, The
(Kardiner), 16
Putumayo, indigenous people of, 30

Quintín Lame, Manuel, 3, 58, 69, 158,
159, 189, 214n84

race: discrimination, 101, 102, 119,
138; fictions of, 37–38
Radin, Paul, 11, 16
Ramos, Alcida, 31, 37, 38, 39, 71
Rappaport, Joanne, 24, 28, 34, 69
Regional Indigenous Council of Cauca
(CRIC), 1–2, 63; birth of, 33, 143,
172–73; documents, 163–89; Marxist groups vs., 71; members murdered, 164; Palechor in, 51, 143–50;
on social identity, 29; struggles
of, 148–51; as union of *cabildos*, 50;
women in, 151–53
resguardos, 44–46, 47–48, 51–52, 56;
boundary-setting, 205n81; identity
and struggles, 60–65; Palechor life
on, 80–88
Ricoeur, Paul, 25
Rojas Pinilla, Gustavo, 119, 121, 122,
211n53
Romero, Oscar, 213n70
Romoli, Kathleen, 58–59, 64
Rousseau, Jean-Jacques, 15

Samuel, Ralph, 17–18
Sánchez, Esther, 34
Schäfer, Dietrich, 41
Schiller, Friedrich, 40–42
Sierra Nevada de Santa Marta, pamphlet, 168–69
slavery in mining, 59
smallpox epidemics, 58
Suárez, Teresa, 1, 71
Swann, Brian, 7

terrajería system, 50–51, 56
Third Indigenous Encounter of Cauca, documents, 6, 57, 170–71, 182–85
Thompson, Paul, 17–18
tinterillos, 48, 69–70
Torres, Camilo, 136–37, 213n69
tradition, role of, 18
Trino Morales, Manuel, 1–2, 17, 149–50
Tunebos. See U'wa people
Turbay, Gabriel, 100, 105, 209n35
Turbay, Julio César, 1
Turner, Terence, 53

Ul, Avelino, 1
U'wa people, 30–31

Valencia, Guillermo León, 129
Vallejo, Enrique, 107–8, 138
Vaupés, indigenous people of, 30
Velasco, Omar Henry, 121
Villegas, Silvio, 106
Violencia, La (1946–1956), 48, 50, 107–10, 211n55
Vivas, Arce, 137
Vivas, Mario S., 107

War of a Thousand Days (1899–1902), 45, 76, 104–5
Warren, Kay, 28–29, 36, 72
Watson, Lawrence C., 13
Watson-Franke, Maria Barbara, 13
Wayúu. See Guajiro people
Wells, H. G., 40
Werbner, Richard, 22

Yanacona people, 6, 33, 52, 59, 159
Yanomami people, 71
Yaví, 2, 186